The Thought at the Back of the Mind

The THOUGHT at the BACK of the MIND

Five Explorations of the Human in the Age of the Natural Sciences

Annette Aronowicz

PICKWICK *Publications* • Eugene, Oregon

THE THOUGHT AT THE BACK OF THE MIND
Five Explorations of the Human in the Age of the Natural Sciences

Pickwick Publications
An Imprint of Wipf and Stock Publishers
199 W. 8th Ave., Suite 3
Eugene, OR 97401

www.wipfandstock.com

PAPERBACK ISBN: 979-8-3852-0715-2
HARDCOVER ISBN: 979-8-3852-0716-9
EBOOK ISBN: 979-8-3852-0717-6

Cataloguing-in-Publication data:

Names: Aronowicz, Annette, 1952–, author.

Title: The thought at the back of the mind : five explorations of the human in the age of the natural sciences / by Annette Aronowicz.

Description: Eugene, OR : Pickwick Publications, 2024 | Includes bibliographical references and index.

Identifiers: ISBN 979-8-3852-0715-2 (paperback) | ISBN 979-8-3852-0716-9 (hardcover) | ISBN 979-8-3852-0717-6 (ebook)

Subjects: LCSH: Literature and science. | Science—Philosophy. | Anthropology—Philosophy.

Classification: PN55 .A60 2024 (paperback) | PN55 .A60 (ebook)

VERSION NUMBER 10/22/24

A variant of chapter 5 was published in a much shorter form as "Marilynne Robinson, *Gilead*, and the Battle for the Soul," *Perichoresis* 15:2 (2017) 41–58.

A much shorter version of chapter 4 was published as "A Poet in the Land of the Sciences. Thinking About Human Nature with Wysława Szymborska," *Bibliotekarz Podlaski* 3/2023: 343–63.

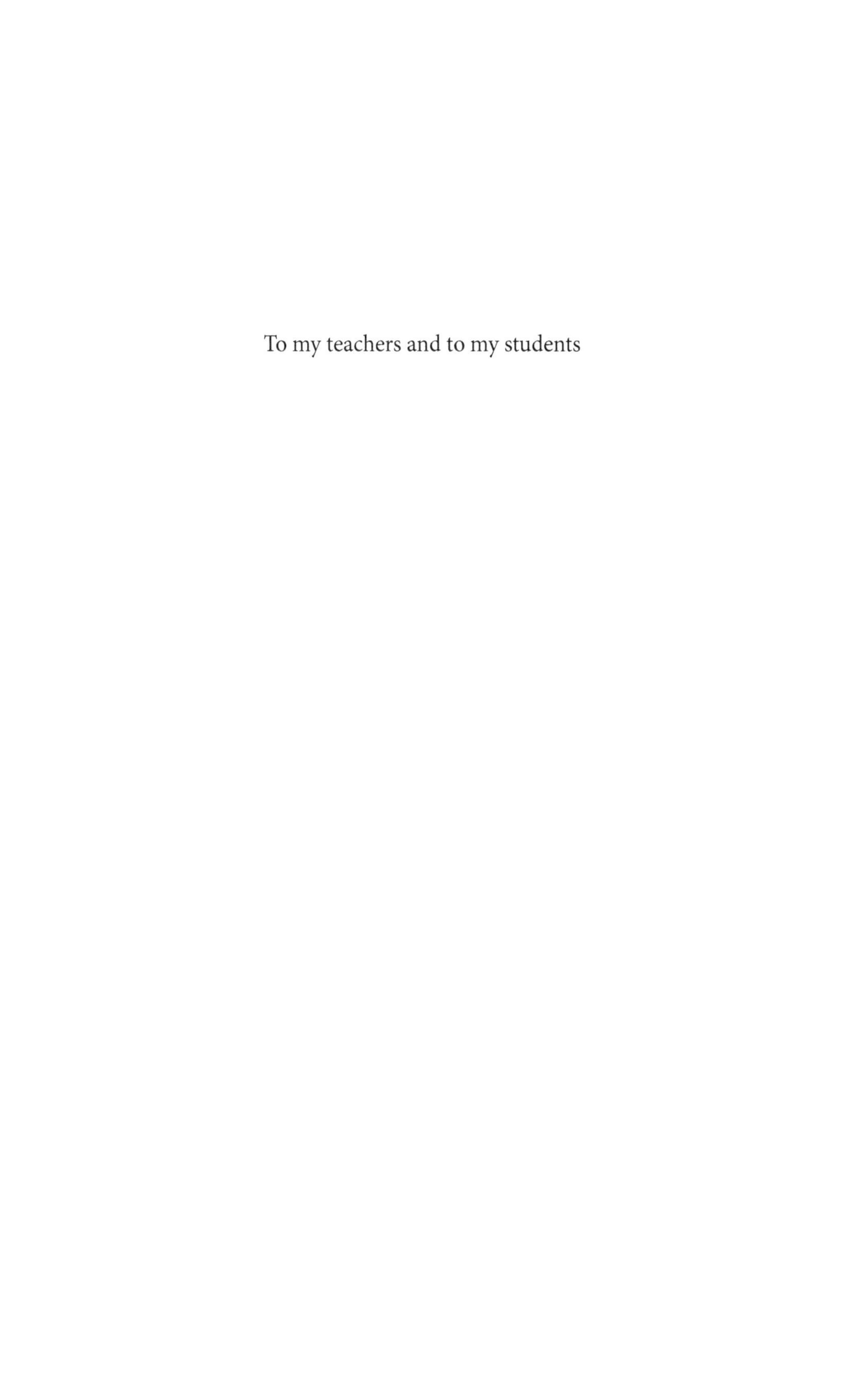

To my teachers and to my students

"This is what is important, this is the one thing that interests me. Don't speak to me of what you are saying. I am not asking you what you are saying. I am asking you how you are saying it."

—Charles Péguy

Un poète l'a dit

Contents

Acknowledgments

THIS BOOK HAS BEEN long in the making. It reflects issues that have been of interest to me from the beginning of my training as a historian of religions at UCLA. I owe the teachers who taught me there, most especially Kees Bolle, a special debt. In the many years I have been a teacher myself, I was fortunate to interact with students responsive to my intellectual passions, and to the ways I practice reading. I am very grateful to them as well. I encountered them in my early years at Stanford University as well as throughout my long career at Franklin & Marshall College. I am most grateful to that institution for allowing me to indulge in my love of teaching in a style that was mine and for providing me with a community of very fine scholar/teachers.

I have limited the alphabetical list that follows to the friends and colleagues who read parts of the manuscript in various stages of its development. They encouraged me, asked helpful questions, challenged me. I cannot thank them enough. They are Lina Bernstein, Sonja Bolle, Almut Bruckstein Çoruh, Catherine Chalier, Stephen Cooper, Joel Eigen, Tamara Eskenazi, Lisa Gasbarrone, Leon Galis, Marian Goad, Matei Iagher, John Modern, Jill Nathanson, Michel Nutkiewicz, Lucyna Aleksandrowicz-Pędich, Paul (Andoche) Praudel, Alison Renna, Carmen Tisnado, Sarah White, Kerry Whiteside.

Lastly, I want to thank Alan Mittleman. He has been both an intellectual sparring partner and a faithful corrector of silly mistakes, many times over. This book owes much to his constancy, his evenhandedness, and his ability to enter into a style of writing and thinking, that while it meets with his own quest, is nonetheless not his own. I am very lucky.

Introduction

The (Romantic) Project

THE ESSAYS COMPRISING THIS volume were written between 2019 and 2023, that is to say, between the birth of GPT-2 and ChatGPT.[1] It is no longer necessary to define these new advances in artificial intelligence, so quickly have they become well known. Still, for the few that remain unaware, these devices can converse, compose poems, produce expository prose and computer code, and might, with further improvements, we are told, compose these very essays if given the right prompt. While the genesis of the idea for *The Thought at the Back of the Mind* precedes 2019 by far (about which more later), the book nonetheless addresses this technology indirectly by addressing the larger context of which artificial intelligence is an instance.

That larger context is defined by an unexceptionable statement of fact. Since at least the latter part of the nineteenth century, the natural sciences have acquired unparalleled authority in our culture as a source of knowledge about the world, including ourselves. The images emanating from physics and biology, for example, now often coupled with those emerging from computer science, make increasingly plausible the prospect that at some point ever closer on the horizon all our supposedly singular features, our defining marks as humans, can be duplicated. This includes, as recent articles on ChatGPT and its competitors and successors describe, not only intelligence but also intimacy, compassion,

1. Seabrook, "The Next Word," 52–63. A few months later, GPT-3 was in the news. See Manjoo, "How Do You Know a Human Wrote This?" We now read about GPT-4. See Metz and Collins, "All the Ways GPT-4 Is Impressive," B1, B6.

creativity, even paranoia and jealousy. The idea is not that these qualities, once performed by a computer program, are the real thing. Most people insist that there is a difference between a human being and a computer program. Many articles on the great gains in efficiency of the latest version of A.I., GPT-4, will point out that this is still not human intelligence. The machines are not good at telling jokes, although they are getting better, we are told, and they do not do well with predictions about the future. They can summarize but not analyze in the human way, says another commentator. There are gaps in A.I.'s ability when it comes to "understanding complex organic forms holistically."[2]

Independently of all these reassurances, these machines evoke fear and wonder. They seem to foreshadow our replacement, or at least a duplication that severely puts in doubt our uniqueness and our secret, so to speak. The author of an article about the difficulty A.I. technology has in reproducing hands gives a momentary sigh of relief. "The machine's failure is comforting, in a way. Hands are a symbol of humanity, 'a direct correspondence between imagination and execution,' as Patti Smith [the American singer/poet] recently wrote. As long as we are the only ones who understand them, perhaps our computers won't wholly supplant us."[3] Only a sentence later, the author envisages a time when this essential difference will be erased as well, and we will look back with nostalgia at a time when we could distinguish some feature as ours alone.[4] Is there any realm we consider strictly human, invisible to an external eye, that a machine cannot detect and duplicate?

As the above presages, I will occasionally resort to newspaper and magazine articles in this book precisely because they testify to what has entered the public realm or is about to enter it. My point is not that the total duplication of the human will ever come to pass. Rather, I mean to underscore that we already live with an image of ourselves as liable to such a duplication through the processes and instruments associated with the natural sciences. Newspaper articles voice our varied reactions to such duplications, which far from being merely theoretical, are part of our daily life, from the automated voices that answer queries on the telephone or computer, to ChatGPT itself. The latter, in just the first months it had been in circulation, already received prompts from ten million users, with a

2. Chayka, "Uncanny Failures," 4.
3. Chayka, "Uncanny Failures," 7.
4. Chayka, "Uncanny Failures," 8.

hundred million people signing up for an account. It, and its competitors, are being adopted by an increasing number of institutions.[5]

An article on A.I. therapists describes one of its latest incarnations. The author, Dhruv Khullar, who is also an oncologist, had, for the purposes of his essay, signed up for "automated mental-health support through a smartphone app, 'Woebot.'"[6] He interacted with it a number of times, noting that it was helpful in talking through his problem, even if he remained aware his interlocutor was not human. Then, one day, after a particularly bad twenty-four hours with a patient whose condition had deteriorated, requiring that he make many phone calls, including to family members who broke down at the news, the doctor/journalist received an unsolicited message from the Woebot on his phone. "I'll be with you every step of the way." The journalist does not tell us why the app responded in that way at that moment. He had not communicated with it about this event. He does speculate that A.I. devices, at some future moment, if not already, would be able to coordinate various data points—in his case, his phone calls and texts during the day, his sleepless night, his pulse rate—from which they will be able to predict his mental state. Even if he chooses not to reveal his distress to anyone, the machine would know, as Woebot seemed to know in the case he described.[7] How uncanny to have one's inner life made transparent to a machine.

In the same issue of *The New Yorker* describing A.I. apps as therapists, we find an article on the status of the humanities on American campuses.[8] The journalist, Nathan Heller, reports on the precipitous decline in the number of students interested in pursuing degrees in English or history. This decline has many causes, of course, but not least is the prestige of the sciences as roads not only to jobs but also to the truth about how the world works, including how the human being works. This is not only a matter of artificial intelligence. Whether it is genetic engineering or techniques being developed to manipulate the microbiome or the electrome[9], our mental life becomes a matter of processes that bypass our consciousness,

5. The actual and possible business impact of ChatGPT and its competitors has received much press attention. For a critical view of the more benign predictions about its liberating effects on workers, see Klein, "AI Machines Aren't 'Hallucinating.'" At the latest count, winter 2023, approximately one hundred million people are using ChatGPT daily.

6. Khullar, "Talking to Ourselves," 16.

7. Khullar, "Talking to Ourselves," 22.

8. Heller, " End of the English Major," 28–39.

9. For an investigation of the scientific quest to view the human from the point of view of electric currents, see Adlee, *We Are Electric*.

best reached through devices that see through us. It has made the classical method of study in the humanities—an ongoing conversation with a wealth of human expressions not transparent to scientific instruments—a hobby at best, a refinement or a luxury for those who can afford it, or an auxiliary to the sciences, as in bio-ethics.

The authors of the two articles cited here, about A.I. therapists and about the decline of the humanities, mainly limit themselves to describing the respective phenomenon of interest to them. Vigorous critique is missing. This is perhaps as it should be. They are reporters whose task is precisely that, to transmit a multifaceted portrait of some aspect of the world we live in. It is the job of others, it could be argued, trained in detecting and questioning assumptions—philosophers and theologians, among them—to reflect and provide us with some external perspective on our humanity. But the real reason for the journalists' lack of critique may lie in the overwhelming presence of the phenomena they are reporting about. What is the point of arguing against an understanding of the human so massively part of our reality, as if it could be dislodged by an argument, no matter how good?

In Khullar's essay on the therapeutic app, for instance, we become aware that the institutionalization of this kind of care has already started. Woebot alone "has counselled nearly a million and a half people, the majority of whom live in an area with a shortage of mental health providers," and there are other mental-health chatbots. The number of users is hardly likely to diminish, given the large population needing to consult with a professional counselor on a regular basis, and the fact that there are far too few therapists to go around. Five billion dollars in 2021 alone were invested in digital mental health start-ups, just the beginning of a much broader enterprise. In counterpoint to this, Heller, in his article about the waning of the humanities, describes at length a 544,000^2 Science and Enlightenment Complex, a part of Harvard University, which reportedly cost a billion dollars, "Wandering the building's hallways, a proud dean told *Harvard Magazine*, is a six-mile hike."[10] No similar investments are being made in the humanities, whose disciplines, in order to raise any money at all, increasingly market themselves as skill sets useful to the sciences.[11] These articles inform us about the world we live in, its dominant trends. If they afford precious little distance toward

10. Heller, "End of the English Major," 35.
11. Heller, "End of the English Major," 36.

them, is this not because it could only amount to a futile exercise in turning back the clock?

It is my intent in this book to provide such a distance, not as a nostalgic act of return to a supposedly better time, but as a way of situating ourselves vis-a-vis our current reality. In each of its five chapters, one author (through my reading), explores what it means to be human in the age of the natural sciences. That is, each explores what is embedded in our technology, in our institutions, in our discourses about the sciences, but also pushes back, although phrasing what it is that they push back against requires a good deal of care. They are quite different from each other, and their main task is to articulate the question of being human in their own inimitable way. Common to all of them is that, although all present arguments, it is mostly through the form or texture of their essays, novels, and poetry that the reality of what they want to defend comes through. It is as if the chief evidence for the singularity of the human lies in the voice of each, so distinct and so elusive. An argument can be refuted; a way of being leaves a mark long after the argument is forgotten.

This in no way precludes argument, and all of the authors included here do argue, but the form in which they do so is significant. The in-between the lines, the humor, the images, the peculiar repetitions that appear in the work of these authors may have the potential to reach what one of them called the area in which "reason and heart overlap,"[12] or what another referred to as "the thought at the back of the mind," a depth from which ideas emanate, which we are generally not fully aware of.[13] If that is the wager, it is not because reaching that spot beyond logic, yet generative of it, will somehow topple the view of the human being that the narratives around the natural sciences and the practices they have introduced into our daily lives have instilled. Rather, my aim is to provide some resources from which we can take nourishment and hope, if we think, as the authors

12. Espagnat, *On Physics and Philosophy*, 446.

13. Péguy, *Œuvres I*, 1415, 1416, 1420, Péguy, *Œuvres II*, 639. In both d'Espagnat and Péguy, I hear echoes of Blaise Pascal, who spoke of truths of the heart, the ones that precede reason, and from which reason takes its direction. These can be first principles, which we simply take for granted when we start to think, like time, number and space, see Pascal, *Pensées*, 28. Truths of the heart can also refer to engaging with others in ways that reason cannot establish or defeat, as in the case of love, Pascal, *Pensées*, 94. At other times, Pascal speaks of feelings, indistinguishable from the outside from fancy, but which operate not as passing moods but as points of orientation for reason, Pascal, *Pensées*, 188–9. References to Pascal will flit in and out of these five essays. Active as a scientist and mathematician in the seventeenth century, he already recognized that a defense of another way of knowing than that proclaimed by scientific reason was in order.

included here do, at least in my interpretation of them, that the vision of the human we inherit from the sciences leaves something essential out, an oversight that exerts a potentially enormous price.

Before I present the five authors in this study, I need to make clear that I am not interpreting them as an expert, as a master of the vast literature already extant about most of them, which would make me a conversation partner in a circle of other masters. This is a worthy task but it is not mine. I have a question that these authors help me to articulate, each in his or her quite particular way. This question is also theirs, but not to the exclusion of other ones, given the richness of their works. If my readings respond to my particular, and peculiar question, this by no means precludes the aspiration to rigor in the interpretations that follow. Close reading, the method I follow, is not just a matter of paying attention to myriad details. Done well, it also highlights possible contradictions, all that does not go in the same direction, all that begs the question. In presenting counter-readings to my own I have included secondary literature on these authors, sometimes present in the body of my text and sometimes in the footnotes. Still, if the topic under investigation is the particularity of the human, the defense of our opacity, the form has to match the content. I do not hide my own reactions, which change as my readings change. Those reactions do not depend on secondary readings.

Who are these five authors? They are, in the order in which they appear in the book, Charles Péguy (1873–1914), French poet, philosopher and essayist; Don DeLillo (1936–), American novelist, short story writer and playwright; Bernard d'Espagnat (1921–2015), French theoretical physicist and philosopher; Wysława Szymborska (1923–2012), Polish poet and essayist; Marilynne Robinson (1943–), American novelist and essayist. Much could be said about each. They are well-known, although in very different circles. I will not give much background about them here, both because some details will become available in the chapters devoted to each, but also because their biography is not as essential to understanding them as their works in themselves. The works I have chosen to interpret were written in the first two decades of the twenty-first century, with the exception of Péguy's, whose writings date to the first decade of the twentieth. Having to make an exception for one or the other is the rule here. They do not easily fit under one rubric. For example, four of these authors are literary figures,[14] but d'Espagnat

14. Péguy and Robinson are also essayists of note. Szymborska, in addition, was known for her weekly quirky book reviews of popular science and how-to books. See

emphatically is not. Three of them oppose some aspect of the narratives around the natural sciences directly, a claim difficult to make for either DeLillo or Szymborska, whose ways of engaging with the natural sciences or the world they have created are not through direct confrontation at all. None of them brings in a religious tradition, Christianity, for instance, as part of their push back against the sciences, with the exception of Robinson. The list could go on, with one or the other author not fitting the proposed category at all.

Despite all these differences, as already indicated, all five grapple with the images of the human wafting over to us from the natural sciences. As a result, similar threads, reflective of their stance, weave their way through my interpretations—the significance of metaphor, for instance; a vein of humor essential to the point the author is making; a reference to transcendence and intuition, as if the authors, who are not indebted to each other intellectually, were echoing each other. To understand the nature of these echoes, it might be useful to refer to Péguy's notion of *recoupement*. He coined the term to mean the unexpected discovery of a phenomenon one had bumped into previously, while investigating an entirely different subject. In his case, for instance, he finds the urge to replace the organic with the inorganic not only when he investigates new building materials but also in his investigation of the humanities' new emphasis on the material causes for human creativity, supposedly a prelude to duplicating it artificially. This appearance of a family resemblance is not the result of any planning. It is a testimony to what all of the authors suggest either directly or indirectly. Everything, at least in a given time period, is interrelated. Eventually, if one pursues one's investigations at sufficient depth into one area, one will discover something that illuminates other areas of it. I am proposing the five works interpreted here as manifestations of the same underlying dense interconnected reality we call our modern world, the world in which the natural sciences hold sway. The authors echo each other in that they each illuminate something central to it. That something central and yet elusive is reflected in what I have called, after Péguy, "the thought at the back of the mind."

Szymborska, *Wszystkie lektury nadobowiązkowe*. For an English translation of a selection of them, see Szymborska, *Non-required Reading*. DeLillo is the one with the fewest writings outside his literary productions but even he has written a few essays. See, for example, Don DeLillo, "In the Ruins of History," *Harper's*, 33–41, written in the aftermath of September 11, 2001.

"Echo" might be the wrong metaphor, however, because the common central point is embedded in quite different events. If one is thinking about the promise of immortality through the advances of the sciences, as DeLillo does in his novel *Zero K,* the light shed on our current reality will be different from the one revealed by the gap between modern physics and "materialism," as d'Espagnat illustrates it in his huge tome, *On Physics and Philosophy*. Quite different chunks of the sciences' influence will come to our attention if one explores the groundlessness of ethics or of consciousness, as Szymborska does in so many of her poems. This, in turn, is at quite a remove from the way a person shaped by the Calvinist tradition encounters modern physics, as Robinson does directly in her essays, and indirectly in her novel *Gilead*. Not only does each author bring to the surface different slices of the natural sciences and the different ways they have of shaping our reality but also the personality of each writer colors the very formulation of the question of being human in these circumstances. I leave it to the individual chapters that follow to illustrate those differences, but, ahead of the game, I would suggest that none presents a fully-fledged counter-narrative to the "materialism" associated with the sciences. It can only be a matter of glimpses into something that eludes the sciences' practices. I am claiming, then, that these five authors offer us a multi-faceted view into our contemporary reality.

This book is simultaneously a foray into a religious sensibility forged in response to the natural sciences. To raise the issue of religion immediately lands us in many difficulties. One would be hard-pressed to know what the word "religion" means, for example, when the authors represented here do not affiliate themselves, at least in these works, with any tradition, except for Robinson.[15] Nor could any of them be considered "spiritual," as in our current popular distinction of "spiritual but not religious." At stake in their work is not an opposition between individual seeking and established traditions. As if this were not enough of a complication, at least two of our authors, Péguy and DeLillo, understand as religious the authority the sciences have gained to shape our daily life. Which is it then? Is the religious sensibility to which these authors give us access "the religion of science" or is it the refusal of that religion?

15. Péguy is known as a Catholic thinker, but he had left the tradition in his youth, returning to it only around 1907 or 1908. Most of the essays I interpret in this volume precede this return. It may very well be that these essays were preparatory to it, but they do not speak in a Christian language and cannot be seen as confessional texts.

The French philosopher and historian Michel de Certeau might be helpful here. In distinguishing what it meant to be a mystic before the sixteenth century from what it meant afterward, he suggested that in the earlier era, the mystic was the one who lived at a profound level the common realities of his or her culture, as expressed in texts, rituals and oral traditions. He or she was the living embodiment of what everyone else also accepted but could neither experience nor express at that depth. In later times, as Christianity increasingly receded from the public sphere, the mystic was seen as the outsider, the unusual and exotic figure, whose experience manifested itself in somatic signs making it difficult to distinguish it from illness. But even so, these somatic signs were not the significant issue. Rather, it was the new disparity between the mystic and the common world of assumptions of the time.[16] The five authors in this book seem to me "mystics" in the pre-sixteenth-century sense. That is, the imagery of the natural sciences has penetrated them, but in a way that profoundly unsettles them as, I believe, is also the case for most of us. The five authors, through their varying expressions, attest both to the authority of the natural sciences to define us, and to the struggle with that authority.

In that struggle two notions of transcendence vie with each other. On the one hand, we want to transcend our limits as humans, which involves dismissing our particularity. We create objects that duplicate our most intimate features, or appear to. We invest in anti-aging research at the (not so far) end of which is the dream of immortality, which in the case of cryonics involves dissolving us into myriad bits, denying us an ineffable essence. We measure our lives by algorithms and statistical averages. On the other hand, we cling to the transcendence that comes only from our limits and our particularity, insisting on its irreproducibility, and impenetrability to an external gaze. This is evident in the very writing of books like the ones interpreted here, for instance, or, even more so, in the proliferation of memoirs; in our unease, expressed in legal and political action, with a world creeping to total digital surveillance, and in many other ways. The desire to transcend our particularity, institutionalized in big science and, increasingly in the educational system that prepares for it, and institutionalized in both our existing devices and in the time and space they create, is threatening to eclipse the desire to cling to our particularity, still institutionalized

16. Certeau, *Le Lieu de l'Autre*, 325–34.

in some of our cultural productions and in parts of our educational and political system. The perceived threat to our particularity is itself part of our sensibility, as evidenced by our five authors.

Phrasing matters in this way immediately calls to mind the Enlightenment/Romanticism split in our culture. Romanticism, as is well known, is an umbrella term for a wealth of related phenomena, but regardless of whether one or the other of the five authors can fit comfortably within any of its manifestations, it is often used today as a label dismissing one's position as old-fashioned or untenable. The sciences have so thoroughly shaped our understanding of how truth is discerned that anyone wishing to suggest that other modes of knowing exist is immediately accused of sentimentalism or obscurantism. The five authors, in my reading, would in this context be resisting the cold objectivity of the sciences, in the name of a mystifying subjectivity. I do not think it is helpful to see these authors as Romantics if by the term is meant simple oppositions such as feelings vs. reason, or subjectivity vs. objectivity, or the organic vs. the mechanical. It would be to distort their work considerably. I also do not want to get into the business of providing counter-labels. One should read their works, outside any labels, and see how they present their questions. If, however, the term Romanticism is seen as an umbrella term for all those thinkers in the modern world who opposed the exclusive authority of the natural sciences to define the human—which would include Husserl and Heidegger, among others, as a philosopher of science recently did[17]—then unquestionably this book, and the five authors it showcases, are squarely on the Romantic side of the Romantic/Enlightenment debate at the heart of our culture.

As the author of the five interpretative essays that follow, I am perhaps most subject to the accusation of being a Romantic. Nothing reveals my true colors as much as the fact that I am making a huge claim—about religion in the modern world, no less. Surely, this is the kind of speculation discouraged by a proper concern for data. And this is precisely what seems to be missing. I am making this claim on the basis of five authors. In the age of huge quantitative studies, a sample of five is ludicrous. My premise, however, is that, as d'Espagnat, the theoretical physicist, suggested, the most important things can only be "grasped," that is, known in a way different from the logic necessary in science, but known

17. Tauber, *Science*, 167.

nonetheless.[18] They are certainly not quantifiable, and do not even appear without the training of an interpreter. That training involves developing an eye for the significant detail, choosing it as symbolic of a larger whole. I am using the word "symbol" in the sense that Péguy gave it, a slice of reality that reproduces the web of meanings of the larger reality of which it is a part. Art, that is, skillful choice, is required to bring out this relationship between the part and the whole.[19] I have chosen each of these authors because their works, from very different angles, reveal a pattern or a conflict that captures our reality. In turn when I interpreted these texts, I chose certain passages, or a metaphor, a repetition, a word choice as indicative of the work as a whole. A symbol in this sense is a part in which a whole is embedded. Five is not a magic number, but at least it suggests the variety within unity that I am aiming to uncover.

Why these five? They happen to have fallen across my path in the course of my life as a scholar, teacher and reader. I have read many books, of course, and completely concur that my choice has an element of the arbitrary in it. I could have included others, even many others. But I have not chosen blindly. These texts are of high literary quality, in four of the cases, and of high analytic quality, in one. This is not my own judgment exclusively. Three of these authors—DeLillo, Szymborska and Robinson—have been showered with the highest literary awards, including, for Szymborska, the Nobel Prize in Literature.[20] Péguy, little feted as an independent artist in his own day, is now considered one of France's great poets, and his prose style, often dismissed in his own time, has also been drawing admiration and reflection. Although parts of his writings are tedious, others are indistinguishable from poetry, in rhythm, condensation and word choice. D'Espagnat is a recognized theoretical physicist, but also the winner of the Templeton prize for his philosophical reflections. Independently of the titles and honors bestowed on their authors, their works impressed me by their density and elusiveness. They cannot be summarized, only interpreted. An interpretation aims not to be a final word but to start a discussion in which its way of addressing a central question is taken seriously. At its best, it is an engaged search for what illuminates our situation as human beings in our very fragile world.

18. Espagnat, *On Physics and Philosophy*, 384.

19. Péguy, *Œuvres I*, 1435, 1449. Péguy, *Œuvres III*, 1151.

20. DeLillo has been the recipient of the National Book Award, and the Jerusalem Prize, among other honors. Robinson, among her other awards, has won the Pulitzer Prize for Fiction and the National Humanities Award.

It might already have become clear that of the five authors helping me formulate my question, Péguy stands out. He is the one with whom I have spent the longest time, starting forty years ago with my dissertation, and continuing sporadically throughout my career. He is, in my judgment, a very keen analyst of what he called "the modern world," although what I touch upon in the essays I examine here, while central to his thought, does not include some other aspects of his critique, his critique of capitalism, for example. Many of the terms he coined became useful lenses in my interpretation of the other authors, and in trying to seize the question driving this inquiry. Among such terms, I have already drawn attention to the term *recoupement* and "symbol" but the title of this study also comes from him, "the thought at the back of the mind." I explain it more fully in the chapter devoted to Péguy, the first of the five. The term takes as its core assumption that reasoning does not start from itself but from the commonly-accepted metaphysical commitments of a given time period, which never fully reveal themselves, even if thinkers spend a lifetime peeling away at some of their layers. When and if they, and we in turn, do catch a glimpse, it is only a glimpse, leaving many other dimensions or manifestations of it in our world unexplored.

I do not pretend in this book to have done anything more than hint at some aspect of this "thought at the back of the mind," a name indicating that which is barely, if at all, within our reach.[21] Following Péguy and some of the other authors in this volume, I have labelled this hidden recess within modern thinking the religion of science. I want to emphasize from the outset that "the thought at the back of the mind" is the very opposite of an ideology, understood as an explicitly acknowledged commitment or stance, usually articulated in contrast to available alternatives, and often associated with the identity of a group. This book is not interested in ideology but in a set of assumptions concealed, at least in part, from those in whom they live. I mean to point to this secret center at two levels. In the first place, in each chapter, I search for that which is buried in the texture of a given author's work, in the way its details and tone and rhythm convey its central organizing principle. In the second place, I aim to catch a glimpse, through these texts, of our multidimensional response to the authority of the natural sciences. The quite disparate, at times

21. Péguy's French original—la pensée *de derrière* la tête—emphasizes this unreachability more than the English idiom, "the thought at the back of the mind." The expression literally means the thought *from behind* the head, as if it is not even in the usual location, in the space reserved for thinking, but outside somewhere.

incongruous manifestations of "the thought at the back of the mind" are also what differentiate it from ideology.

In making Péguy more than just one of the five, but a guide in the exploration of the other four, I do not in the least mean to diminish the original contributions of DeLillo, d'Espagnat, Szymborska and Robinson. None repeats what Péguy says. They illuminate a topic he may have brought to light but quite differently from him. Part of the difference lies in the highly particular personalities involved here, and the particular chunks of the world to which they have been most exposed. But part of the difference inevitably stems from the fact that Péguy lived and wrote a full century earlier. Those hundred years do not count in some ways and do count in others. On the one hand, we see from the many echoes between his writings and that of the others that we are still living in the same historical period, if viewed from the point of view of the authority of the natural sciences. The fact that the positivism Péguy was both exploring and resisting is no longer in vogue does not mean that the image of the sciences as the royal, not to say exclusive, path to knowledge about ourselves and the world at large has diminished. Including Péguy in this study thus permits us to see the problem as preceding, and by a long shot, the current scientific breakthroughs. Dismissing any knowledge not obtained through the scientific method does not start with his own era either, as he is at pains to point out, in his analyses of mid-nineteenth-century thinkers, and their predecessors. On the other hand, our particular placement in the first three decades of the twenty-first century requires analysis of phenomena that Péguy could not have imagined. I have tried at the beginning and end of each chapter to signal both its starting point in Péguy's questions as well as the divergences from his way of responding to them. Each essay stands independently as well, and can be related not only to Péguy but to any of the other authors. Each author, I can only emphasize again, is a full-fledged thinker in his or her own right. I have left the discovery of the echoes between them to the reader.

In taking my inspiration from a master thinker whose work is irreducible to a thesis; in my close reading of texts, as if everything depended on the texture in which ideas are expressed; in affirming the particularity of each author, as if context, although important, is not sufficient, I am unabashedly defending a certain practice of the humanities. Along with conveying whatever these five artists and/or thinkers have to tell us about our world, this book aims to adumbrate the metaphysical assumptions about self and cosmos that undergird the status of the humanities as conveyors of an irreplaceable knowledge about reality. The five authors I interpret here may open a path to a renewed formulation of these assumptions, or, if that is too much to ask, at least to a new, invigorating look at our predicament.

Context

It is customary to place one's work in a broader context of thinkers addressing the same issue. This would lead me to utter despair since the effect of the natural sciences on our sense of who we are as humans has been at the center of so many works. But, true to my understanding of *recoupement,* of echoes that appear in unexpected places because the underlying reality the works reflect is the same, I would like to point to two contemporary authors who do not speak about the natural sciences at all, or at least do not situate their work in a struggle with them. *Recoupement* is always a bit of a surprise. The first author is the journalist Rachel Aviv, who in her book, *Strangers to Ourselves,* reflects, on the basis of five case studies, about the elusiveness of mental illness. The second is the historian Sarah Shortall, who in her book, *Soldiers of God in a Secular World,* speaks about the theological categories deployed and articulated by a group of twentieth-century French Catholic theologians, whose innovations became known as "la nouvelle théologie."

The *recoupement* between this book and Aviv's lies in the emphasis on the particularity of each person whose story she tells, *a particularity unexplained.* She repeats throughout her book that our narratives about mental health, whether they stress biology and proffer drugs or whether they stress "insight" and proffer talk therapy, too easily place a mentally ill person in a pre-established category, without paying attention to what does not fit that category. The five people with mental illness at the center of her book, to each of whom she devotes a chapter, had a story to tell that was unclassifiable, and when, in some cases, they did accept the classification given to them, it became a kind of substitute for their own immediate experience to which they ceased having access.[22] Aviv admires Roland Kuhn, a Swiss psychiatrist, who, in the mid-twentieth century, was part of the phenomenological school of psychiatry, "that aimed to study the experience of mental illness on its own terms—without the

22. Aviv, *Strangers,* 184, 186.

interference of preexisting theories."[23] "'Only when this happens,' Kuhn wrote, can there be 'a true relationship between patient and physician, a relationship between two human beings.'"[24] It was crucial, in his mind, that a person's reality find expression in an exchange not determined by a prior grid of therapeutic terms.

Consonant with her accent on particularity, Aviv interweaves her own self throughout her book. She spells out that her question emerges not from the documents alone but from her history. She had stopped eating for two weeks when she was six. The many possible explanations she finds for her childhood behavior, shifting as she reads more, along with her own memories of that time, never comfortably coincide with the label of anorexia that she was given once hospitalized. The label and her singularity do not coincide. Of course, it is not only her childhood experience that accounts for her stress on particularity. It also intersects with her readings. She names William James's "unclassified residuum," that which fails to fit a closed and completed system of truth,[25] early on, and it clearly influences her desire to find the particular that does not correspond to the current system or systems of understanding mental illness.

The source of one's particular question and one's particular method for approaching it is never a simple matter to locate. I am sure that in my case being the child of parents who had lived through the Second World War intersected with my choice of intellectual influences. My teacher, Kees Bolle, who had been an adolescent during the war in Holland, had the atrocities of those events firmly lodged in his approach to the study of religion. Far from a neutral exercise, the study of religion was meant to illuminate our world, catching again and again the image of the human in it. He stressed that as historians of religions, to do justice to any other time period required simultaneously becoming aware of our own reigning hidden assumptions about "real reality." I inherited from him, among many other points of method, the willingness and even the responsibility to ask big questions. I have also spent much time as a reader and interpreter of the French philosopher, Emmanuel Levinas. As is well known, he devoted his philosophy to the defense of the particularity of the other person, the responsibility for whom establishes my own irreplaceable "I. " Not the least

23. Aviv, *Strangers*, 46.

24. Aviv, *Strangers*, 46. Kuhn's phenomenological approach did not exclude treatment through drugs. In fact, he experimented with various drug treatments.

25. Aviv, *Strangers*, 25

of his influence on me was his hermeneutic, his method of interpreting Talmudic texts, about which I have written elsewhere.[26]

In Sarah Shortall's masterful study of Henri de Lubac and fellow Jesuit and Dominican theologians who came of age after the separation of Church and State in France in 1905, I detect echoes of my preoccupations as well. I would like to call the point in common with her "nonideological thinking." She emphasizes that the central categories that these theologians used—Incarnation and the Kingdom of God, for instance—became lenses through which they came to see their role as Christians to be that of critics of the ambient culture.[27] Those terms, whose meanings come to light in contact with specific events, made them critics of whatever in the current political world posed a threat, on their reading, to furthering the personhood of every human being (Incarnation) or the brotherhood of mankind, (the Kingdom of God). The fluid meaning of these terms led these new theologians to quite disparate, sometimes contradictory political engagements. Some, for example, after the Second World War, made common cause with Communist Party activities among workers, others emphatically did not.[28] Shortall urges historians not to reduce religious ideas of the type she is engaged with here to political ideologies. They can function that way but they do not necessarily do so, and, in the case of her theologians, these ideas working in a multivalent and unpredictable way, defied party loyalties, even that to the empirical Church.[29]

Like Shortall's theologians, my authors' expressions cannot be understood on the basis of party interests vying for State power. When Péguy rails against the positivistic assumptions of the early twentieth-century French State, and the way its politicians control education, it is not because he would like to put the Catholic Church back in charge. His is a critique of a metaphysical overreach of the party in power, the imposition of a positivist worldview on all schools, hiding behind the authority of the natural sciences. Similarly, none of the authors presented here is in the "anti-science" camp. The works I have chosen to interpret neither advocate nor oppose a State policy regarding vaccines or global warming or some other issue. Their critique of the natural sciences, if critique is the right word, is directed at the narratives about the human

26. See, for instance, the two introductions to Levinas, *Nine Talmudic Readings*, ix–xxxiv; xxxvii–lxxxi.

27. Shortall, *Soldiers*, 7, 144, 168.

28. Shortall, *Soldiers*, 8, 51.

29. *Shortall, Soldiers*, 7, 139–41.

or about the reality that emanate from them, not at this or that scientific finding. It is not even directed against the so-called scientific method, just against its application to areas in which it does not belong.

In a way that crisscrosses with my own, Shortall's work also scrambles the line between secular and religious. "[S]ecular and religious thought have never been as separate as we might expect," she concludes her opus.[30] She means by this that these theologians' ideas were not in a silo, but in constant interaction with secular philosophies, each borrowing from the other.[31] They were brought "into dialogue with a range of interlocutors, from Jean-Paul Sartre and Maurice Merleau-Ponty to Martin Heidegger and Alexandre Kojève . . . and *both* theology and secular philosophy were reshaped in the process."[32] Given this, Shortall wants theology to be taken as part and parcel of the historical fabric, and not studied separately or, as often happens, ignored. The historian studying religious phenomena should thus perform "a certain, critical, disruptive function in relation to the ideological secularism that so often underwrites the categories of historical analysis."[33]

It might be difficult to detect *recoupement* with my own work here. After all, I do not argue for the importance of theology and my work does not involve, again with the exception of Robinson, authors confessing Christianity. I do, however, scramble the distinction between secular and religious by placing someone like Robinson side by side with someone like DeLillo, who shies away from any specific religious allegiance, or at least who articulates none through his main characters. We all live in the same world, which makes it possible to set a scientist like d'Espagnat, who suggests the existence of a Veiled Reality on the basis of the implications of quantum physics, next to Szymborska, the poet who has no truck with such notions, and yet whose encounters with quantum physics lead her to articulate a transcendence of her own. Only an ingrained secularism, itself with a complicated history, would make us want to put them into a secular vs. religious camp.

Undeniably, this book differs from Shortall's in that I do not provide an elaborate context for the five authors interpreted here. In fact, she

30. *Shortall, Soldiers*, 258.

31. *Shortall, Soldiers*, 2.

32. Shortall, *Soldiers*, 10.

33. Shortall, "Lost in Translation," 285; She expresses a similar thought in Shortall, *Soldiers*, 258.

insists on two contexts and the dialectic between them.[34] The first is the historical period in which her theologians were living: changes in seminary education, the rise of various social and political movements, the Second World War and beyond, all with an eye to her theologians' participation and reactions. Of equal relevance is the second context, the long textual tradition from which these theologians drew, both the Church Fathers and Thomas Aquinas. I provide neither kind of context, that is, neither the social and political context in which the authors were writing, nor the longer textual tradition of which they are a part.

Part of the difference lies in the fact that I am much more of an essayist and text commentator than a historian in the vein that Shortall illustrates. But the choice of method goes beyond personal proclivities. In my view, the five authors in this study are consciously writing within a certain historical moment, which they bring to light. They may, in fact, do more to illuminate it than political or intellectual history might do alone, although, to be sure, interpreting their work does involve awareness of the concrete events to which they are reacting. Don DeLillo, for instance, was not writing in a void, but in a world in which billionaires' quest for immortality through science/technology and the huge amount of research being done on anti-aging in prestigious institutions is very much a reality. I supply some information on that political and economic context. It is DeLillo, however, who makes us think about this context as a context to begin with.

But if I do not consistently refer to political or social events external to the texts, this by no means signals a refusal of context as such. It is merely that the context I choose to underscore in each author is the authority of the natural sciences. That is what they are responding to, that is what forms them, and *that is what they make visible to us in a way we would not see otherwise.* If one is a historian of religions, as I am, this broader frame is the relevant background against which we situate ourselves, "the thought at the back of the mind" we have in common. To point to "the thought at the back of the mind" is simultaneously to underscore the wealth of expressions emanating from it.

In contrast to Shortall's contextualization, nothing in my interpretation of these authors, with the exception of Robinson, resembles a return to foundational religious sources. If I have not placed a great deal of emphasis on tracing the authors' genealogy, it is because I want to suggest

34. Shortall, *Soldiers*, 11.

that in the case of four of these authors, they are homeless in this respect, that is, no longer in direct contact with the religious imagery of a particular tradition, or, at best, with an oblique contact to it. This is precisely the context of interest. Many of us have become homeless in that specific sense as well. These authors are of interest, though, because, while homeless, the central concern of each—the particularity and irreducibility of the human, the sheer inexhaustibility of the real, as it reveals itself in daily life—can find echoes in traditional religious texts, and probably, through indirect and unintended routes, can be traced back to them. The inverse is also true. That is, the themes evoked by these writers can help renew and invigorate classical religious texts.

Regardless of whether these five authors' emphases can be traced back to traditional religious texts, the problems they raise, as already mentioned, transcend the religious/secular divide. The images emanating from the natural sciences seep into our daily life, no matter whether we are Christian, Buddhist, Muslim, Jewish or call ourselves secular. The objects around us and the discourse surrounding them challenge our status as humans, whether we profess a particular religion or not. Neither our dreams of wellbeing nor our fears of apocalypse can be separated from the natural sciences, regardless of affiliation. We live in a time measured by scientific devices and operate in a space defined by images coming from those devices. Whether we want to or not, they shape our inner life, a term itself suspect in today's discourse about the human.

More on the Religious/Secular Divide

This project had originally started, about a decade ago, with a work of Czesław Miłosz, the great Polish poet and essayist. I do not include *The Land of Ulro* here, although Miłosz does play a significant role in my chapter on Szymborska. It may seem an inadmissible omission, since what he, following William Blake from whom the term "the Land of Ulro" originates, describes in that book is very close to what I describe as the situation we find ourselves in. We are imprisoned, he says, in a view of ourselves that makes it practically impossible to defend our particularity as humans, even if we still feel impelled to rise in its defense. For him, the paradigmatic figure who expresses our plight is Dostoevsky. His heroes "are inhabitants of the Infernal City, the land of the disinherited, in which all are reduced to specters, to phantoms of the abstract intellect . . . and Dostoyevsky, internally riven, corrupted by the 'scientific world-view', wages a desperate war."[35] But the tonality of Miłosz and the tonality of my five authors, as much as they vary from each other, do not match. The authors in this volume do not exhibit despair, and remain surprisingly feisty, even if they acknowledge that their feistiness will not by itself defeat the dominance of a certain view of the human. Perhaps a description of DeLillo's work characterizes them all: "pessimism of the intellect but optimism of the spirit."[36]

I, the interpreter of these five authors, also differ from Miłosz. He draws too solid a line between secular and religious, seeing modernity mainly as a departure from Christianity, a departure he bemoans. He turns exclusively to Christian authors, even if their theology is heterodox, in his search for a viable alternative. I, on the other hand, do not take the line between religious and secular very seriously in regard to the question at hand. It might very well be so-called secular thinkers and writers that will help us, a group he tends to dismiss *en masse*.[37] In terms of the problem delineated here—the authority of the natural sciences to define the human—good formulations and good resistance do not lie in a particular camp, in a particular vocabulary or in particular institutions.

One might reply that all the authors in this volume are of Christian provenance, even if their works are not oriented by Christian teachings. That is true. But no one is secular in a void. The term, if it means to delineate a historical phenomenon, and not the end of history, always means something in relation to a specific tradition. In our historical moment, the term secular strongly denotes a departure from an otherworldly transcendence, an entity beyond nature, or a world that awaits beyond this one, associated with Christianity. In this sense, these authors are secular. This does not mean, however, that transcendence—understood as a relationship to what is other par excellence, that which cannot be assimilated to our concepts—disappears, even if it no longer wears its name. These authors allow me to draw attention to the transcendence emanating from

35. Milosz, *Land of Ulro*, 123–4.

36. Duvall, "Introduction," 4.

37. Milosz, *Land of Ulro*, 157. "In the literature of the mid-to late-twentieth century, no one would presume to challenge the laws of physics, biology, psychology, sociology, and so on; they are flatly taken for granted . . . Granted literature serves not only as a tool of cognition; but to surrender one's awareness in advance, to regard the disease as not a disease, is to assent to one's own decadence."

the natural sciences, as well as the groping for transcendence of another kind, glimpsed in the most ordinary of activities.

Even if this work reveals mostly a Christian/post-Christian problem, to some degree it has been exported everywhere, given the global nature of the reach of the narratives about the natural sciences, and the global transformation of daily life it has engendered. This does not mean that the terms of the discussion are always the same. If I were to phrase the significance of these five authors, I would simply say that they help us to see. That is, they give us a way of noticing and responding not only to the phenomena they themselves discuss but to others that they have not. This includes noticing forms of articulation and resistance which stem from other secularizing processes.

Conclusion

I would like, in lieu of a summary, to end with a short story I read recently, as if only the multiple meanings embedded in works of fiction or poetry can do justice to the self's elusiveness, opacity or transcendence—my heavy and clumsy expressions—to which the five authors in this volume have hinted. It will involve a detour through a veterinary clinic, only to come back to the central point about the human at the end.

Rivka Galchen's "How I Became a Vet" is about a veterinarian, a young woman, quite peculiar, or "weird," as she puts it.[38] She describes herself as someone who has spent her life alone, growing up on an isolated farm with her father, and continuing to live in a world of her own beyond that. Her peculiarity did not prevent her from jumping through all the hoops required to become a veterinarian, no small feat. In the story she tells, the manager of the emergency animal clinic in which she has worked for twelve years has just told her that she needs to go for a two-week retraining, with no guarantee that she will have her job back upon completion. She had reached the magic number: twelve negative reviews, defined as a numerical score of three or below. These reviews come from distraught or irate owners, unable to accept a difficult diagnosis about their pets. The protagonist of our story loves animals, has been around them all her life, and is quite gifted in putting them at ease, facilitating treatment. But the animals are not the ones who write reviews. The manager, in making his

38. Galchen, "How I Became a Vet," 57.

decision, takes neither of these factors into account. It is difficult even to call it a decision. The numbers have spoken.

I should be embarrassed to pick this incident out as particularly significant for our reflections about the authority of the natural sciences. How heavy-handed and tendentious. Numerical evaluations have to do with business practices and not with scientific research, except, of course, for the pale imitation of objectivity involved in this kind of quantification, an image we do inherit from the sciences, through no fault of their own. These derivative images are always at once independent of the day-to-day work of natural scientists and yet bear the authority derived from their practices. That is their mode, floating free of the sciences and yet attached to them. When I described the authority of the sciences earlier as embedded in our daily life, it is to these kinds of phenomena I alluded, the inoffensive quantitative evaluation one among many.

We remain far from the natural sciences again in the rest of the story, if intuition as a mode of knowing is left out of the scientific method. The protagonist, after her dismissal, decides to investigate a mystery that has intrigued her profoundly. At the clinic she had treated three dogs in a row, who had jumped out of their respective owners' car at exactly the same spot, near a bridge. After her dismissal, she goes to the site and tries to guess what might have made the dogs behave so uncharacteristically. It takes some doing, placing herself in the same position as the dogs, for instance, which requires that she climb down a muddy slope, attempting to enhance her awareness of smell. She suddenly understands the reason. A family of minks had made their home in the mud below the bridge. The dogs were driven out of their minds by their scent.

Discovering the reason for the dogs' leaps leads her to an epiphany she describes in the last dense paragraphs of the story. Two expressions taken from her father's Anabaptist teachings become key. The dogs, she hears her father saying in her mind, committed an error of the heart, driven to their injuries by the scent of love.[39] Humor makes its appearance, since one hardly thinks of dogs unceremoniously pursuing their instinctual responses to smell as subject to Christian categories, either love or error as opposed to sin. It is part of her "weirdness," perhaps, that for her these categories are broad enough to understand the dogs, to make room for them. She is overjoyed to discover that they were not suicidal, as some in the clinic had speculated. They had been moved

39. Galchen, "How I Became a Vet," 61.

by desire. Perhaps this has something to do with the second expression she uses, a teaching her father enjoined on her, the duty of joy. He had taught her, she says, that joy is the only proper response to receiving the gift of life. Sometimes it misfires, as in the case of the jumping dogs, thus the expression "error of the heart."

I would like to see in this story two types of illogic, the illogic of the quantification system and the illogic of the heart. We may not always see the illogic of the former. Quantified reviews of performance are ubiquitous. They have become a natural part of doing business, in the order of things. Some of us might still shrug or get impatient, but we know we can do nothing about it, and, just maybe, the numbers have some merit. After all, a business serves at the pleasure of its customers. The protagonist, from her own description, does not have the soothing manner required with distraught clients or does not know how to deflect their anger. Improvement of her performance on the job rests on just such client reports, we are told.

Lost in that sensible reasoning is the fact that there is absolutely nothing rational about those numbers. They came into being, to give one example in the story, because a pet owner takes offense that his parrot has been diagnosed with a disease caused by sexual contact. "'The bird had no bird lover; it was a solo bird,'" the owner insists, even though the protagonist tries to explain to him, to no avail, that the particular kind of chlamydia involved here is a different strain altogether.[40] There is nothing rational either about the manager's decision to dismiss the protagonist. Would someone with better social skills necessarily be as good as the protagonist at treating the dogs, cats and parrots in her charge? Why twelve? What is rational about that number? The arbitrariness makes one dizzy, but it is the illogical logic of our world. Errors of the heart are, of course, also not rational. They proceed from an urge, she calls it love, that we cannot control, or control badly. Her own urge to understand the dogs' behavior can be seen in this light. Her manager reprimands her for it.[41] It is enough to simply treat the contusions and broken bones. Anything else is a mere distraction. Why would she need to climb down a steep, muddy hill, driven by the urge to understand them? Yet her urge to understand gives her joy, and it involves, in the case of the "suicide dogs" using her intuition, based on years spent with dogs.

40. Galchen, "How I Became a Vet," 58.

41. Galchen, "How I Became a Vet," 60.

We live in a world in which both these illogics exist, the quantifying illogic and the illogic of the heart. In the world of the quantifying logic, she concludes, "We have to make our own rules and our own judgments, and not curse ourselves or others for the way we arrived in the world."[42] The story concludes with such a judgment. She now knows that she really is a veterinarian, on the basis of her new understanding of the duty of joy, and calls the minks as her witnesses. "Though I had been a veterinarian for many years, that was when I became in the eyes of the minks and myself, a true vet."[43] She is deriving her sense of herself and of what it means to be a vet in ways other than through the distortions of the evaluative survey.

Her phrasing nonetheless is definitely on the odd side. Calling the minks as her witnesses? Becoming a vet because of the duty of joy? We can go on interpreting what she means but what if we stopped at "odd" as at the center of it all? What is wrong with "odd?" It certainly is not, in this case, a refusal of order, or of reason. On the contrary. In a world so easily derailed by the error stemming from desire, she says, ". . . we need to build a higher railing on the bridge, or otherwise devise a way to spare these dogs from injury." Caught in a system of numerical evaluations based on a misreading of the word "chlamydia," if one manages to be odd and reasonable at once, it is a precious gift, even a source of joy. One has the duty to recognize this.

Even if we stick to this reading alone, so many matters call for further investigation. What are those religious terms doing there at the end? The protagonist had explicitly rejected her father's religion at an earlier point in her life. "I came to the conclusion that my father had made an error. It was the wrong time period to be an Anabaptist, I told him. The sect didn't make sense anymore, I said."[44] What does her return to these expressions mean? Is it significant that Galchen, the author, chose Anabaptism as the protagonist's father's religion? After all, it is a tradition that takes its distance toward the ambient culture, and resists it. Not to mention that even if we spend much more time interpreting the young woman's epiphany about the "suicide dogs, " it would not end what we could say about it. Her language does not allow us to rest comfortably in one reading.

42. Galchen, "How I Became a Vet," 61.

43. Galchen, "How I Became a Vet," 61.

44. Galchen, "How I Became a Vet," 57.

The five authors I interpret in this volume are odd in the sense described above, in the protagonist's vocabulary, "weird."[45] It is my hope that their weirdness propels us to epiphanies of our own. In a world hurtling toward containing us within the content spewed out by ChatGPT and its successors, we have no choice but to be weird or at least to take comfort from those who are. More is at stake than our splendid individuality. If we are lucky we get a glimpse, each time from another angle, of "the thought at the back of the mind."

45. In the podcast "The Culture Creating A.I. Is Weird," *New York Times*, May 2, 2023, Ezra Klein interviews the writer Erik Davis. Their use of the word "weird" inspired me to focus on this word in Galchen's story.

CHAPTER 1

Reason and Intuition in the Age of the Natural Sciences

Charles Péguy's Essays of 1904–9

Preface: Introducing Péguy

THE INFLUENTIAL FRENCH THINKER, Charles Péguy (1873–1914), whose meditations on the natural sciences will be the subject of this chapter, was in his lifetime primarily known as the editor of a bi-weekly literary and political review, *Les Cahiers de la Quinzaine.* In his role as editor, he solicited the work of others, but also frequently contributed his own commentaries on contemporary events. His training as a philosopher shaped his observations, many of which became famous, not only in France but in Europe. His refusal to fit into the ideological camps of his time made him into a controversial figure, and he has remained so to this day. Just to give one example, some contemporary scholars consider him a nationalist and a reactionary, while others praise his prescience, his keen understanding of the dangers of total centralized control, emerging decades before that phenomenon declared itself in its full colors.[1] Once one reads him, it is difficult to remain neutral about Péguy.

1. For a presentation of Péguy as the inspiration behind the French Resistance, see Bastaire, *Péguy contre Pétain.* Sarah Shortall, in her brief excursus on him in *Soldiers,* 94–96, presents him as proposing "a heady mixture of philosemitism, socialism,

Quite a few of his essays were not published in his lifetime. This is the case for most of the ones I will turn to here, written between 1904–9.[2] They are less well-known today than some of the other works published posthumously, perhaps because of their very subject matter: a critique of the status of the natural sciences in the modern world, a critique likely to puzzle, if not offend many readers. Péguy objected primarily to the use of the scientific method within the humanities, specifically within the study of history and sociology. No one better than Péguy, in my estimation, can show us that what one reads, how one reads, and whether one reads are all keys to the tensions and cracks within an entire world. But he did not stop at the appropriation of the scientific method in the humanities. Rethinking the humanities requires rethinking the inherent limits of the natural sciences themselves.

Péguy is certainly not the only critic of the hegemony of the natural sciences. Famous names, Martin Heidegger, Jacques Ellul, Hans Jonas, Lewis Mumford, to name just a few, immediately come to mind.[3] One would have to place at their head Henri Bergson, who, unlike the others who wrote after Péguy's death, had an enormous influence on his thought.[4] Were all these authors merely repeating each other's points, there would,

nationalism, and antimodernism," which, although inspiring both Vichy and the Resistance, she goes on to cite mainly as a source for those who supported Vichy. Maguire, on the other hand, in *Carnal Spirit* presents Péguy as a very careful thinker, who saw, very early, the problems plaguing us today. Maguire names the many people in many different traditions of thought that see in Péguy a rampart against the worst tendencies of the modern world.

2. These essays were published from 1953–5. In a more complete edition, they appeared only in 1988. In a sense, the cut-off between these essays and earlier and later ones is artificial. Already in an essay written before "Zangwill" but also from 1904, "Pour la rentrée," Péguy speaks, even if very briefly, of the cult of Science, Péguy, *Œuvres I*, 1391, but I would maintain, the style associated with Péguy really begins with "Zangwill," the first essay of the ones we examine here. In his essays after 1909, many themes treated here come back. In the earlier essays discussed in this chapter, however, the status of the natural sciences remained the central topic. In the later essays, Péguy's critique shifts increasingly to capitalism, closely allied with the rise in status of the sciences, as even these essays indicate. His later essays also dwell on Christianity, which gets hardly any development here.

3. One could claim that technology rather than the sciences themselves becomes the targets of these thinkers' inquiry. Since modern science is both the source of technology and impossible without the instruments provided by technology, the two are difficult if not impossible to disentangle.

4. Péguy attended Bergson's lectures, knew him personally, and even placed his family in Bergson's care when he went off to the front. Bergson, in a letter to Péguy, even claimed that Péguy took him to places he had wanted to go himself but did not. See Robinet, *Péguy entre Jaurès, Bergson et L'Église*, 222.

of course, be no reason to read them all or to add Péguy to the list. Péguy's great contribution, maybe his greatest, is to show so insistently that the critique of the status of the natural sciences, of their authority, cannot be captured by an argument made correctly by this or that author, once and for all.[5] The power of the natural sciences is institutionalized in state and industry and embedded in the practices of daily life. Since these are endless and varied, what can be said about them is also endless and varied. Certain thinkers and artists capture this endlessness in one of its dimensions, making it possible for others to discover it in their own multiple ways. Péguy is one such artist and thinker.

Despite the relative obscurity of the essays of 1904–9, I am, of course, not the only one who has noticed their importance. Among others, the philosopher of science Isabelle Stengers has remarked upon their astonishing power to confront present-day issues.[6] Bruno Latour, anthropologist of science and philosopher, has argued that Péguy has gotten to the heart of our current globalized world, a century early.[7] Several contemporary American literary scholars have also commented on their relevance to today's debates and realities.[8] My own interpretation of Péguy is related to theirs. Like them, I think that he has put his finger on a key aspect of our modernity. Since I am a historian of religions, however, I am perhaps more interested than some in explicating that modernity as a religious phenomenon, a central aspect of Péguy's reflections on the natural sciences. I am also more concerned than some with the form of Péguy's essays as an essential conduit to his meaning, although Péguy's style has drawn a great deal of attention. That form, I argue, makes present a counter-religious meaning, a point I shall return to in the conclusion.

5. Péguy, *Œuvres III*, 1449–56, in which he argues against some Catholic opponents of Bergson who maintain that the problem of positivism is now solved.

6. See Stengers, "La thèse que Péguy n'a jamais écrite," 32–67. She is especially impressed with his discussion of competence, and the return to sources of knowledge other than the Western scientific one. See the discussion of competence below.

7. Latour, "Nous sommes des vaincus,"' 8–18, does not limit himself to these essays. He argues that Péguy has captured the notion of time that undergirds all aspects of the modern world. See also, Latour, "Charles Péguy: Time, Space and 'le Monde Moderne,"' 41–62. Schmidgen, "Materiality of Things," argues that Latour's own work in the anthropology and philosophy of science has been directly influenced by Péguy, whose essays were partly the subject of his doctoral thesis.

8. See, for example, Roe, *The Passion of Péguy;* Maguire, *Carnal Spirit*; Milbank, "Foreword," xi–xxxviii; Ward, "Introduction," 1–25.

Many of the essays of 1904–9 are unfinished, stopping short of the treatment that Péguy might have given them, had he wished to publish them. This should not deter readers from engaging with them. In the first place, although Péguy frequently reminds his readers that he is only at the very beginning of his inquiry, that he intends to pursue his themes further in the future,[9] he also comes to the realization that being at the beginning is simply where he will always be. "*Tout ce que je sais, c'est le commencement*," he says in a later essay.[10]

It is worth pausing here for a minute to reflect on what he means. In the first place, always to be at the beginning brings to mind what he calls the geological method, to which we shall return later in this essay. The geologist has to work layer by layer, discovering new dimensions in each investigation. For the researcher into the status of the natural sciences, each phenomenon reveals the whole in a new way. Secondly, being at the beginning means searching to formulate the right question, whose formulation shifts as the object of study changes.[11] Both these ways of staying at the beginning require a good deal of effort, undoing mental habits built over a long time. As a result, the basic frame of an inquiry cannot be acquired once and for all. How can one have such a static structure, in which everything can be made to fit, when, each new phenomenon forces one in a different direction? Being at the beginning is to recognize the necessity of starting over, or of digging ever deeper into the nature of the problem one is facing.

Despite the open-ended nature of these essays, that is, their changing topics and directions, they nonetheless cohere around certain themes. Many of these writings were intended as a preparation for a doctoral thesis Péguy planned to submit on the status of the "scientific method" in the disciplines of history and sociology.[12] In fact, the last of these essays is

9. Péguy, *Œuvres I*, 1449–50, Péguy, *Œuvres II*, 633, 640, 808, 831. For a description of the progress of the thesis, see Burac, "Notices, notes et variantes," in Péguy, *Œuvres II*, 1546–8. Despite years of work, Péguy never submitted it, turning to other writing instead.

10. Péguy, *Œuvres II*, 961.

11. Much later, in speaking about the works of Descartes and of Bergson, he says, "A great philosophy is not the one that resolves all questions once and for all but the one who poses them," Péguy, *Œuvres III*, 1269. All translations from the French are my own.

12. See also Burac's note introducing "Notes pour une thèse,"in Péguy, *Œuvres II*, 1546–8. One of the essays leading up to it is entitled "De la situation faîte à l'histoire et à la sociologie dans les temps modernes," (Of the status given to history and sociology in modern times), Péguy, *Œuvres II*, 481–518.

entitled "Notes pour une thèse," a most peculiar set of notes, but they cohere both internally and with the previous essays. Péguy's lack of a system bespeaks a willingness to stray from what appears to be the topic in question only to return to it from an unexpected side. This straying reminds one of Blaise Pascal's famous pensée, already noted, in which he speaks of the truths of the heart. Truths of the heart can only be expressed in digressions, each digression pointing to the central truth in its own way. What are the truths of the heart? Those not established by reason—first principles like time, space, number, and realities like love.

> The heart has its order, the mind has its own, which uses principles and demonstrations . . . This order [of the heart] consists mainly in digressions upon each point which relates to the end, so that this shall be kept always in sight.[13]

Taking my clue from Péguy, I do not pretend to do anything but remain at the beginning myself. From these writings, over an oceanic thousand pages in length, I wish to start out three times, each time exposing Péguy's method of analysis from another angle, related but also not continuous with the others. In the first foray, I will present him as making an explicit argument: *the natural sciences have gained the status of a religion*. But even here, at his most expository, digressions come to subvert the straight path of an argument, making it branch out in many directions, as if uncontainable in the frame of an argument to begin with. In the second foray, I will comment on the formal elements structuring these essays, indispensable to his argument, chief among them, his humor.[14] Much of it depends on the sudden interruption of what seems seamless and impersonal logic, but his humor cannot be reduced to that. In the third foray, I explore Péguy's understanding of intuition, his use of it indebted to Bergson's thought, which he contrasts with "the scientific method." Intuition, in these essays, is not only a topic to explore, but also a practice on display from the beginning.

All three of these sections explore Péguy's understanding of human reason, its proper deployment and its limits. To put it another way, the three forays together point to his emphasis on the recalcitrant nature of reality, that is, its refusal to fit our instruments and concepts, Yet, this

13. Pascal, *Pensées*, 94.

14. Péguy's humor has been noted by many of his readers. See Burac, *Sourire d'Hypathie*, in which the author divides Péguy's humor according to genres; Labouret, "Humour," 160–163.

reality, always slipping through our fingers, is most intimate to us. Immediate access to it, Péguy argues, is what defines the human. "Metaphysics also is of the human being and of humanity. And it is even undoubtedly what makes them themselves."[15] To forget this, he claims, is both comical and dangerous. Illustrating this central point, which does not sit easily within a thesis, will be the task of this chapter.

Part 1: The Argument

Science as Religion

Occasionally, in his voluminous writings of this period, Péguy refers to the status given to the natural sciences in his time as "the religion of science."[16] Since in Péguy's time, in this respect still like ours, religion was perceived to be what science was not, what science had risen to defeat, the term carries a particular punch.[17] In the age of science, it was widely thought, no longer would human beings be blinded by beliefs based on authority. All would be fact-based. Science would dispel the irrational fantasies, the mythologies that have plagued the human race. Only science, maintained Marcellin Berthelot, the famous French scientist and statesman, "could provide the foundation for doctrines freely accepted by the citizens of the future, in contrast to the coerced and

15. Péguy, *Œuvres II*, 629.

16. Péguy, *Œuvres II*, 504, 560, 594, 647, 1192. Sometimes, he associates science with both religion and metaphysics, using them in the same sentence, as in 560, 647, 1192. At other times, he speaks of the attitude toward science as a superstition, 601, 842, 1192. The three terms cover different ground, although, in Péguy's usage, they intersect at points.

17. The opposition was between revealed religions, most especially Christianity, and science. See Carnino, *L'Invention de la Science*, for a study of how the opposition froze into place in France by the mid-nineteenth century. See also, Harrison, *The Territories of Science and Religion*, for a history of how the two terms finally came to be in opposition in the nineteenth century, with science as offering a unique and privileged access to truth, an idea still present in the twenty-first century. An example of a late twentieth-century opposition perpetuating the one from the nineteenth century can be found in Jacob, *Of Flies, Mice, and Men*, 107. "As a matter of fact, the history of science is in a way the history of the battle of reason against revealed truth." Despite this very common contrast, it was not uncommon for nineteenth-century proponents of science to call science a religion, worthy of veneration, precisely because, following Auguste Comte, it relied only on empirical data, and thus had freed human beings from the speculations of earlier times. See, Lalouette, "La glorification de la science au xix siècle," 431–3.

blind faith of the naive believer."[18] By calling the attitude toward science a religion, Péguy was aiming to show that the status the natural sciences had acquired rested on unproven foundations, had led to the spinning of mythologies of their own, and hinted at some of the features of revelation. In short, the modern adherence to the natural sciences as the exclusive path to truth involved naive belief.

It would be a mistake, however, to interpret Péguy's reference to the religion of science as an intention to "prove" that science was a religion. That is, he does not first define religion and then show that his contemporaries' veneration of science fits this definition. Rather, his musings about the status of the natural sciences make us rethink what we mean by religion, enlarging its meaning beyond adherence to the established churches or adherence to beliefs. He goes about this project by meandering and digressing but always returning to the same key points. I shall reflect upon his mode of argument in a later section of this essay. For now, it is these key points I would like to investigate. In the first place, Péguy wishes to lay bare the aspiration to transcend the limits of the human condition at the core of the narratives about science. In the second place, he wants to show how these narratives, rather than remaining pure ideas, become embedded in the practices and objects of daily life.

Transcendence: The Quest for Omnipotence and Omniscience

In the first essay Péguy fully devoted to the topic of science as religion, "Zangwill," he went back to two of the greatest proponents of science and of the transpositions of its methods to the humanities, Ernest Renan and Hippolyte Taine, highly honored and highly influential nineteenth-century historians. They had made fervent followers of the professors who taught Péguy, and they, in turn, instilled great enthusiasm for the scientific method in his generation.[19] It is with Renan's youthful text, *The Future of Science* that Péguy begins. Written in 1848, it was published only in 1890, at which point Renan appended a preface from which Péguy quotes:

> In a century, humanity will know approximately what it is possible to know about its past; and then it will be time to stop . . . The

18. Lalouette, "La glorification de la science," 440.
19. Péguy, *Œuvres II*, 504.

> history of religions is already explained in its most important branches. It has become clear not through *a priori* reasoning but through discussions of so-called testimonies that there has never been, in the centuries known to man, either revelation or a supernatural event. The *process* of civilization is known in its general laws. The inequality of races is established.[20]

Péguy points out that Renan, in his praise of what science has accomplished to date, is claiming no less than omniscience for its practitioners. In a mere century, we will know everything. We have already established that a transcendent source of truth independent of human reason—revelation—does not exist. Our science has seen through claims to the contrary. We now know how civilizations evolve and which race is higher and which race lower.

The other foundational historian, Taine, echoes this claim to omniscience. In his book about the seventeenth-century French writer Jean de La Fontaine, *Les Fables de la Fontaine*, careful never to interpret the meaning of any of these witty poems, he begins his analysis with the spirit of the indigenous inhabitants of France, the Gauls, a product of physical causes. He names the sky, the soil, the climate, the food.[21] When he does get to the fables themselves, he breaks their composition up into mechanisms, again ignoring what any given fable might be communicating. Taine's method arises from the presupposition that human beings produce poetry in approximately the same way as silkworms produce cocoons and bees their hives.[22] The historian just needs to find all the causes and mechanisms involved in the process. This exhaustive analysis enables conclusions as to how any creative act comes to be, whether it be beehives or poetry.[23] Unveiling the secret of creation, Péguy argues, is a pretense to omniscience rivaling that of Renan.

For the proponents of the scientific method whose writings Péguy examines here, omniscience does not seem to be enough. From a late work of Renan, *Dialogues and Philosophical Fragments*, he excerpts the following passage:

> An extensive application of the discoveries of physiology and the principle of selection could lead to the creation of a superior

20. Péguy. *Œuvres I*, 1416.
21. Péguy, *Œuvres I*, 1398.
22. Péguy, *Œuvres I*, 1405.
23. Péguy, *Œuvres I*, 1405–6.

> race, having a right to govern not only in the sciences by the very superiority of its blood, brain and nerves . . . Nature brings forth viable products only in general conditions; but science could extend the limits of viability. It is up to science to take creation beyond the point at which nature has left it . . . [24]

In a later passage, Renan imagines a future era in which "animals are replaced by higher mechanisms . . . In the same way that humanity came out of the animal realm, divinity will come out of humanity."[25] In other words, thanks to science, human beings will be able to control nature to such an extent that they will take over the evolutionary process, and turn themselves into gods. As the above passage states, this does not mean that all human beings will be so endowed. A chosen few will rule over the rest. In a later passage, Renan speculates that the masses will sacrifice themselves for the goals of the sciences.[26]

Taine sounds milder, but only in appearance. In his book on La Fontaine, he states that the material causes leading to the production of the fables, while now still approximations, will soon be accompanied by "statistics and the precision of experiments."[27] He is cheered by the fact that an anthropological society has just been founded in Paris, whose members' research into anatomy and physiology will make us understand how different races resulted from different geographies.[28] Péguy points out that this claim to knowledge of all causes is inseparable from the project of reproducing what is known. "In the order of the physical sciences, the chemical, the natural sciences, to know exactly, entirely, the prior and external conditions that determine phenomena is to have on hand the very production of these phenomena."[29] Taine, unlike Renan, who put off the creation of superhuman entities into a future realm, is already crediting contemporary anthropologists with this power. They will know the physical causes that resulted in a given race, enabling them to control the process as they choose.

It is here that Péguy first introduces a reference to transcendence. The God of Christianity, for instance, was a god who knew all and could

24. Péguy, *Œuvres I*, 1421.

25. Péguy, *Œuvres I*, 1422.

26. Péguy, *Œuvres I*, 1410.

27. Péguy, *Œuvres I*, 1410.

28. Paligot, "Médicine," 453–7, discusses how the attempt to identify racial types dominated nineteenth- and early twentieth-century French anthropology.

29. Péguy, *Œuvres I*, 1440.

do all. The proponents of science take pride in having done away with such a god. But, in transferring to the scientist omniscience and omnipotence, if only as a project to be realized in due time, they have made themselves into the very gods that they deny exist.[30] Because of their emphasis on duplicating creation, Péguy insists that they have taken on the status not of the gods, but of the Christian God himself. They have given themselves the attributes "not of one of those tiny wooden gods of the old Hellenic regime . . . but very precisely of God. Of a God like that of the old Christian regime, a creator-god, all powerful, all-knowing."[31] He calls this desire to transcend the human condition, to become God, the secret desire of the modern world.[32]

Secrecy and Embeddedness

Examining in what way the religion of science works in secret will bring us to Péguy's second key point—the embeddedness of this religion in daily life. But before we get to this, one might ask how much it really matters that a couple of prominent historians and their followers attribute eventual omniscience and omnipotence to the practitioners of the scientific method. Péguy freely admits that no historian of his generation would approve of Renan and Taine's claims to omniscience and omnipotence, maintaining in the case of the first that he was too much a philosopher, that is, an unscientific speculator,[33] and in the case of the second that his method was still too imprecise, and his public too general. Péguy maintains that these historians are more wedded to Renan and Taine's dreams then they are willing to admit but, even so, it just extends the circle of foolishness. At best, thinking of oneself as God is a mere rhetorical figure. Can anyone take such an expression literally? The fact that genetic engineering and artificial intelligence repeat the dreams of controlling the creative process seem to make the claim more literal. But we are getting ahead of ourselves.

30. Péguy, *Œuvres I*, 1445. Peguy, *Œuvres* II, 1415. The claim that human beings have divinized themselves in the modern era is not infrequent. One thinks of Fyodor Dostoyevsky and Friedrich Nietzsche, for instance. Péguy's presentation of academic historians and sociologists as gods unaware of the status they have given themselves retains an element of humor.

31. Péguy, *Œuvres II*, 855.

32. Péguy, *Œuvres I*, 1422.

33. Péguy, *Œuvres II*, 843.

To a degree, Péguy, especially in this first essay, "Zangwill," does emphasize the foolishness of these claims to divinity.[34] Human beings are so fallible that they remain completely unaware of their most basic premises. He often alludes to the miracle associated with the advent of modern science.[35] The story disseminated throughout the French educational system, which the proponents of science controlled, is that before modern science, human beings were all benighted, but with its arrival, everything changed lock, stock and barrel.[36] This happens to contradict the very path to the truth that the scientific method inculcates—the discovery of material causes. The scientific method alone, like revelation, seems to have entered the world without material antecedents or at least cannot be reduced to them. The miracle chased from nature by science simply reappears in the practice of science itself. Whereas historians can limit the meaning of the works of geniuses and saints to the environment that caused them, their own method, with all the assumptions embedded in it, is the only one that stands above time and place.

Péguy points out that every civilization has seen itself as being at the final stage of history. The proponents of science are in good company, except they do not know it. "What is interesting, what is new is that modern humanity thought itself well protected against such weaknesses by its science . . . as armed, warned, guarded as the modern world was, it was precisely in the oldest human error that it fell, as if by accident."[37] The proponents of science, placing themselves above the myths and illusions of former times, merely reflect every other civilization, each of which has proclaimed the same confidence in having arrived at the end. Not to be aware of this does not augur well for omniscience.

On another level, however, he does take the narrative about omniscience and omnipotence very seriously. The proponents of science control both the State and the educational system, meaning that the narratives' penetration into minds happens early and spreads very widely. By 1900, a generation of students steeped from elementary school on in those narratives elect to political office those who repeat these narratives.[38] The

34. Speaking about these claims, Péguy says that in the face of something so infantile and naive, "tears of tender pity are more likely to flow from one's eyes," than any other emotion, Péguy, *Œuvres II*, 829.

35. Péguy, *Œuvres II*, 652, 829–30, 856.

36. Péguy, *Œuvres II*, 712–3, 1087–8.

37. Péguy, *Œuvres I*, 1419.

38. Péguy, *Œuvres II*, 713, 957, 1049.

same circular pattern occurs at the university level. University professors often hold government office, and government officials appoint university administrators, since the university is a State institution.[39] The University controls all appointments to professorships and to high school teaching positions, and control all curriculum.[40] Péguy referred to this symbiosis of political representatives and professors as "*le parti intellectuel*."[41] They spread the narratives about science way beyond a narrow circle, translating it into near total control of intellectual life.[42]

Péguy claims the religion of science has penetrated the world we live in at such depth that even its proponents are not aware of its full dimensions. One of the proofs of this depth of penetration is that even those who oppose the religion of science are imbued with its assumptions. He reflects on the noted historian of literature, Ferdinand Brunetière, one of his teachers at the École Normale, the prestigious training ground for the French professorate. In 1895, Brunetière wrote a famous pamphlet, "The Bankruptcy of Science," claiming, against widely held opinion, that science could not answer questions regarding morality or the final purposes of human beings. Only religion could do that.[43] Nonetheless, Péguy marvels, Brunetière continued to use the scientific method in the study of literature, *after* his manifesto, introducing evolutionary theory as a way of grasping the whole span of literary forms, each of which evolves in ways akin to the mechanisms of biology.[44] Despite his repudiation of science in the realm of morality and metaphysics, only causal, material explanations could explain human creativity. This signaled that the thirst for omniscience could function without the full awareness of the person it inhabited.[45] Péguy calls such a hidden impulse "the thought at the back of the mind" (*la pensée de derrière la tête*).[46]

39. Péguy, *Œuvres II*, 718.

40. Péguy, *Œuvres II*, 684, 699.

41. Although references to the *parti intellectuel* are numerous throughout these and other essays, Péguy also dedicated two long essays to the topic, Péguy, *Œuvres II*, 519–565, 678–774. His use of the term extends to a style of thinking rather than to a political party, but it also refers to a political power not recognized as a party as such.

42. Péguy, *Œuvres II*, 698.

43. See Lalouette, "Banqueroute," 480–481, for the context in which Brunetière wrote.

44. Péguy, *Œuvres II*, 588–590.

45. Péguy, *Œuvres II*, 589–90.

46. Péguy, *Œuvres I*, 1415, 1420, Péguy, *Œuvres II*, 639.

The religion of science, then, operates in such a way that it eludes the full awareness of its practitioners, remaining, as it were, a secret from them. But it is secret also in that it is the center from which everything else emanates. Its manifestations are everywhere at once, varying in such a way that we might not notice the link between them. In the course of his writings Péguy draws attention to some of these manifestations of the religion of science. We have already seen that it affects how one reads and what one reads: the scientific method turns us into seekers of causal explanations rather than for meaning. It affects one's notion of time—before science and after science. But it also affects daily objects. He mentions, for example, military knapsacks and military formations;[47] new interchangeable objects—lamps, brakes, industrial machinery;[48] new building materials such as steel.[49] These objects signal a new way of thinking, a new relationship between human beings, and of human beings to nature. In the case of the new knapsack, Péguy objected not to its newness but the way it was created and imposed from above. It was designed, he satirizes, "on the basis of the multiplications and divisions of days and men," and then approved "by a commission of old generals who tested it by wearing it on their back for three and a half minutes."[50] It lacked only one advantage, which was the essential quality of the old knapsack: wearability. Péguy's barb has a serious underside. He protests against what he calls the "scientific disdain for any traditional reality, familiar, memory-based, in common use."[51]

In the case of the new building material, steel, Péguy appreciated the skill and precision it took to produce it.[52] Nonetheless, he felt it introduced and embodied a host of attitudes different from those expressed in working in wood or stone. It was the difference between matter that one beats and matter that one carves,[53] the former signaling a control over nature and a brutality of a different order than the latter. In addition, products associated with steel are interchangeable in the way wood and stone products are not.[54] This brute force exerted over nature, the inter-

47. Péguy, *Œuvres II*, 748, 779–87.
48. Péguy, *Œuvres II*, 969.
49. Péguy, *Œuvres II*, 946.
50. Péguy, *Œuvres II*, 749.
51. Péguy, *Œuvres II*, 603.
52. Péguy, *Œuvres II*, 950.
53. Péguy, *Œuvres II*, 946.
54. Péguy, *Œuvres II*, 959–65.

changeability of the products represented by steel, and the practice of replacing human experience with the result of an intellectual construction unrelated to it, as in the case of the knapsack, pointed to the *hidden center* of the religion of science, the thought at the back of the mind: the secret desire to control and replace the organic world with an artificial one, permeating both thinking and practice.

The religious nature of science lay not, then, merely in its proponents' claims to transcend the human condition but also in the way the religion of science becomes a world, a web of multiple meanings, all referring to each other. Péguy uses a strikingly negative image, which at first seems to convey the opposite, the death of a world. He speaks of the spread of volcanic ash over a city. At first, as the ash just begins to fall, we welcome the novelty. "A speck of ash is nothing and the first fall of the first specks were joyously received. What beautiful skies, they said, those beautiful falling ashes make . . . It was beginning to be boring that that stupid sky was blue. And the trees. It was really getting difficult to bear, all that green, all the time that the leaves of the trees were green."[55] But in no time, the world is covered with ash, snuffed out of existence. And yet, despite its association with death, Péguy sees the religion of science as strangely alive. "It is a meaningful sign that an infinite hollowness, an infinity of hollowness . . . really balloons out to infinity like fullness, becomes almost an infinity, like a world, real, like a belly of fertility."[56] In other words, the artificial and inorganic have taken on the properties of the real, expanding to infinite manifestations. There is no end to the artificial forms that the religion of science brings into being.

Overflow of the Argument

This imagery is alarming in its negative appraisal. Is Péguy not engaging in a mythology of the end of time himself? Besides, if the narratives around science are as powerful as he describes, lodging as religion, that is, as "the thought at the back of the mind," what chance does anyone have to escape the grip of these narratives, if one agrees with Péguy that they are dangerous? I will return to both of these questions. For now, it is too soon, simply because the main lines of his argument can hardly do justice to its many branches, which are not asides at all. In what

55. Péguy, *Œuvres II*, 937.
56. Péguy, *Œuvres II*, 937.

follows, I will tackle only two such asides which really aren't, just to give a very partial illustration of the many ramifications necessary to understand Péguy's explorations of the religion of science. One might ask, for instance, supposing that science has indeed turned into a religion, why Péguy's hostility to this particular one? Was not Christianity just as controlling of its environment, just as much part of daily life—marking the landscape and the styles of thinking of people? In short, was it any less totalizing in its effects?

Péguy freely acknowledges the parallel. The Church used to control education, for example, much like the proponents of science in his day. Péguy's objection was not that the Church/State alliance had been severed. He welcomed the separation between the two. Rather, he objected to the fact that the State had simply replaced one set of dogma with another. He quotes a Minister of Labor, who in his speech in the Senate, declaims to loud applause that the anticlerical government he represents has finally freed the people: "We have torn from the soul of the people the belief in another life, the belief in deceiving and unreal visions."[57] But, asks Péguy, should a government be doing this? "We have the disestablishment of the Churches. When will we have the disestablishment of metaphysics?"[58] The Labor minister thinks of himself as without metaphysics, of course. He is secular. But the secularity he is promoting does not institute freedom of thought. It operates, as the quotation shows, on the premise that there is nothing beyond this world. This is a valid methodological assumption in the natural sciences. But to make this a statement about what is really real is to mistake assumption for fact, and metaphysical assumption at that, since it is a claim about what reality really is—only matter. This governmental imposition of a metaphysics, without even acknowledging that it was doing so, Péguy considered tyranny.[59] Under the guise of liberating people from power, one simply imposed one's own domination. Modern proponents of science, in other words, in their association with State power, were just like the clerics they had replaced.

Looked at from another angle, however, the religion of science is more dangerous than what preceded it, not because of the contents of its metaphysics but because of the circumstances into which it was born. One of the key features of the modern State is its unprecedented

57. Péguy, *Œuvres II*, 552.

58. Péguy, *Œuvres II*, 564.

59. Péguy, *Œuvres II*, 589.

centralization of power.[60] The Church had controlled education at a time when formal education had been restricted primarily to a small elite.[61] In France, universal elementary schooling began in 1881, and therefore the modern French educational system[62] had control of what every school child in France was learning at any given hour, quite unlike the much more limited prior control of the Church. The spread of the religion of science was not even a matter of France only. Because of the nature of modern capitalism, and its ties to both the State and the sciences, the religion of science spreads globally, making it increasingly difficult to find pockets of people elsewhere in the world where it does not penetrate. "It is precisely because of this that the modern world runs a risk that the other worlds did not run . . . could not run because of former ways of organizing life in separate cellular units."[63]

The combination of centralization and sheer global spread means that the sanctions against those who want to critique the narratives around the natural sciences are very great. Previous regimes also had severe sanctions, sometimes lethal, against the critics of their metaphysics.[64] But the nature of the modern ones is that they strangle those critics all the while giving the appearance of a complete freedom of thought. The main means is economic, which may not sound like much in comparison to the death penalty, but the inability to find work or to find an outlet in which to publish creates an inability to make a living. It thus prevents intellectuals and academics from thinking outside the prescribed lines, imposing on them an inner censorship, that is, preventing them from even imagining other possibilities when it comes to the narratives surrounding science. If they did do so, and made the results public, a boycott, unprecedented in its reach, would be organized against the possibility of being heard, condemning them to isolation, financial destitution and hunger.[65]

If the religion of science were operating as a metaphysics—without resorting to State power for its enforcement—Péguy would consider it merely one possible, if not particularly attractive approach to reality,

60. Péguy, *Œuvres II*, 164–5.

61. Péguy, *Œuvres II*, 1100–1101.

62. For a comprehensive study on the development of the modern French educational system in the course of the nineteenth and beginning twentieth centuries, see Ringer, *Fields of Knowledge*.

63. Péguy, *Œuvres II*, 467.

64. Péguy, *Œuvres II*, 514–5.

65. Péguy, *Œuvres II*, 515.

among others. The proponents of the religion of science are infinitely entitled to their metaphysics, he says.[66] It is their refusal to accept the narratives and premises with which they operate as metaphysical in the first place that he finds dangerous.[67] In "Zangwill," his first full essay on this topic, he still speaks of a debate between the proponents of the scientific method in the humanities, and those who deny that those methods are valid in that area.[68] But he will soon turn to the metaphor of war.[69] There is no common ground upon which to meet if the truth, from the beginning, becomes a matter of fact already verified by the only acceptable method. One can debate with someone who will accept one's way of collecting evidence, even if not the evidence itself or the conclusions one draws from it. But if the method of acquiring evidence is excluded in principle, then there can be no expectations of eventual agreement or disagreement. One's mouth has been shut.

Another aside which is not one: Is not what Péguy referred to as the religion of science restricted to those who transpose the scientific method into the humanities and social sciences, what we might call scientism today? To a great extent, this is indeed what he found most dangerous, revealing the urge to control and manage human beings from above, not granting validity to their own experience.[70] In the case of the natural sciences, on the other hand, Péguy maintains that the scientific method is the only one available to it. "It cannot do anything else."[71] He also claimed that it is the contemporary natural sciences that provide us with a way to push back against the claims made in their name.[72] Much of what he argues about the natural sciences is indeed inspired by the writings of the reputed physicist, chemist and mathematician Pierre Duhem, and the engineer Georges Sorel, renowned as a political thinker and a philosopher, but also well versed in modern physics.[73] He

66. Péguy, *Œuvres II*, 562.

67. Péguy, *Œuvres II*, 618–19, 647.

68. Péguy, *Œuvres I*, 1449–50.

69. Péguy, *Œuvres II*, 839–40, 1044. Latour speaks of him as engaging in military campaigns rather than in the writing of books, Latour, "'Nous sommes des vaincus,'" 15. That is, each of his essays, in illustrating again and again a method of reading, is a battle in the larger war.

70. Péguy, *Œuvres II*, 629–31.

71. Péguy, *Œuvres II*, 627.

72. Péguy, *Œuvres I*, 1432.

73. Péguy, *Œuvres II*, 652–53. The *Cahiers* (14 Oct., 1907) published an article by Sorel, "Préoccupations métaphysiques." Much of what Péguy says of the importance of

also cites the famous mathematician Henri Poincaré to support some of his own points,[74] as well as Émile Duclaux, the biologist under whom he had studied.[75] All of this should not obscure the fact that, for Péguy, the humanists' extolling of the scientific method as the only path to truth arises from premises within the natural sciences themselves, premises embodied in their foundational texts and echoed by many of their current practitioners. Does not the scientific method in the humanities "correspond to an internal tendency of modern science itself . . . I mean, the real tendency of real modern science?"[76]

Péguy's central reproach against the natural sciences is that while their practitioners and proponents claim to give up on metaphysical questions—on questions of what is ultimately real and on questions of meaning and purpose—as outside the purview of the scientific method, they are in fact doing two contradictory things at once. In the first place, they do not merely set these questions aside but dismiss them as not worthy of inquiry since they cannot be settled through their methods.[77] But, secondly, at the same time, they simply substitute their findings as definitive answers to the questions they claim they are not asking. In other words, a mechanistic, materialist universe becomes not the limitations of what their experiments allow them to see but a description of all of reality.

instrumentation in the acquisition of scientific truth, for example, can be found in it. Burac, "Notes," in Péguy, *Œuvres II*, 1452. He had also solicited several articles from Duhem for the *Cahiers*. Burac, "Notes," in Péguy, *Œuvres II*, 1459. Some of the limits of the work of natural scientists no doubt come from Duhem. As Stephen Toulmin characterizes Duhem's thought, "Scientific hypotheses and theories are merely intellectual instruments that human thinkers construct and use to relate together their limited observations of nature," Toulmin, *The Return to Cosmology*, 11.

74. Péguy, *Œuvres II*, 1179, 1190–93. For a clarification of how Péguy understands Poincaré, see Péguy, *Œuvres II*, 1554.

75. Péguy, *Œuvres II*, 1134–69.

76. Péguy, *Œuvres II*, 640.

77. Péguy, *Œuvres II*, 623–5. For an illustration of a more recent dismissal of all that is not a result of the scientific method, see the biologist and Nobel Prize winner in Physiology or Medicine, Medawar, *The Limits of Science*, 60. "It is not to science, but to metaphysics, imaginative literature or religion that we must turn to questions having to do with first and last things. Because the answers neither arise out of nor require validation by empirical evidence, it is not useful or even meaningful to ask whether they are true or false . . . *The failure of science to answer questions about first and last things does not in any way entail the acceptability of answers of other kinds*; nor can it be taken for granted that because these questions can be put, they can be answered. So far as our understanding goes, they cannot." (My italics) In other words, if something cannot be answered through the sciences, it cannot be answered satisfactorily at all.

> This idea in the depth of modern science, of substituting itself fundamentally for metaphysics while appearing to refuse to engage with it only through a pretended modesty . . . is a false modesty. For the thought at the back of the mind of modern science is to substitute itself for metaphysics, to eliminate it, no doubt, but in another sense than what it says. It gives itself the appearance of eliminating it through a great show of respect . . . [but]This idea of modern science is to substitute itself for metaphysics—entirely—to take its place completely and entirely.[78]

Péguy gives an example of this substitution in his discussion of the "as-if" central to the scientific method.[79] Direct observation of nature is often not possible for many reasons, including the presence of too many variables. Scientists create experiments in which they bracket out the multiple dimensions of the real, always messy and not easily fitted into a hypothesis. This method, creating a model as if it were reality, produces results through the mediation of an instrument. "Causation is not simple causal operation, a direct causal relation of the causing to the caused, but an indirect causal relation of the causing to the caused through the mediation, the usage of a mechanism, and thus one must always take the mechanism into account."[80] The result the mechanism produces cedes a truth about the material world under investigation but Péguy insists that it does not give us the truth about what the material world really is.[81] The fact that the scientific method leads to automobiles and other goods and theories does not erase the difference between what can be known and produced as a result of controlled experiments and what is really real.[82] An infinite

78. Péguy, *Œuvres II*, 623.

79. Péguy, *Œuvres II*, 615–18, 879–80.

80. Péguy, *Œuvres II*, 1119.

81. Péguy frequently differentiates between *le vrai* (the true), accessible to the scientific method, and *le réel* (the real), not accessible to it. Péguy, *Œuvres II*, 613, 624, 627, 632, 972. The *vrai* is a product of hypothesis in the way the *réel* is not. Stephen Toulmin, *The Return to Cosmology*, 242, describes a distinction quite similar to it, which reigned in the sciences, but with the opposite valuation, "The veracity or correctness at which the onlooker aims rests on the accuracy and scope of the expectations he has about things—it is a one-way kind of knowledge possessed by a spectator." He contrasts it to a kind of knowledge which is reciprocal, "possessed by a participant who cannot detach himself from the action and view it from the outside, like a mere spectator." The view of the spectator would align with what Péguy meant by *vrai* and the view of the participant with what he meant by *réel*.

82. For a very good discussion of this difference, see Jensen, "La Vérité scientifique," *Monde Diplomatique*. See also Noë's description of the functioning of a fMRI machine and the distance between the images of neural activity and actual neural activity, Noë,

difference separates the two.[83] Erasing that distance is what he sees as the sleight of hand operative in the natural sciences themselves.

One of his examples of this sleight of hand is the way Darwin's theory of evolution crossed the line between biology and metaphysics. It started out, Péguy says, "as a genuinely scientific hypothesis, verified like so many others, by a certain number of facts or coinciding with them . . . a natural naturalist hypothesis that made it big scientifically and that certainly merited it."[84] What started out as a theory to explain physical phenomena in the biological realm then turned into a thesis that explained everything, without any acknowledgment that a switch to metaphysics had taken place. As a result, the certainty available to scientific findings—limited to a specific verifiable realm, tested through experiment—is now extended to realms in which that kind of test and verifiability do not exist. Stating that literary forms or that societies operate on the law of evolution, for example, cannot be so verified. Nor is the claim that all is material, and thus determined by the law of cause and effect, verifiable. The theory of evolution, when it claims to explain all of reality, keeps the certainty of science but refuses to accept the uncertainty of metaphysics.[85] It refuses to recognize that it has crossed the line, making secure what cannot be secured in that way.

Perhaps one of Péguy's most daring forays into the natural sciences involves mathematics, the jewel in the crown of scientific methodology. As he himself admits, the terrain here is the most difficult, both because one can get stumped easily, given the specialized language, and because, in his day, it is rarely explored either historically or philosophically. This is precisely what he begins to do, asking whether the notion of equality in classical Greek geometry is the same as the concept of equivalence and interchangeability, the latter notions predominant in modern mathematics.[86] He concludes that interchangeability and equality are not at all the same, but that in any case, neither represents the real world, in which no two things are interchangeable, and in which no two things may even be equal.[87] Once again, the formal model is not the concrete reality.

Out of Our Heads, 20–24. For another analysis of the discrepancy between fMRI results and brain activity, see Tallis, *Aping Mankind*, 76–78, 82.

83. Péguy, *Œuvres II*, 632.

84. Péguy, *Œuvres II*, 587.

85. Péguy, *Œuvres II*, 587–8.

86. Péguy, *Œuvres II*, 965–972, 978–9.

87. Péguy, *Œuvres II*, 985–6.

Whether one agrees with Péguy that "modern science awakened the number sleeping in reality . . . and that reality was not in the numbers,"[88] or whether one holds that reality and number coincide, and/or that numbers reveal the deeper reality, this is a metaphysical question, not at the same level as the mathematical operations themselves. When a mathematician makes one or the other claim, he makes it as a philosopher. Péguy's intent here, as in his earlier explorations of the "as-if" crucial to science, is to separate metaphysical claims from the positive knowledge about specific aspects of the world that mathematics and the natural sciences cede. The philosopher does this by paying close attention to concepts taken for granted by the practitioners of a given discipline and thinking out their implications. Philosophy, that "soft" humanistic science, is, in fact, the one that deals with the heart of the matter, that which the supposedly "hard "disciplines bypass.[89]

Reflections on Péguy's Critique of the Religion of Science

Looking back on Péguy's critique of the religion of science, we have a picture more complicated than it might at first look. We might be tempted, given the way he began and the greater time he spends in general on the transposition of the scientific method into the humanities, that this was his only target. It was not. Humanists such as Renan and Taine, and their latter-day followers are in fact reflecting ideals and presuppositions embedded within the natural sciences themselves. Its practitioners do not limit themselves to the "as-if" world, leaving aside speculation as

88. Péguy, *Œuvres II*, 1207. A similar attempt to distinguish between Greek conceptions of geometry and the ones undergirding modern science, in relation to Edmund Husserl, is discussed in Gasché, "Universality and Spatial Form," *Science and the Life-World*, 116–35. As early as Galileo, a "'surreptitious substitution [Unterschiebung] [took place] of the mathematically substructed world of idealities for the only real world, the one actually given through perception, that is ever experienced and experienceable—our everyday life-world. (*Crisis*, par. 9h).' Husserl submits that this substitution of idealized nature for the prescientifically intuited nature is of the order of a disguising or covering over and replacement of the life-world," Gasché, "Universality," 135. It is an ethico-philosophical error, Gasché interprets Husserl to say, Gasché, "Universality," 135.

89. Péguy, *Œuvres II*, 494–6. Péguy already uses the distinction between hard and soft science. His humanities professors had taught him, even if they did not say it directly, he says, to view philosophy, literature and the arts as something soft and the sciences as something hard, rigid, rigorous. Péguy, *Œuvres II*, 838.

to the real one, but substitute it for the real one. Péguy speaks of the *coup de pouce*, the shove of the thumb, that makes of the results of a constructed experiment a description of the real.[90] He was afraid, not of this or that artificial substitution, but of the project of wholesale substitution itself, of wanting to remake creation as a whole. He asks himself "whether science could constitute itself against nature, against creation as a rival power,"[91] making our age not atheistic but auto-theistic.[92] He cautions that it is too soon to tell, modern science being too recent a phenomenon.[93] Nonetheless his apprehension, as evident in the imagery of the whole world covered with ash, is palpable.

Complicating the picture yet more is that at times Péguy speaks quite favorably about the natural sciences. It is from them, it may be recalled, that a push back against the narratives around the sciences might originate. He also has no ax to grind with the method of obtaining knowledge in the natural sciences. Laboratory experiments, hypotheses, "as if," are all necessary to wrest knowledge from nature. In addition, in a section to which we shall turn later, he speaks with admiration of scientists who have reached the level of what he refers to as competence. Since we know that in his eyes the present-day humanities are themselves fully implicated in the narratives surrounding the sciences, they are in no way preferable to them. This would mean that Péguy directed his objections to the *narratives around science*, to the claims that the scientific method gives us a direct and exclusive access to reality, and not to the practice of science itself.

This is undeniable, but we are not out of the thicket of complications quite yet. I want to go back to the image of the ash covering the whole world, and of the sky no longer being blue and the leaves no longer green. On the one hand, he uses these images as figurative language for the artificiality, the man-made constructions replacing the organic at the center of the dreams of the religion of science. He did not literally mean that the sky and the leaves were changing color. But where does Péguy's metaphor come from? In the late nineteenth century the sky and the leaves of its trees did change color in places of greatest industrial pollution. As for the ash, this was certainly the case in mining towns, in some cases,

90. Péguy, *Œuvres II*, 834.
91. Péguy, *Œuvres II*, 1210–11.
92. Péguy, *Œuvres II*, 855.
93. Péguy, *Œuvres II*, 1210–11.

dark at noon.[94] His metaphor is not mere figure of speech but points to a concrete reality, revealing the enormity of the phenomenon. Even though it would be an anachronism to attribute an environmental concern to Péguy, ash-covered cities were already part of his world. In our own time, environmental devastation makes these metaphors lose their merely figurative quality. We speak not only of pollution, with entire cities like Beijing and New Delhi covered in unbreathable particles, but also of the rapid disappearance of forests, with no leaves left to turn brown. In the Second World War, a mere forty years after Péguy wrote, two large cities turned to ash as a result of nuclear bombing.

My point is not so much that Péguy was right about the consequences of the natural sciences but that the tension between the literal nature of these images—the destruction of the physical world—and their metaphoric range—the suggestion that the world is in the process of becoming totally artificial—is also the tension between Péguy's attitude toward the practice of science and the religion of science. They are separable and yet they are also not separable. The religion of science, the narration of eventual omniscience and omnipotence, can be separated from the affirmations of individual scientists who do not hold to this narration at all. Yet it is reinforced by their scientific inventions, which embed themselves in daily life. Those scientific inventions not only transform and modify nature on a planetary scale but also, in the process, transform the organic into the inorganic.

To see Péguy exclusively as a prophet of doom, however, is to come to a premature conclusion. Something in the form of his writing shows a path forward, allowing his readers both to take the religion of science seriously and to begin to shake it off. Hoping to illustrate this, I will turn now to some formal aspects of his writing.

94. Péguy, as a university student, helped gather funds for the miners of the city of Carmaux, a mining town in southern France. The reference to darkness at noon is to Butte, Montana, founded as a mining town in the later nineteenth century, and called the richest town on earth, because of the huge amount of metals, especially copper, which were extracted there. The environmental effects continue to this day.

Part 2: The Form

Geology and Geography or How Best to Conduct One's Reason

In the middle of an unpublished essay dating from 1907 ("Un poète l'a dit"), Péguy interrupts himself to address his friend, the writer and frequent contributor to the *Cahiers* Daniel Halévy. "Here I go, my dear Halévy, letting myself be pulled along, not resisting this pull sufficiently, and not even resisting this pull at all."[95] He expresses his temptation in terms of the contrast between geology/geodesy and geography. Rather than continuing to pursue his geological and geodesic investigations into the status of the natural sciences, slowly, and one layer at the time, he has switched to geography, drawing a map of the entire surface area, detaching the main lines of his argument from any specific investigation. For several pages, Péguy proceeds to illustrate what he means by the geographic method, listing a central thesis and a whole flurry of sub-theses, splitting the logic into finer and finer distinctions, in an attempt to grasp all the dimensions systematically. Since he goes on to claim that switching to the geographical method was a reckless and foolish move, in effect revealing his defense plans to the enemy,[96] one might well want to know both why he considered it dangerous and, if so, why he switched to it all the same. After all, what could be dangerous about a thesis—on the hidden metaphysical assumptions of the proponents of the scientific method—which he had made quite explicitly many times before?

It must first be pointed out that it is the formal, systematic manner of presenting his thesis about the sciences, not his thesis itself, that Péguy finds dangerous here. When engaged in what he calls geological investigations, he had proceeded by analyzing one phenomenon at a time: practices in the humanities at one moment, those in the military at another, those in the building trades at yet another, examples among many others. Each time his reasoning arose out of the material he studied and not just from the implacability of a formal logic. Such a way of reasoning led to multiple connections at once, as the image of geodesy might suggest. The new habits of reading, for example, connect to both "scientifically designed" knapsacks and to building in steel, revealing a coherence unlike

95. Péguy, *Œuvres II*, 839.

96. Péguy, *Œuvres II*, 839–40.

the coherence of a formal, linear argument. Proceeding in this way is to shed new light on a whole never exhausted by its parts.

It just so happens that a whole not exhausted by its parts describes the religion of science. It cannot be defeated by even the most correct argument because it is a reality, and thus a world in which everything relates to everything else. The force of the religion of science lies in its thickness, its multiple interweaving threads, its many layers, and not in the linearity of argument alone. It defeats anyone who proceeds to encompass it all in one thesis. But, if that is so, why does Péguy spend several pages arguing in this manner anyway? Perhaps, in laying out his central thesis and its logical derivatives in a systematic manner, Péguy is simply acknowledging how the mind works. The thinker is always tempted to capture it all at once, by means of logical distinctions, blithely ignoring the very dimensions that the argument cannot get at. To think is to notice this unwarranted controlling thrust. Given free rein to it for a while is one way to keep it in check.

A faint humor accompanies this entire section, partially produced by the hair-splitting and convoluted distinctions that he makes in order to capture his argument.

> Speaking the language of metaphysics, then, our central proposition will be that the central enemy proposition is that the modern historian, in the first degree, that the modern sociologist, in the second degree, *is able* in the first place, and in the second place *does succeed*, in establishing a representation, a repertory of the event, which is a repertory, in the first place *infinite*, in the second place *universal*, being an exact repertory and nothing else than a replica, or more exactly a second edition, of the event, itself infinite and universal, being the language, the development, the unfolding, being the event of reality itself. Then. Secondary propositions or derived propositions included in this central proposition . . . no less important.[97]

He soon gives up on this formal endeavor, but not before he has claimed that "we will attach ourselves to this metaphysics. We will recognize it. We will debone it . . .We will first have to show that it is, and then what it is. We will start then by showing that it is. We will continue by showing what it is."[98] The excessive formality might evoke a smile, in my case, a laugh.

97. Péguy, *Œuvres II*, 841.

98. Péguy, *Œuvres II*, 843.

I would like to submit that Péguy's real argument in this section is about the proper way of conducting one's reason, in general, but also more specifically, in response to a phenomenon such as the religion of science. Reason requires the geological method, that is, thinking afresh with each event, without a prior hypothesis, allowing it to lead where it does. But something else is also necessary, most especially in the current context: speaking in one's own voice, complete with its idiosyncrasies. Style is key. "This is what is important, that is the one thing that interests me. Don't speak to me of what you are saying. I am not asking you what you are saying. I am asking you how you are saying it."[99] Style, in Péguy's usage, does not mean aesthetic refinements, but the particularity and even oddity attached to the speaking voice. Against an embodied reality, in this case, the religion of science, only a human being who appears not as disembodied logic but as embodied in his or her particular way of speaking, has a chance to make a dent. Since humor permeates Péguy's writing, sometimes implicit like a tone of voice, sometimes explicit, as in a turn of phrase, I will now turn to it as one of many stylistic features interwoven with his arguments. It must be said, as this section has already illustrated, that humor here does not induce Homeric laughter. Nor does it lie in the telling of jokes. It functions as a peculiarity of phrasing, a faint irony, or exaggeration to the point of absurdity.

Humor and Reason

Return to La Fontaine

We recall that Péguy began his meditation about the religion of science by turning to the historian Hippolyte Taine's book on La Fontaine's fables. Not only did the sky, the earth and many other material factors cause these fables to arise but also the seventeenth-century poet's manipulation of literary mechanisms—meter, grammar, logic, musicality etc.[100] At the end of his book, the historian once again returns to the importance of the natural world, in this case the French countryside, in the creation of French poetry.

> This is how the mind reproduces nature; the objects and the poetry of the external world become the objects and poetry of

99. Péguy, *Œuvres II*, 820.

100. Péguy, *Œuvres I*, 1398.

> the internal one. One should not conjecture too much, but in the end, it is because there is a France, it seems to me, that there has been a La Fontaine and that there have been Frenchmen.[101]

Péguy retorts: "My God, yes; only there is a France for everyone, France shines upon everyone, and yet all Frenchmen, while they remain French, are not La Fontaine."[102]

That retort, after the many pages listing the causes that led to La Fontaine's fables (it takes Péguy at least three pages to list them all), is comical in its very brevity. Part of the humor lies in how obvious his observation is. It is precisely this obvious point—that not everyone produces a great work of art—that the proponents of the scientific method were trying to debunk. La Fontaine was merely reflecting his environment, subject to the same causes that affected all his countrymen. Since material causes are key to the material world, and since only the material world exists, human beings too can be leveled to common denominators. But the gap between La Fontaine and his fellow seventeenth-century Frenchmen remains. Taine, using the scientific method, comes to certain conclusions, but one is permitted to point out, as a simple layman, that some really big problems remain unsolved.

Despite appearances, Péguy's quick retort was not intended to solve the problem of creativity in favor of some splendid independence of the artist from external influences. "My God, yes," Péguy says, completely agreeing that we are shaped by our environment. It matters that La Fontaine was born in France.[103] It just fails to explain why the same environmental factors did not act in the same way on everyone. There is only one La Fontaine. Since Taine also mentions all sorts of technical devices—grammar, logic, musicality, word choice, meter—neither should we understand Péguy to be denying, in pointing out the singularity of La Fontaine, the significance of a common set of poetic devices. Very frequently, especially in the later writings, he delights in discovering the technical elements in the poetry of Victor Hugo, among others.[104] These elements of craft do

101. Péguy, *Œuvres I*, 1411.

102. Péguy, *Œuvres I*, 1411.

103. Péguy had an enormous amount to say about the inescapability of being from a certain time and place. See, for example, his meditation on having been born in France in the immediate aftermath of the Franco-Prussian war, *Œuvres II*, 137–40. His major works are all meditations on time and memory.

104. Both the essays "Victor-Marie, Comte Hugo," and "Clio—dialogue de l'histoire et de l'âme païenne" are constructed around text interpretations. See Péguy, *Œuvres III*,

not add up, however, to a recipe that others can apply to become creative themselves. He cites a poem of La Fontaine, in which the speaker, an old man nearing death, asks his sons to separate a set of darts tightly bound together. Each tries but fails. Only he is able to separate them, only he has the secret of what holds them together.[105] This applies both to the secret of personality and to the secret of great works of art. When it comes to those great works, Péguy says, "One absolutely cannot see how they were made. They are a given, like life itself."[106]

A hundred years later, we have art works—musical compositions, poems, and essays, produced by computer programs—and robots who engage with humans in conversations. Neither the indivisible yet varied whole that constitutes a human being nor that of a great work of art is taken as a given. Each is viewed as a series of mechanisms or processes that can be duplicated. This is not the place to evaluate the status of these artificial creations, but rather to point out that they reveal what Péguy detected as the desire to duplicate reality at the heart of modern science. It in turn raises the question of whether humor—so dependent on quirks of personality, on specific contexts, on timing and placement—eludes being broken down into parts that can be put back together again. If so, humor, an indivisible yet varied whole that cannot be replicated, would testify *without the need of argument* to the limits of a method such as Taine's.[107] Humor cannot be defeated by argument,

161–345, 997–1214. Especially in the case of the poetry of Hugo, the attention to rhyme scheme, word usage, and variants of his work take up a good part of Péguy's discussion.

105. Péguy, *Œuvres I*, 1413.

106. Péguy, *Œuvres II*, 498.

107. There have been recent scientific studies of humor. See Provine, *Laughter.* Provine admitted, in a 1996 *American Scientist* article, that the science of laughter was still far from worked out. We don't know the genetic source of different sounds produced by laughing people, for example. Quoted in Carey, "Robert Provine." Carey also mentions a Humor Research Lab at the University of Colorado, Boulder, whose director, Peter McGraw, authored a book, "*The Humor Code: A Global Search for What Makes Things Funny.* Not unexpectedly, there are also numerous books on how to write jokes. Most recently, it appears that ChatPGT, the A.I. program, can write jokes "but it does not show that it understands what will make someone laugh. 'It does not grasp the nuance of what is funny,' said Oren Etzioni, the founding chief executive of the Allen Institute for AI, a prominent lab in Seattle," Metz, "In Pushing Frontiers of A.I," *New York Times*, A1, A14. A full-page article discusses the merits of ChatGPT as a source of jokes, see Zinoman, "Are Comedian Bot Ready to Kill?" Of course, Péguy's humor does not fit in the genre of jokes, and would be difficult to understand on the basis of the laughter it produced, should it have produced any to begin with.

much like the narratives about science cannot be defeated by argument. It creates a distance that argument cannot remove.

Return to Mathematics

Another instance of Péguy's humor occurs in the midst of his exploration of the language of mathematics, among his most arid pages. One wonders whether Péguy has followed his own advice here. "The daring of incompetence is everywhere the same and speaking of what one does not know will always remain the human being's favorite occupation."[108] His own mathematical education did not extend beyond his admittedly very good lycée. But Péguy is not pretending to perform mathematical operations. He is focusing on an ubiquitous mathematical concept, equality, and asking questions about the different meanings it has acquired in the course of mathematical history. Much reasoning ensues, involving two pieces of wood aligned on top of one another, and how the notion of equality involving superposition differs from the notion of equality involving interchangeability, expressed by points on a grid.[109] Just as the reader's eyes are beginning to glaze over, Péguy interrupts himself. "To make myself clear (*Je m'explique*): I am, do believe me, very embarrassed to find myself, to be in the midst of all these difficulties."[110] He then proceeds to explain the two pieces of wood superimposed on each other all over again. This is even more convoluted than his previous explanations because he has just discovered another dimension of the contrast he wishes to make. He apologizes again.

> To make myself clear (*Je m'explique*): I am myself very embarrassed, I find myself very unexplained (*inexpliqué*) [as to how I] find myself in the midst of these difficulties. I am myself difficult, unrewarding, difficulty-ridden (*difficultueux*). But that is because these difficulties are there. And we have come upon them.[111]

After so many attempts to distinguish between equal, equivalent and interchangeable—logical abstractions—a most particular person suddenly rears his head. This person insists on apologizing not once but

108. Péguy, *Œuvres II*, 1103.

109. Péguy, *Œuvres II*, 966–79.

110. Péguy, *Œuvres II*, 979.

111. Péguy, *Œuvres II*, 980.

twice, and in such an ungainly syntax, that explaining why he is sorry appears to require as many distinctions as the problem of the two pieces of wood. Not only is he difficult, presumably to read, but he is also *difficultueux*, exhibiting a special facility for getting himself into difficulties. As if this were not enough, in the next sentence, he is very unexplained, which from what follows, seems to mean that that he can't explain why he finds himself in such difficulties, why he finds his way to them. The final sentence flips all the difficulties on their head. It is no longer a matter of his limitations alone. He reached an impasse because he has touched on a real problem. That is, there are so many dimensions to the real world that one cannot get to all of the relationships between equality, equivalence and interchangeability. As soon as one discovers a contrast, something from the real world intrudes to blur it. Thinking about such matters practically guarantees that the thinker will run into trouble very quickly. Reality is tricky. "The more one advances . . . in the knowledge of reality, always mysterious, often sneaky, the more naturally one lands in difficulties, perhaps inextricable, as well as in complicated propositions."[112] But since the relations of mathematics to the concrete world in which we live affects us all, we have no choice but to use our reason and then realize it can only get us so far. I would read Péguy's apology here as a reminder that thinking is not the work of logic alone, but also a matter of intellectual honesty. This honesty comes not from logic, but from a commitment to truth that precedes and accompanies it.

Explaining the Returns: Repetition

A few pages later, Péguy insists that he never repeats himself, that his one great success is that he has never repeated himself. He repeats the point that he never repeats himself for quite a while.

> It is perhaps the only rule that we have followed since the beginning of our studies . . . never to repeat ourselves. And in fact we have succeeded . . . In fact we have succeeded in never repeating ourselves. We have never repeated ourselves. Not even once. And this is already a great result. And we are not going to start today. It is not at our age that we will start."[113]

112. Péguy, *Œuvres II*, 900.
113. Péguy, *Œuvres II*, 983.

It is unnecessary to point out how often Péguy repeats himself as he proclaims that he never does and that he will not start today. On the surface he does nothing but repeat himself, not only at the level of the words in his sentences and their return at periodical intervals, although even here, there is variation rather than identity, but he also repeats himself on the level of his main theme. Let us, for brevity's sake, and quite inadequately, articulate it as the utter disregard for the limits of what we can know in what he calls the religion of science. But each time this theme appears, it comes from another direction and illuminates a previously unnoticed aspect. Péguy's retort to Taine, for example, and his own investigation of mathematics both point to limits. In the case of the historian, he points to the limits of mechanistic explanations for human creativity. In the second instance, he suggests the limit of mathematics' reach, unable to grasp the non-interchangeable, but the limits also lie in the philosopher's inability to encompass all the complexities involved in demonstrating the limits of mathematics. Rather than repetition, then, we have an intersection between points, what, we recall, Péguy calls *recoupement*.[114] "The path from which one enters the house . . . the side from which one comes in . . . count[s] a great deal for the very value and the content and the meaning."[115] One ends up in the same house, but the direction one takes to get to it changes what one sees along the way. This intersection is all important, revealing an inexhaustible center from which the thinking, in all its variety, proceeds. We are back to Pascal's order of the heart, and also, of course, to the thought at the back of the mind.

Return to the University

I cannot resist giving one more example of humor at work, illuminating limits from yet another starting point. Péguy states that despite the French university's attempt to be modern, to be "with it," it nonetheless fluctuates between being fifty to five hundred years behind the times. He then makes it more precise. It is sometimes more than five hundred years behind, but never less than thirty.[116] He goes on to illustrate his preposterous claim most soberly. The word "science," for example, is used in humanities faculties, he claims, in ways long discarded in the

114. Péguy, *Œuvres II*, 579, 804, 828, 870, 940, 984.

115. Péguy, *Œuvres II*, 854.

116. Péguy, *Œuvres II*, 907.

labs of the science faculties themselves.[117] He gives as another example of a lag the teaching of Romanticism, all the rage in his literature classes at the École Normale, long after it stopped being a living movement among artists themselves.[118] A third instance involves Karl Marx, introduced at the Sorbonne in 1895, thanks to the German literature professor, Charles Andler, who provoked a scandal by doing so. Péguy claimed Andler had managed to reduce to a mere fifty years the usual five-hundred-year delay of the university.[119]

The discrepancy between being fifty years behind and five hundred year behind, and then the added precision that the real delay might be between thirty and five hundred years, might make a reader smile. Is Péguy poking fun at the inevitable imprecisions of numerical precision? "Everyone knows that numeration, number, make for the beginning of science," he had once quipped.[120] Or, rather, is he poking fun at the inability of statistics to encompass how both numbers could be right, but on qualitatively different levels? The university's general conservatism, dating five hundred years, makes it consistently thirty to fifty years behind. The point, however, is not the accuracy of Péguy's evaluation of the university but his play with the authority of numbers. He deploys quantification against the very institution, the university, that, in its latest attempt to be "with it," is promoting it. We are back to Péguy's emphasis on epistemological limits, but from another angle. Not only can quantification not grasp key qualitative differences but also those who wield numbers do not have immunity from the same quantification that they deploy on others, to which they will surely object, as if this simple reversal had never occurred to them.

These are just instances of what I have called Péguy's humor, appearing so frequently that it is difficult to separate it from his arguments. Beyond the point he is making in every instance, his humor always involves a person who intrudes into the thinking process, interrupting its course. The sudden presence of this quirky individual adds layers that the logic of his argument alone cannot get to, adding a play of meanings unavailable without it. Never is the reader allowed to forget that a specific, fallible person lies behind what might otherwise appear as totally disembodied knowledge. Perhaps Péguy's fear that resorting purely to logic, what he

117. Péguy, *Œuvres II*, 909.

118. Péguy, *Œuvres II*, 908.

119. Péguy, *Œuvres II*, 918–20.

120. Péguy, *Œuvres III*, 268.

labeled the geographical method, was dangerous lay in that, whatever the force of the argument, he was resorting to the same abstract method as the enemy, handing him a victory by ignoring the concrete, multiple dimensions that argument ignores.

Part 3: Intuition and Reason

In the previous section, I chose four passages, among the many that are sprinkled throughout Péguy's voluminous writings. Why these four? Why humor? I bumped into these passages as I was reading along. They arrested my attention before I knew why they were important, which took me quite some time to figure out. Péguy characterizes this as proceeding according to the intuitive method: "To choose, this is the great word . . . to choose is to take a short cut, how to choose, then, in the indefiniteness, in the infinity of the real, without some intuition, without some direct apperception, without an inner grasp."[121]

Direct apperception does not mean we come to what we choose from the ocean before us as if we were empty slates. In my case, I was trained as a historian of religions for whom humor of a certain sort is always meaningful.[122] This does not mean that I was specifically looking for it or that I knew ahead of time what each instance of it meant. Rather, my training functioned more in the nature of "the thought at the back of the mind," guiding my thinking, but not present as an explicit theory or thesis I was testing. Perhaps when Péguy refers to intuition as "inner grasp," as he does in the above quotation, he is referring to this guiding thought, not analyzable into parts,[123] which makes us capable of seizing the guiding thought in someone else's writings, its beating heart, what permeates it as a whole.

Intuition is unmediated, but it cannot arise without a background. In the case of reading texts, it requires a great deal of training, and also a long experience of putting that training to work. Péguy had an enormous amount to say about the training that might lead to intuition, especially in regard to reading texts.[124] I will restrict myself here to three

121. Péguy, *Œuvres I*, 1449.

122. See Bolle, *Freedom of Man*, 35–72, in which Bolle discusses the importance of humor as a category for understanding key religious expressions such as myth.

123. Péguy, *Œuvres I*, 1413.

124. Some of the most important, and beautiful, passages that Péguy wrote about the art of reading occur in a later essay, perhaps his greatest, "Dialogue de l'histoire et

interrelated aspects. The first precondition relates to what he says about his professor of Latin, Charles Édet. He was a stickler for detail, "untiringly teaching accuracy, slowness, exactness, precaution, reading closely." It involved conceptual clarity, not confusing "unreal with potential," for instance, and linguistic command, the ability to weigh the worth of different translations.[125] Édet taught precision, *justesse*, which is inseparable from justice," says Péguy.[126] Secondly, it is not enough to learn the mechanics (and ethics) of good reading practices, as in this first prerequisite. One must also acquire familiarity with the contents of a variety of texts, an intimacy with passages lodging deeply in the mind, like the many lines of poetry that Péguy tells us are always floating in his head.[127] These texts constitute a kind of memory, of which one is not even aware, but which comes out at crucial moments. While reading a contemporary article on physics, for example, one may recall, as Péguy did, some classical Greek nomenclature. In remarking on the affinity between the cosmologies of the classical Greeks and modern cosmologies, Péguy cautions that this sort of parallel can only occur "for one who knows how to read. That is for one who knows a bit of history and philosophy."[128] Intuition implies a prior wealth of knowledge. It arises from it.

Thirdly, intuition requires what Péguy calls, "*un travail continu dans la matière*,"[129] spending a long time with the matter at hand, that is, the specific object of one's study. Intuition requires immersion, impossible without an investment of time. Péguy's first choice of the matter at hand—the works of Renan and Taine—resulted from his long familiarity with

de l'âme païenne," Péguy, *Œuvres III*, 1006–20. In the context of interpreting Homer, he speaks of reading as more than "entering into." It is a sympathy, a friendship, a faithfulness, even a love. One must enter as if to go to the source of the work and literally collaborate with the author. "Reading is the act in common, of the one reading and the one read," Péguy, *Œuvres III*, 1007. It is not a passive receptivity but a collaboration and a cooperation, Péguy, *Œuvres III*, 1008. It is a contract in which we become responsible for the future of the work we read, Péguy, *Œuvres III*, 1020. The ethical dimension of the act of reading is reminiscent here of the writings on hermeneutics of the French Jewish philosopher Emmanuel Levinas. See "Of the Jewish Reading of Scriptures," "The Name of God According to Some Rabbinic Texts," "Revelation in the Jewish Tradition," in Levinas, *Beyond the Verse*, 101–50.

125. Péguy, *Œuvres II*, 371.

126. Péguy, *Œuvres II*, 372.

127. Péguy, *Œuvres II*, 903.

128. Péguy, *Œuvres II*, 649–50.

129. Péguy, *Œuvres II*, 964.

them. They had been the object of his youthful passion.[130] Even more so, his reflections on the passages he cites would be unthinkable without his long exposure to the thought of both Blaise Pascal and Henri Bergson, whose influence, singly and together, permeates so much of what Péguy writes.[131] As already shown, Pascal's thoughts on the limits of reason, about the truths of the heart, are reflected in Péguy's form, although the influence goes beyond this. As I will show presently, Bergson's thought about intuition and about the limits of the scientific method appear not as separate ideas but as the background against which Péguy thinks, although he also often quotes them explicitly. He takes these thinkers to realms of daily life and thought that they did not themselves consider, demonstrating thereby the creative power of their influence.[132]

What makes intuition direct, then, if it depends on so much prior knowledge, and requires so much prior immersion? It bypasses a deliberately constructed hypothesis. Memory shows up as if without us. We did not even know it was there. In that spontaneous rising up lies the directness of intuition. That directness can only be highly personal. No one has the same memory as anyone else. But, emphatically, arguing for the intuitive method is not tantamount to arguing for an individual insight arising as if unrelated to any prior influence. The books one has read deeply, for example—although memory is not limited to them by far—are an important component of one's uniqueness. Intuition, as we have seen, also does not imply a lack of precision or doing away with skills. Choosing what is significant depends on a prior body of painstakingly acquired knowledge. Neither does intuition reject logic, proof and exposition. It *precedes* them, grasping a whole immediately, through the choice of a significant part. Logic and reason follow in explicating the part's significance to the

130. Péguy, *Œuvres II*, 504.

131. For Pascal, see Péguy, *Œuvres II*, 209, 804–10, 857–70. Péguy had also, in his very early essays, referred to Pascal in his very titles, "Lettre du Provincial," "De la grippe," "Encore de la grippe," "Toujours de la grippe," in Péguy, *Œuvres I*, 287–99, 401–75. For Bergson, see Péguy, *Œuvres II*, 659–66, 864, 1163–4. The last of the essays he wrote before his death were on Bergson. For two recent studies of Péguy's relation to Bergson's thought, see Riquier, "Péguy Bergsonien," 149–78; Milbank, "Foreword," xi–xxxv.

132. In the process, Péguy also modifies the tradition in which he works. In the case of Pascal, he refuses the notion of progress that is suggested by the famous image of later generations standing on the shoulders of giants, and therefore seeing further. In the case of Bergson, he puts much more emphasis than Bergson on the decay that accompanies the passage of time.

whole, careful to avoid ready-made categories.[133] It is intuition, then, that Péguy opposes to the "scientific method," and its claims to break down and replicate, with no remaining whole. He is, in fact, arguing that the practitioners of "the scientific method" renounce what they are themselves practicing. Once they have started to express what they see, they have made choices.[134] These choices are determined by "the thought at the back of the mind," and do not emanate from simple objectivity. For this reason, among others, Péguy tells us that he avoided the distinction between objectivity and subjectivity like the plague.[135]

This is both his argument about intuition, and the way he proceeds. Quite a few other features of Péguy's writing direct us to this whole which precedes the parts. One thinks of his practice of quoting at length, pages at a time, a habit that he remarks will get him in trouble for copyright infringement, if he does not contain himself.[136] If he were allowed, he confesses, he might not be able to control himself and quote the entire book.[137] From these long citations, he usually focuses on a line or two, from which his own thinking takes off. Why did he not cite just those two lines? Perhaps, leaving so much untouched is the point. One's choice emerges from a vast sea of meaning, which it does not exhaust.[138]

Another feature of his style is his wariness of definitions.[139] For instance, he barely defines "intuition" beyond what I have already cited, and yet, I submit, intuition is present in one form or another everywhere in his writings. Each time the term explicitly appears, the context provides another angle on its meaning, but, more importantly, even when a term does not appear, the reader can infer a connection with a passage in which it does appear explicitly. For example, when Péguy speaks about his Latin teacher's attention to detail, he does not mention intuition. But surely, one cannot help noticing that when he speaks of the direct access

133. Péguy, *Œuvres III*, 1254–6.

134. Péguy, *Œuvres I*, 1449.

135. Péguy, *Œuvres II*, 631.

136. Péguy, *Œuvres I*, 1419. In fact, he had gotten into trouble with the publishing house Calmann-Levy several times for citing texts to which they owned the rights. See Burac, "Notices," Péguy, *Œuvres I*, 1845.

137. He does go on to reproduce Renan's text for at least twelve pages, in small print, most of them uninterrupted by his commentary. Péguy, *Œuvres I*, 1421–32.

138. Péguy, *Œuvres I*, 1438. In a later text, after a lengthy interpretation of Homer, the voice of history says, "Do not fear that I have *gobbled* up your Homer. It is an inexhaustible flood, and the more one takes, the more there is left," in *Œuvres III*, 1168.

139. Péguy, *Œuvres II*, 964.

of intuition, he cannot mean the refusal of a prior education in careful reading. Linking explicit and implicit passages to each other requires deep familiarity with the whole of a text. Péguy's reluctance to define central terms forces both the author and the reader to work in the geodesic method, tracing multiple, non-linear interconnections.

The Importance of Voice

Rather than to continue illustrating other ways that Péguy both deploys and elicits intuition, I would like to turn to a single passage that complicates our understanding of intuition considerably. On its basis, it might not be too bold to state that intuition comes into play exclusively in response to a human expression. In order to catch what he might mean, we need to return to the importance of style. "Don't speak to me of what you are saying," he had said. " I am not asking you what you are saying. I am asking you how you are saying it."[140] He then continues:

> It is the tone, it is the style, it is the resonance of what you say that I await, and when I hear it, I listen. Because that comes from you, because that comes from the human being himself, because only this exists, with the only precondition, with the only reservation, that you exist, that you are . . . Only this could prove it, only this could be a proof . . . If you do not exist, if you are not, you will be a human being without a style. You will not even be able, for this too is an art, to turn a corner on a bicycle with any style.[141]

The immediate context of this passage is Péguy's polemic with the historians and sociologists of his time, who ignored the texture of a text in favor of mechanistic, causal explanations, and who dismissed style as "subjective."[142] They would catalogue ideas according to who had expressed them in the past. Péguy is arguing that ideas are not things but

140. Péguy, *Œuvres II*, 820.

141. Péguy, *Œuvres II*, 821–2.

142. Péguy speaking of the humanities at the university, quips. "For it was understood that to have style was a slight on one's honor," Péguy, *Œuvres II*, 1058. Ringer, *Fields of Knowledge*, 227, reports that Gustave Lanson, a professor of literature at the Sorbonne, one of the proponents of the scientific method whom Péguy occasionally names, stated that a business report seemed a better model for writing about literature than a literary essay. Lanson also thought of literary criticism as "subjective," as opposed to the objectivity of literary history. He advocated for the control of "personal" reactions. Ringer, *Fields of Knowledge*, 256–7.

living voices that change meaning depending on how they are said. The "how" makes it enter into the world of meaning, gives it life.

I would like to read "only this exists" in a stronger sense, however. Only what is communicated through a human voice is real, provided that human voice is inhabited by what it is uttering. This does not mean enthusiasm or even conviction. The idea must arise out of one's life, formed by the passage of time, "because it is a matter of your own life, of your own existence, of your own being."[143] The last sentence in the passage is unexpected. What does the riding of a bicycle have to do with anything? It adds the element of an idea emerging from the life lived from another angle. Turning a corner on a bicycle with style implies a long practice of riding one and freedom from the mere mechanics of it. Style is indeed a kind of freedom, born from the pleasure one takes in an activity, so familiar that one can play with it. The very insertion of that bicycle in this passage is a feature of Péguy's style. An idea so expressed, through the vehicle of a particular person, is our conduit to the real.

The centrality of human expression flits in and out of Péguy's writings. In a series of dense pages, he argues that metaphysical certainty exists only in relation to our knowing of human beings, whom we grasp intuitively.[144] That is, only human beings convey to us what is real, because the real cannot be grasped through a concept but only through an intuition. We are present to ourselves and others are present to us with an immediacy, with a directness that does not exist in regard to matter. We know astronomical movements and mechanical equivalences, for example, differently from the way we know human beings.[145] The former requires instruments and measurements. Only in the case of human beings, do we simultaneously shed an inner light and clarify our own inner selves.[146] To accept as the sole model of knowledge the knowledge of matter is to cede our own intimate presence to ourselves and of others to us, "that certainty of grasp which in ourselves, through ourselves and on ourselves we have of human beings and of humanity."[147]

These pages are among the most abstract in Péguy's essays. One can nonetheless hear echoes of a distinction between understanding and explaining, associated with the German philosopher of hermeneutics

143. Péguy, *Œuvres II*, 822.

144. Péguy, *Œuvres II*, 632.

145. Péguy, *Œuvres II*, 632–3.

146. Péguy, *Œuvres II*, 632.

147. Péguy, *Œuvres II*, 629.

Wilhelm Dilthey. But, I would submit, the accent in Péguy's expression, the "how" of it has a special urgency. He is not serenely discussing different jurisdictions—the humanities limited to the domain of understanding, and the natural sciences to explanation—but exposing a danger. Our immediate presence to ourselves and others to us is what makes us human. It is a given, not explainable by something else, a whole not exhausted by its parts. It is precisely the access to this inexhaustible whole, already there when we begin to think, which he refers to as metaphysics. It is our distinctive characteristic as humans. "Metaphysics is also of the human being and of humanity. And it might even be what is proper to it."[148] I take this to mean that denying reality to that immediate access to ourselves, prior and indivisible, is to dehumanize us.

This, for Péguy, is not a neutral stand but a position with enormous and potentially devastating consequences, not only for the particular human being but for our ability to come into contact with the real to begin with. For, if I understand Péguy correctly, when it comes to knowing the real, *only understanding particular human beings through the medium of our own subjectivity give us access.* Observations of objects through the medium of instruments and hypotheses gives us much useful, partial knowledge, but they do not reveal our reality as it really is. In other words, although he does not use these terms, those who deny the validity of intuitive grasp deny not merely subjectivity but objectivity as well.

This may explain the centrality of reading texts, including, it goes without saying, those of scientists who write in a non-technical language,[149] in Péguy's writings, almost all of which have their point of departure in the works of others. He does not treat these texts as an assemblage of parts, but as symbols, that is, "a part of reality, homogeneous and homothetical with a whole of reality, and representing suddenly, through an enlargement of reality, made through art and reality, that immense whole of reality."[150] Each text is a piece of our reality, reflecting it from one angle. A symbol here is not a concrete object standing for an abstract idea. It is a concrete whole reflecting, from one angle, the larger whole of which it is a part. Art, whether on the part of the author or of the reader, means apt choice, concentration on a part in which the whole

148. Péguy, *Œuvres II*, 629.

149. Péguy was a frequent reader of *La revue générale des sciences*. At various points, he interprets Bacon, Pascal as scientist, Newton and Darwin. See Péguy, *Œuvres II*, 618, 1225–6, 1228.

150. Péguy, *Œuvres I*, 1435.

is reflected. The author chooses to focus on a part of the inexhaustible world he or she lives in. The reader chooses a part of the rich world of a great text to illuminate its meaning as a whole. A sentence, a word can illuminate a world.[151] "To choose is an artistic technique . . . to choose is to take a short cut; and the short cut is one of the more difficult artistic techniques." Neither for the author who composes, nor for the reader who interprets[152] is there is a prescribed place to choose. Intuition, within the constraints of memory, is free.

The link between great texts and reality is even more explicit in a later essay. Now that he has finished his formal schooling, Péguy tells us, he spends all his time apprenticed "to the masters and to reality, to authentic masters and to the head master reality, that is, today that I am spending my life in looking around and in reading texts."[153] He underscores this equivalence when, yet later, he refers to works of genius. They arise when the author in question becomes so permeated by a nascent reality and manages to convey it so powerfully that the work becomes permanently associated with that reality, and enters the memory of mankind.[154] Not all texts need to be works of genius. He considered neither Taine nor Renan in that category, and yet they were symbols of the nascent religion of science. Whether works of genius or not, texts are bridges to the many aspects of the real.

Although Péguy's emphasis is on texts, he often speaks of other kinds of human expressions as symbolic, that is, as parts of reality revealing a whole: haystacks, roofs, railroad tracks, military formations, public ceremonies, the layout of fields in the countryside, the city of Paris, events, works of art. Nonverbal expressions exist in relation to the verbal ones. The movement of cattle and carts on French country roads bears some resemblance to the rhythm of French classical versification, revealing a similar sensibility.[155] Which precedes which? They coexist. Still, Péguy's overwhelming reliance on verbal expression, from the beginning to the end of his oeuvre, suggests that human speech best illuminates the reality that is already there. But the relation can also be reversed. What one sees around oneself illuminates the expression. It is not enough to read. One must look around.

151. Péguy, *Œuvres III*, 1151.

152. Péguy, *Œuvres I*, 1449.

153. Péguy, *Œuvres II*, 902–3.

154. Péguy, *Œuvres II*, 1165.

155. Péguy, *Œuvres II*, 1007–14.

Intuition in the Sciences

As we might expect, as with so much in Péguy's writings, the question of the human voice, of intuition and of access to the real, as if it were not complicated enough, gets yet more complicated. In his later writings of this period, he makes room for intuition in regard to the practice of the natural sciences. A new category when thinking about knowledge, the category of competence, comes to the fore.[156] It is the third and highest level of knowledge in the realm of the natural world, reserved for the scientist who has so internalized his field of study that it no longer appears to him only as separate principles and discrete practices. As an example of what he means by competence, Péguy cites in full a speech given by the biologist Émile Duclaux to the future professors of the newly established Universités populaires, whose purpose was to provide instruction not to university students but to workers.[157] He cautioned the professors to imagine their field as a whole, and not just the separate principles and practices they teach sequentially. Much science and mathematics, Duclaux says, are taught in such a way that one does not see the forest for the trees. "Notions of the whole are missing, to such a degree has one been hypnotized by compartments and divisions."[158] The result is that, facing concrete situations, the scientists lack a flexible understanding, and are unable to address what faces them effectively.[159] Duclaux urges the instructors to try to shed light on the problems facing the workers in the everyday world, not through technical know-how as such, which they already have, but through giving them a perspective on their practices, making them able to make links they would otherwise not have made. This requires an understanding of a fluid whole which can be expressed differently in different contexts.

Competence resembles intuition in many ways, although Péguy, at least in an earlier text, does not use the term, speaking instead of an internalization of the scientist's knowledge so deep that his or her choices in the face of particular problems become as if spontaneous, similar to what precedes humanists' choices.[160] He does use the term

156. Péguy, *Œuvres II*, 1134–46, 1162–81.

157. Péguy, *Œuvres II*, 1146–61.

158. Péguy, *Œuvres II*, 1155.

159. Péguy, *Œuvres II*, 1155.

160. Péguy, *Œuvres II*, 1199–1201, 1213.

intuition in discussing the work of certain scientists in a later essay.[161] Yet he does not put the knowledge of matter and the knowledge of human beings on the same level. The immediacy of access to the object of knowledge is missing, in the case of the scientist. In investigating the material world, the scientist is outside his subject matter, and has to set up all sorts of equipment to get to it. If only he could be inside in the way that a human is inside being human, he would happily give up all his machines.[162] Intuition can come into play only between human beings, and not between human beings and objects, even if the scientist at the level of competence sees the whole of his field and not just parts. At one point, Péguy suggests "that no matter how much a scientist owns his science, it is never the way an artist owns his art. There is an immediate touch (*atteinte*) in art which is eternal, definitive, achieved once and for all, which does not occur in the sciences. A Rembrandt owns color, light, and shade, as a painter, in a way that a scientist specializing in optics cannot."[163] Scientific knowledge is always provisional and mediated by hypothesis in a way that artistic knowledge is not, even if both attempt to capture nature. It is not the same kind of capture.

If we turn for help to Bergson's notion of intuition, to which Péguy was heavily indebted, things do not necessarily become much clearer, at least as concerns its status in the natural sciences. On the one hand, in his *Introduction to Metaphysics*, Bergson denies that intuition has a place in the natural sciences at all. Intuition requires that the object one is trying to know, both one and multiple, have an inside that we can penetrate immediately as a whole. "By intuition is meant the kind of intellectual sympathy by which one places oneself within an object in order to coincide with what is unique in it."[164] Scientists cannot perceive objects from the inside, as an indivisible whole. They operate through concepts, breaking the whole into parts, reducing to the smaller unit, the analytical method. Given this, intuition would be limited to the understanding of human beings, as Bergson goes on to say, "There is one reality, at least, which we all seize from within, by intuition and not by simple analysis. It is our own personality in its flowing through

161. Péguy, *Œuvres III*, 316.

162. Péguy, *Œuvres III*, 321–2.

163. Péguy, *Œuvres II*, 1214.

164. Bergson, *Introduction to Metaphysics*, 23–24. A very similar opposition between intuition and the scientific method also appears in Bergson, *Creative Evolution*, 189–90.

time—our self which endures.[165] Our own personality has the capacity to grasp others immediately, from the inside, as when we identify with someone else or with a character in a novel.[166]

On the other hand, Bergson claims that knowledge of the natural world in the modern sciences arose through intuition. "Modern science dates from the day when mobility [or duration] was set up as an independent reality." How exactly intuition arises is not crystal clear. He mentions Galileo and his desire to capture motion not through already-established concepts but through observation of actual objects. He would not have resorted to this method without an intuition about motion, but, again, how he got it is not further specified in this text.[167] Whatever its origin, it is incontrovertible, for Bergson, that intuition disappeared of necessity from scientific investigations as scientists went on to make their analytical concepts the only arbitrators of the real, in the process, turning mobility into immobility.

> Intuition of duration . . . quickly turns into fixed, distinct and immobile concepts . . . Men of science have fixed their attention mainly on the concepts with which they have marked the path of intuition . . . Gradually they have blotted out all difference, in positive science, between the natural and the artificial, between the data of immediate intuition, and the enormous work of analysis which the understanding pursues around intuition.[168]

It seems, then, that the natural sciences, in their essential daily operations, exclude intuition, a knowledge of the whole, by definition. Their mode is analysis, breaking the object up into parts, comparing, reducing.[169] Yet the sciences would not have arisen without an intuition that precedes their methods.

This may account for Péguy's insistence on a broad education in philosophy and classical and modern literature for scientists, claiming that the greatest discoveries often came from scientists who were thus educated.[170] The humanities become a bridge to the realm of intuition for the scientists, who, of course, develop that intuition through extended

165. Bergson, *Introduction to Metaphysics*, 24.
166. Bergson, *Introduction to Metaphysics*, 22.
167. Bergson, *Introduction to Metaphysics*, 54–55.
168. Bergson, *Introduction to Metaphysics*, 54–55.
169. Bergson, *Introduction to Metaphysics*, 24.
170. Péguy, *Œuvres II*, 1221, 1224.

practice with the matter of their particular discipline. Humanists, for their part, cannot ignore scientific findings. They must stay informed about the findings of the natural sciences, as they are conveyed in a language accessible to a general audience, as one more area upon which to exercise intuition.[171]

At this point, all the adjectives Péguy used—difficult, *difficultieux*, difficulty-prone—apply to my attempt to see how intuition fits in the natural sciences, according to Péguy, and certainly according to Bergson. Beyond the clear fact that it appears in the natural sciences but not through its methods, it is difficult to say more. We can nonetheless insist on some nonnegotiable points in Péguy's understanding of intuition: It is what makes the humanities and the arts what they are. It defines them. In deploying it, the humanities and the arts touch a whole that cannot be divided into parts, although each act of understanding reveals that whole from another aspect. That whole presupposes an education that provides the wealth of knowledge antecedent to making intuitive choices. Most importantly, the intuitive method is also a metaphysics, presupposing the very whole it seeks. It is thus a counter-metaphysics to that of the religion of science, affirming what that religion denies—the centrality and uniqueness of consciousness, understood as a fluid whole not amenable to instruments meant to locate an object divisible into parts.

Conclusion

Péguy is our contemporary in that the narratives reducing the human to component parts or processes are more powerful than ever. What makes him even more our contemporary is that the attempts to counter those narratives seem as futile as in Péguy's time, if not more so. I will point to just two examples. The very thought that education in the humanities should be centered on prolonged conversations with central texts, both ancient and modern, is often dismissed today as a ploy of a nationalist or racist agenda, intentionally obstructing the real force of the world, power dynamics, and thus perpetuating injustice by not attempting to change them.[172] If, on top of this, one would suggest that scientists themselves

171. Péguy, *Œuvres II*, 1231.

172. As an illustration of how politicized a curriculum of classical texts is in 2023, see Goldstein, "Florida Colleges," *New York Times*, A22. The test was not created to promote a conservative agenda but has gotten trapped in Florida politics. The article mentions that the test includes some contemporary authors, even if the majority is from earlier periods of Western history.

need to be exposed to classical texts, both contemporary and ancient, including the classical texts of scientists themselves, as background nourishment for their work as scientists, one has gone even further beyond the pale. To forge a language that argues otherwise, without falling into the camp of reactionaries or fools, remains a daunting challenge, even if there are glimmers of change on the horizon.[173]

In yet another way as well, we seem to have lost a language of critique, of distance. The duplication of features we associate as unique to human consciousness—programs that can recognize faces, engage in conversation, compose verse or computer code, and most recently, exhibit paranoia and jealousy—is all around us. We may still be surprised when a program is able to imitate one more feature we thought exclusive to humans, and we may still attempt to find arguments for our uniqueness. But the assumption that we are merely replicable processes dominates through the very objects that surround us, suddenly alarmingly like ourselves. The point is not so much that we are any closer than we ever were to finding the secret of creation, but that the idea that we are indeed almost there has become the "thought at the back of the mind," functioning even without our awareness.

Péguy, for his part, did not think the war against the religion of science was lost. Even if he knew that the battles of the day could only end in defeat, new underground forces were being born.[174] Reality has a way of playing tricks. It is certain to change, only we do not know how. In the meantime, the task is to keep seizing that whole, that thought at the back of the mind, and to keep on trying. He wrote thousands and thousands of pages, always in that same inimitable style. As already mentioned, much of what he wrote was not published in his lifetime. "In the end," asks Robert Burac, the editor of his complete works, "was it not more important for Péguy to write than to publish all that he had written?"[175] We might think of it as a daily purification, like a prayer. He spoke of his religion "as the absolute respect of reality, of the real as it is given to us, as it comes."[176] Respecting it lies in the effort to locate it every day anew. This

173. Emma Green, *Old School*, 12–18, reports on a growing classical education movement, mostly associated with conservative causes, but now also including other schools, whose founders wish to improve lower-income students' education, perceived to be inadequate in the public-school system. Still, the subtitle of the article is telling, "have the liberal arts gone conservative?"

174. Péguy, *Œuvres II*, 589–91, 1032–4.

175. Burac, "Avertissement," in Péguy, *Œuvres II*, xix.

176. Péguy, *Œuvres II*, 604.

daily thinking from scratch on the basis of what appears on our horizon does not seem like much of an attack against an enemy who held all the important fortifications. The important thing was not to win the argument, but to keep embodying the metaphysics, keeping its reality present for oneself. In the process, one leaves behind writings or other forms of expression for the time when the current narratives around the sciences will loosen their grip. One practices daily not only for oneself, then, but as a hope for the future. The religion of science is, after all, but one metaphysics among others, not the final truth to which we have arrived.

I want to conclude with an article I just read about ChatGPT. The author underscores that it produces impressive results. When he asked the device to provide a summary of Theodor Adorno and Max Horkheimer's book on capitalism and ideology, the result, he reports, was more than adequate. "[I]t gives me a shockingly good answer, including details faithful to that notoriously difficult text."[177] But he also points out what many people have already, the flatness of A.I. language. "What GPT systems spit out is language, but averaged out around a selected center of words. It's a mush . . . but ironed out and set to the most middling version of itself."[178] This flattened expression, reproduces dominant ways of thinking, what the author refers to as ideology. Péguy's emphasis on intuition was precisely a counter point to this flattening out, to what the author of the article also refers to as "kitsch," "the predigested," "the pathways better-travelled than others."[179] For Péguy, to think is to immerse oneself again and again in a text, in an event, without knowing what might come out ahead of time. Péguy's style, so quirky and filled with an odd humor, embodied something always in the making, imperfect, groping. The power of his thought cannot be separated from that style. Is style enough to get beyond ready-made thinking, that is, thinking in ready-made categories, and can it give us a peek beyond the categories that rule our world? Not in itself. A.I. can imitate style, to a degree. But Péguy's works do not depend on style alone. Their meaning depends on an interpreter who can see the hidden connections in his thought and express them in his or her particular style. The central point remains hidden, and keeps on remaining hidden, throughout the chain of interpreters. Style is but a vehicle, but an essential one. The humanities are best defended by insisting on this hiddenness, and on

177. Weatherby, "ChatGPT," 3.

178. Weatherby, "ChatGPT," 3.

179. Weatherby, "ChatGPT," 4.

a form adequate to preserve it. Much more is at stake than merely an academic discipline, as Péguy never tired of pointing out.

CHAPTER 2

Immortality

The Religion of Science in Don DeLillo's *Zero K*

Preface

In the previous essay, I had claimed that the questions Péguy raised about the natural sciences in the early twentieth-century remain very much with us in the first decades of the twenty-first. Don DeLillo's *Zero K*, published in 2016, does much to illustrate this continuity.[1] Although countless differences in sensibility and style separate the American novelist from the French philosopher, both authors expose the promise of transcendence embedded in the narratives emanating from the natural sciences, and explore the secret penetration of these narratives into our everyday life. This is to say that, in both cases, we confront the religious status the natural sciences have acquired in our world, its status as the thought at the back of the mind. The point of intersection between the two authors also extends to the way they invoke, not only through argument but also in the very form of their writings, a different kind of transcendence, inexorably tied to human limits.

1. DeLillo, *Zero K*, 2016.

Introducing DeLillo

I had mentioned in the introduction that background information about the authors in this book is not essential for understanding their works. In the case of DeLillo, that background information is scarce, in any case. Although he has given interviews regularly, he very rarely reveals anything about his life. Rather, he makes clear that he wants to maintain his distance from our culture of celebrity and mediatization in order to insure his independence as a novelist. "We're all a beat away from becoming elevator music," he tells one of his interviewers."[2] Preserving that very endangered distance becomes the very aim of his writing.

We nonetheless can glean some details about him from the interviews. He was raised in the Bronx, in an immigrant Italian-American family, attending Catholic schools and Fordham University. This Catholic background hardly provides direct access to his novels, however. As one interpreter puts it, even if scenes in his novels point to a sense of a mystery communally experienced, they are inseparable from an ironic reading.[3] In addition, "[W]hat happens remains discursively unsecured by any theological vocabulary."[4] *Zero K*, the novel in question here, comes late in DeLillo's oeuvre (he was born in 1936), making him eighty at the time of its publication. It too fits the pattern described above. It is marked by a transcendence that eschews its name, not visibly grounded in Catholic theology.

Two other features characterize DeLillo's works. The first is the role language plays in it, which we shall see ourselves in the second half of our analysis. It is not merely his tool, but also a central theme.[5] Playful and varied, language, in its very form, points to a way out of what entraps us, despite our expressed doubts about the possibility of escape. "DeLillo's affirmation of language seems to point toward a spiritual force at odds with the skepticism of his characters."[6] The second feature of his works, often noted, is his prescience. DeLillo has an uncanny knack for noticing the cultural mood, the cultural turn, the way our sense of reality now coincides with what we see on our multiple screens, for instance. The wonder lies in the specificity with which he manages to capture the

2. Begley, "The Art of Fiction," 95.
3. McClure, "DeLillo and Mystery," 176.
4. McClure, "DeLillo and Mystery," 168.
5. Cowart, "DeLillo and the Power of Language," 151–65.
6. Duvall, "Introduction," 8.

phenomena in question. The signs he notices are there for everyone to see but most of us have not looked or have not found the language to convey our situation. His novels speak just ahead of some phenomenon that becomes part of the common mental landscape. The one that follows *Zero K*, for instance, *The Silence* (2020), his last to date, seemed to anticipate the utter silence that follows a global disruption of our technology, as if presaging the eerie quiet during the corona virus pandemic, much like the industrial-level chemical spill in a small American town in *White Noise* anticipated such disasters since, including the vocabulary used to discuss it and the way people reacted to it. *Zero K.* is no exception, as we shall see it. It too reflects and articulates a reality in the making, the huge investment in a technology promising immortality.

Zero K's Real-Life Context

Zero K centers around a practice still restricted to a very small number of people—cryonics—the freezing of the brain upon death at exceedingly low temperatures in the hope of eventually resurrecting the person thus frozen through scientific means. A few months before the publication of *Zero K*, a long front-page article appeared in *The New York Times* on precisely this topic. "A Dying Young Woman's Hope in Cryonics and the Future" chronicles the story of Kim Suozzi, who, upon discovering that she had a fatal form of brain cancer, opts to have her brain frozen as a prelude to a possible scientific resurrection. She had first encountered the idea of scientifically-induced immortality through an assigned text, *The Age of Spiritual Machines,* in one of her college classes. In this best-selling book, its author Ray Kurzweil, at one point chief Engineer at Google, predicts that by the middle of the twenty-first century, human beings will be able to upload their brains into computers and live indefinitely. Kim and her boyfriend Josh raised the requisite funds for the cryonics procedure and for storage, $80,000, through GoFundMe. Shortly following her death, a team of nurses rushed to her bed to prepare for the eventual process, part of which Josh watched from the observation deck at the facility to which Kim was taken.[7]

A little over a year later another article on the same topic appeared in the same newspaper.[8] This time the story revolved around a

7. Harmon, "A Dying Young Woman's Hope."

8. De Freytas-Tamura, "Last Wish of a Dying Girl."

fourteen-year-old girl, almost ten years younger than Kim Suozzi, who also chose to undergo the cryonics process after having been diagnosed with a fatal cancer. In her case, a lawsuit was involved, since her father did not want to grant permission for the procedure. (Kim's father had also been opposed but Kim was already an adult.) The judge ruled in favor of the adolescent. Her grandparents raised the funds, approximately $46,000 in this case, and her body was eventually shipped for storage in a facility in Michigan, reportedly one of three such facilities in the world. Amy Harmon, the author of the first article, speculated that given the increased research on the brain and on brain preservation, "the question the couple [Kim and Josh] faced may ultimately confront more of us with implications that could be preposterously profound."[9]

We might be tempted to think that DeLillo, in exploring the phenomenon of immortality through science, as he does in *Zero K*, is tapping into a brand-new reality, at best only decades old. It turns out that it goes back to the very founding documents of modern science. The seventeenth-century philosopher Francis Bacon, credited with formulating the scientific method, in *The New Atlantis*, his last book, "predicted that men would one day create a new species and become as gods."[10] Reading Péguy makes us aware that this hope remained alive and well in the nineteenth century. In one of his late writings, Ernest Renan speculated that human beings, as science progresses, will take over the reins of evolution from nature, creating a superhuman being, a deva, into whose consciousness all consciousnesses will be brought back to life.[11] In the writings of the milder Taine, the goal of the scientist was to exhaust all the factors involved in a given act of creation.[12] Although Taine limited himself to poets, his procedure, meant to follow that of biologists, does not seem so far removed from that of neuroscientists today who work on miniscule layers of the brain with the idea of putting the whole brain together, in all its details, creating from scratch, as it were, with the idea of replication not far behind. An article announces this aim in its very title. In "The Neuroscience of Immortality: Mileposts on a Long and Uncharted Road," its author investigates the various steps that scientists claim would

9. Harmon, "A Dying Young Woman's Hope."

10. Quoted in Noble, *The Religion of Technology*, 67.

11. Péguy, *Œuvres I*, 1421–2.

12. Péguy, *Œuvres I*, 1398–1403.

have to take place if, within a century or so, "our minds are to continue functioning after death."[13]

In our own time, even if the choice for scientific resurrection is restricted to a very small number of people, it nonetheless lives in a much broader universe of scientific endeavor than we might expect. One can bump into it accidentally, as I did when reading an article on an apparently unrelated topic, the controversy surrounding the oldest person known to date, Jeanne Calment, who has been validated to have died at the age of one hundred twenty-two.[14] Two Russian scientists, a gerontologist and a mathematician, have contested that she was indeed one hundred twenty-two, relying on the former's experience as a gerontologist/geriatrician, and the latter's experience as a statistician. Lauren Collins, the author of the article, roams far and wide, interviewing scientists in France, Russia and the United States, combing through records, reading histories of age registries and validations in the process. It is a fascinating story, revealing international competition for claims to have the oldest person alive, the uncertainty of establishing even so seemingly simple a fact as a person's age, the claims of local knowledge versus distant statistical assessments, and much else. Not least interesting, however, is the fact that the story also lives, even if indirectly, within the claims of immortality through science.

We find out, for instance, that one of the parties involved in the controversy is Aubrey De Grey, a computer scientist with a specialty in artificial intelligence and a doctorate in biology from Cambridge University. His role in the Calment controversy is limited to insisting that the blood sample that the supercentenarian gave to a French scientific research institute be made public. Ostensibly, the blood sample could settle the controversy about Calment's identity and age, but his interest also lies in conducting various experiments upon it that might further the project with which he is associated. Chief science officer of the SENS (Strategies for Engineered Negligible Senescence) Research Foundation whose goal is to reverse the aging process, he claims "that there are human beings alive right now who could live to more than a thousand years."[15] In 2019, SENS held an anti-aging conference in Berlin, to be repeated in future years, with hundreds of international participants.

13. Harmon, "Neuroscience of Immortality."

14. Collins, "Living Proof."

15. Collins, "Living Proof."

De Grey edits *Rejuvenation Research*, a respected academic journal in the field of gerontology.

His missionary zeal for the idea that we can vanquish death through technology certainly makes him an outlier in the scientific community but that does not mean that he is not supported financially. The Silicon Valley mogul Peter Thiel has invested at least five million dollars in SENS, and De Grey much more than that, having inherited considerable wealth.[16] SENS itself invests in startups that produce anti-aging products, and also makes it its business to match other venture capitalists with promising start-ups in this area. De Grey's Mountain View outfit no doubt pales in size when compared to comparable projects at Google, which has a division named "Calico," an acronym for the California Life Company, whose stated goal is to solve the problem of aging, with 1. 5 billion dollars in the bank.[17] Bill Maris, "who hatched the idea for Calico, has said it is possible that people could live for 500 years."[18]

One could conclude that this kind of ambition is limited to Silicon Valley promises, with little wider repercussions. The Russians who dispute the age of Jeanne Calment seem to have much more pedestrian concerns. They contest her age because of what they consider to be evidence of incompetence or fraud. Valery Novoselov, the geriatrician and gerontologist, does not think that the photos and described behavior of Jeanne's older years match those of any known supercentenarian. Nor do the statistical studies carried out by Nikolai Zak, the mathematician, make the age of one hundred twenty-two plausible. We know from other sources that up to 98 percent of claims to be over one hundred fifteen years old do not pass the validation process. In the years since Calment's death, no one has lived to be that old, and the three years separating her from the next oldest person represent an enormously long time in the supercentenarian world. In addition, Zak has tried to draw attention to what he considers inconsistencies in the validation process which cast suspicion not only on Calment's age but also as to whether she was not in reality her daughter.[19] Both Novoselov and Zak appear as colorful characters under the journalist's pen, but neither seems particularly interested in achieving immortality through technical means.

16. Collins, "Living Proof."
17. Regalado, "Google's Long Strange Life-Span Trip," 3.
18. Regalado, "Google's Long Strange Life-Span Trip," 12.
19. Collins, "Living Proof."

Appearances can be deceiving. Although Novoselov, the head of the Gerontology Chapter of the Moscow Society of Naturalists, attached to Moscow State University, seems at first to have the goals of most gerontologists and geriatricians, to study ways in which human beings can live longer and healthier lives, his ambition reveals itself to be much greater than just a healthy and long life.

> The population is aging very fast, and I believe that we need to focus our efforts on developing and testing the interventions that would effectively bring aging under medical control in humans. There will be 2 billion people who are sixty years old and older by (2050), which is one fourth of the global population. How are we supposed to cope with the overload on our healthcare system without powerful therapies that can address the underlying mechanisms of aging, and thus prevent and cure age-related diseases?[20]

To bring aging under medical control sounds very much like indefinite life span, and the anti-aging movement. Nikolay Zak, the mathematician, has been interested in life extension for some time, doing research for the Gerontology Chapter in Moscow and belonging to the Lifeboat Foundation, an organization whose stated mission is to avert or at least help human beings survive a host of potential global catastrophes, and one of whose branches also involves anti-aging research.[21]

But even if the circle of those interested in reversing aging now expands beyond De Grey (and Kurzweil) to include Novoselov and Zak, (connected, by the way, since De Grey has held the title of International Adjunct Professor at the Moscow Institute of Physics and Technology), they still represents a fringe element in the scientific community, even if some of the parties involved are attached to well-known and/or well-funded institutions, such as, informally, Moscow State University in the case of Noveselov, and Google Research, for Kurzweil. Academics at large prestigious American universities are involved in anti-aging research both at Google Research and independently of it. An organization mentioned in the article about Jeanne Calment is the Gerontology Research Group,

20. Milona, "Valery Novoselov."

21. The online site Lifeboat.com announces anti-aging news such as the following: Undoing aging 2021 is not only open to the scientific community, but also welcomes startups, investors, the general media, and all interested members of the broader rejuvenation movement. The conference will feature a student poster session showing the work of innovative undergraduate and graduate students in the field of damage repair.

founded in 1990 primarily by scientists from UCLA and Caltech. One of the main functions of this organization is to create an international data base of all known supercentenarians. But, as a Smithsonian magazine article indicates, the ultimate purpose of the Gerontology Research Institute is to slow down the aging process itself, "to reverse aging through the application of scientific research knowledge."[22] And in a breezy article in the *New York Times*, "Is There a Ceiling on Life Expectancy," the journalist cites a number of researchers from prominent universities, "whose goal is to tackle the various causes of aging in the coming years."[23] These include scientists at the Albert Einstein School of Medicine, Harvard and the University of Illinois. None of these specialists would claim that their research is to make humans immortal. As the historian Yuval Noah Harari comments in his best-selling book, *Homo Deus*, "The vast majority of scientists, doctors and scholars still distance themselves from outright dreams of immortality, claiming that they are trying to overcome only this or that particular problem."[24] But he disputes that their dreams are as modest as all that, arguing instead that in the twenty-first century "human beings are likely to make a serious bid for immortality."[25]

Harari's book is itself a sign that scientific immortality is in the air. He sees in its pursuit the logical and inevitable outcome of a scientific point of view in which death becomes merely a technical problem that we can and should solve.[26] At times, he seems to adopt this vision as his own. At others, he proclaims his agnosticism as to the dream's actualization. In any case, he maintains, that "even if we don't achieve immortality in our lifetime, the war against death is still likely to be the flagship project of the coming century. Our ideological commitment to human life will never allow us simply to accept human death. As long as people die of something we will strive to overcome it."[27] This book has sold over two million copies, and has been translated into at least thirty languages. It means at the very least that these ideas are penetrating a much larger public than that of gerontology labs.

22. Nuwer, "Keeping Track of Oldest People in the World."

23. Bakalar, "Is There a Ceiling on Life Expectancy?" See also, Zimmerman, "Biotech Start-Up," B3.

24. Harari, *Homo Deus*, 24.

25. Harari, *Homo Deus*, 21.

26. Harari, *Homo Deus*, 21.

27. Harari, *Homo Deus*, 28.

My point throughout is not that all scientists are working to make us immortal, but that the hope that science will save us from death floats in our culture, at once peripheral and mainstream, and that that hope is accompanied by finance and brick and mortar research centers. The search for immortality is institutionalized, in other words. This becomes even more clear if we stray away from gerontology research per se and into brain science and artificial intelligence. If we are regular readers of mainstream newspapers or journals, we are bombarded daily with articles about computers that read faces, that develop taste recognition in food, compose music, write essays, converse with us and console us, diagnose diseases, and who knows what else. Behind these feats, and, in addition to them, are major investors in brain research, such as the United States government, under the Obama administration, which granted 4.5 billion dollars to the National Institutes of Health, with the stated goal to arrive at a "comprehensive mechanistic understanding of mental function" by 2025.[28] The European Union has also invested billions of dollars into a Human Brain project, among many other investors.[29]

None of these institutions makes even the slightest mention of immortality, it is true. But is not the goal of understanding the brain as a whole, a prelude to duplicating it? Ilya Sutzkever, former chief scientist at Open AI, a cofounder along with Elon Musk and Sam Altman of this research institute whose products include computer programs that aim at duplicating human creativity such as GPT-2, -3 and now -4, speculates that "researchers can't disallow for the possibility that we will reach understanding when the neural net gets as big as the brain."[30] Altman himself surmises that "there is absolutely no reason to believe that in about thirteen years we won't have hardware capable of replicating my brain."[31] Since, for these scientists, the brain is the mind, and the mind holds the key to our identity, replicating our intelligence in silicon form will make humans immortal, even if not in our current body, in some hybrid form. if you are Kurzweil and think we can upload our own intelligence on to a computer frame and live on forever, as in Renan's vision of the deva of the future, brain science promises individual immortality as well.[32]

28. Harmon, "Neuroscience of Immortality."

29. Harmon, "Neuroscience of Immortality."

30. Seabrook, "The Next Word," 63. On GPT-3, and its powers, see Manjoo, "How Do We Know a Human Wrote This?"

31. Friend, "Sam Altman's Manifest Destiny," 10.

32. Kurzweil is just one of the better-known contemporary spokespeople for

It is this heady atmosphere, at once completely implausible and yet already here, that DeLillo explores in *Zero K*. Rather than simply introducing us to cryonics, the novel introduces us to the world this dream is in the process of making. He makes us aware of its massive nature. It is not as marginal and dream-like as we might think. He also makes us aware of our bewilderment as the dream becomes part of the reality in which we live. Both of these aspects—the penetration of the project of immortality into our lives and our bewilderment that this is so—point to the religious dimension of the natural sciences, at once as Péguy described it, and yet with a new face.

Part 1: The Religion of Science

Faith-Based Science

The main character in *Zero K*, thirty-four-year old Jeffrey Lockhart, discovers that his stepmother Artis, who is terminally ill, has chosen to undergo the cryonics process. Her brain will be severed from her body and frozen, in the expectation that future scientific advances will bring her back to life. A couple of years after his wife's procedure, Jeff's father, Ross, makes the decision to have his brain frozen as well, even though he remains in relatively good health. Shortly before Artis is frozen, Ross summons Jeff to an undisclosed location in the desert, the site of the cryonics process. This huge structure, most of which is off-limits to Jeff, and thus whose length and breadth he has no way of fathoming, is called the Convergence, not only the name of the place but also of the time when human beings will achieve immortality. DeLillo's choice of this name may not be haphazard. It refers to the term that scientists in the world outside the novel use to indicate the joint endeavors of nanotechnology, biotechnology, information technology, and cognitive science, also referred by the acronym NBIC.[33]

---

immortality through the advances of artificial intelligence and other sciences. An earlier prophet announcing eternal mind in silicon form is Hans Moravec, who argues for not only replication but also enhancement in his books *Mind Children* (1988) and *The Age of Mind: Transcending the Human Condition through Robots* (1995). For a description of how modern electronic computer technology and the idea of immortality grew up together, see Noble, *The Religion of Technology*," 143–71.

33. Dupuy, "Cybernetics is Antihumanism," 236–40. A similar reference to the use of the term Convergence in the scientific community occurs in Liogier, "Transhumanisme," 561.

Through Jeff, we are introduced to the perspectives of those who, like his parents, choose cryonics, as well as of a motley crew of spokespeople who promote it. But *Zero K* is also, even more than a description of the advocates of cryonics, a phenomenology of our disorientation in the face of it. Jeff's reactions to the Convergence bring into language and awareness our own muddled reactions when we read, for instance, about the two young women who chose to have their brains frozen or when we encounter in our daily reading of the newspaper the many achievements of artificial intelligence seemingly making superfluous, if not now, then in a near future, the very journalist who has written the story. Our disorientation speaks to the displacement of the categories that order our world. Our very grip on reality is affected.

A case of this disorientation occurs early in the novel when Ross explains to his son that after a period in cryonic suspension the mind and the body will be restored to life. Jeff points out that the belief in immortality has a venerable religious pedigree, casting doubt on the scientific credentials of cryonics. Ross admits to the religious nature of the whole enterprise. This time, because the god is technology, he says, the promise is "real, it's true, it delivers."[34] To affirm the erasure of the line between metaphysical longings and science, Ross calls the Convergence "faith-based technology."[35] Jeff is thrown off guard. "I was disoriented. This was the morning of my first full day here and this was my father across the desk and none of it was familiar—I'd be on my way home before I'd be able to absorb any of it."[36] Later, after having spent a couple of days at the Convergence, he says, "They were drenching me, out-thinking me, these several days, this extreme sublifetime. What was it beyond a concentrated lesson in bewilderment?"[37]

Jeff's bewilderment is at least in part the result of a crossing of mental wires. Faith and science/technology are usually defined against each other. Faith signals a commitment that cannot be verified by the usual empirical means. Science, on the other hand, in our common parlance but also in its founding documents, is synonymous with empirical evidence, with the refusal to arrive at conclusions without such evidence, with the refusal to accept something as valid on the basis of belief alone. But nothing in the sciences thus far constitutes empirical verification that we can

34. DeLillo, *Zero K*, 9.

35. DeLillo, *Zero K*, 9.

36. DeLillo, *Zero K*, 8.

37. DeLillo, *Zero K*, 153.

conquer death or even extend lifespan much beyond what it has always been. We can prevent or cure certain illnesses and thus extend the average lifetime of human beings, in some cases considerably, but once human beings outlive those illnesses the outer edge of mortality has remained basically the same as in earlier times. But even if we could live much longer than we currently do, the claim that we can reconstruct a brain that would function as mind, with all the requisite self-consciousness and individual particularities of a person, is, despite all the money that has been poured into brain research, a very far stretch indeed.[38]

But were the task of simulating the activity of a human brain achieved, the very assumption that the secret of life is exclusively a matter of a reconstructed brain, detachable from a body, is itself contested within the scientific community. As one scientist voiced his objections, "A brain requires a network of nerves and a metabolism. It requires vocal cords and oppositional thumbs. The brain must evolve in natural environments rich in semiotic and semantic meanings. It requires the nurture of families, communities, civilizations from which it acquires language, tools and purpose. The brain, much like the genome, does absolutely nothing by itself."[39] Another neuroscientist argues that neurological activity is merely a necessary but not sufficient condition to understand consciousness, making neuroscience, which deals with the brain, incapable of studying mind.[40] There is the not completely irrelevant fact that no brain detached from a body has ever been anything else but the symbol of death, as in the skulls of yore.

Ross, Jeff's father, is very aware of this lack of empirical evidence, thus his term "faith-based technology." But from his point of view, technology has done so much that we could not have anticipated that it becomes easy to believe that it can achieve anything, immortality included. It is worth turning to Pascal's famous wager to elucidate this. We might think that Ross and others who believe in immortality through the natural sciences are simply making a bet on what is probable and what is in their self-interest. If immortality does not occur, they would be dead

38. Alva Noë, philosopher and experimental psychologist, begins his book, *Out of Our Heads*, xi, with the following remark: "After decades of concerted effort on the part of neurosciences, psychologists, and philosophers, only one proposition about how the brain makes us conscious—how it gives rise to sensation, feeling, subjectivity—has emerged unchallenged: we don't have a clue."

39. Grassie, "Millenianism at the Singularity," 259.

40. Tallis, *Aping Mankind*, 92–94.

anyway, and so what do they have to lose? But in Pascal's Wager, while the person the philosopher is trying to convince admits that the logic of Pascal's argument is impeccable, he still cannot believe in God. Pascal then advises him that if he really wants the faith upon which immortality depends, his interlocutor needs to pray, fast and behave in general as if he were pious. Eventually these ritual practices can open the heart to faith.[41] In the case of Ross, who gives himself up to cryonics before he is terminally ill, it might very well be the practices of science, which include our daily ritual handling of its products and our daily exposure to the narratives floating around them that lead to the same result. They induce faith, even if now the faith is in the salvific powers of science itself.

The very bulwark against a world beyond the realm of reason and the senses, science, has become the main source of dreams about a world beyond empirical proof, religion. The dreams do not seem to stop at immortality. Thanks to experiments on vision, for example, we will be able to see not through a glass darkly but face to face, penetrating into layers of reality inaccessible to our present sight, Artis tells her stepson.[42] "[O]ne of our objectives is to establish a consciousness that blends with the environment," an expert pronounces.[43] It is none too clear what this could signify but the lack of clarity is the point. We are entering, through the natural sciences, into a transcendent, wholly other realm we could not possibly understand in our current lowly state. Scientific research will "stretch the boundaries of what it means to be human—stretch and then surpass."[44]

The spokespeople Jeff encounters at the Convergence are quite aware of their defiance of both the evidence and of the normal operations of reason. "We think of ourselves as transrational," they say.[45] They had to create this underground site in the desert, far away from everything, "in order to separate ourselves from reasonableness, from this burden of what is called responsible thinking."[46] If to be reasonable is to assume that everything living must die, to be transrational is to declare, "Death is a cultural artifact, not a strict determination of what is humanly

41. Pascal, *Pensées*, 121–25.
42. DeLillo, *Zero K*, 47.
43. DeLillo, *Zero K*, 64.
44. DeLillo, *Zero K*, 71.
45. DeLillo, *Zero K*, 128.
46. DeLillo, *Zero K*, 71.

inevitable,"[47] a statement that Jeff overhears in one of the seminars he is privy to attend, as if he were in the presence of both De Grey and Kurzweil who have made the same claim. If to be reasonable is to accept the difference between animate and inanimate, between life and death, then to be transrational is to refuse it. In the innumerable corridors of the Convergence, Jeff is continually running into bodies, in pods, in piles, standing alone. He cannot tell whether they are mannequins or flesh and blood. He refers to them as "the dead, or maybe dead, or whatever they were, the cryogenic dead."[48] In one instance, he encounters a nude human figure with no head, resembling a Greek or Roman statue. His guide explains, "This is not a silicone-and-fiberglass replica. Real flesh, human tissue, human being. Body preserved for a limited time by cryoprotectants applied to the skin."[49] The fact that the body is headless does not seem to challenge the notion that it will be revived as a human being someday. At the moment, it is "preserved," neither alive nor dead. If distinguishing life from death is so basic that we cannot even imagine a world without it, in the Convergence that distinction ceases to be operative, except as a folk survival from a prior age.

It is important to underscore that faith-based technology is not only an internal state, a belief. It is also a massive external reality, expressed through a huge network of institutions. The Convergence is not one thing but a complex of different disciplines. These disciplines are funded not only by billionaires like Ross but also by national governments, drawing on the intellectual and financial resources of the entire world. The very name Convergence suggests this meeting of everything—capitalism and science, the local and the international, the present and the future. One of the stated goals of the Convergence is to build the future, becoming as it were its first instantiation. In its erasing or blurring the line between being processed and dying, between animate and inanimate, the Convergence is building a world on a new basis, as the artificial garden that Jeff encounters in the desert symbolizes. In this new Garden of Eden, as he is told to consider it, all the vegetation is plastic or fiberglass, "museum quality."[50] This is the future that is already here.

At this point, if not earlier, a reader might point out that DeLillo is describing an imaginary reality in *Zero K*, not the future which is already

47. DeLillo, *Zero K*, 71.

48. DeLillo, *Zero K*, 74.

49. DeLillo, *Zero K*, 231.

50. DeLillo, *Zero K*, 122.

here. In the ordinary world, the difference between animate and inanimate and life and death go unchallenged. One could respond that the promised and actual inroad of artificial intelligence, the very ways of defining death as brain death are blurring that line[51] but this would go beyond what DeLillo's novel is suggesting. He is not claiming that the world we live in has already turned into the homogeneous and artificial environment of the Convergence. Much of the novel takes place in New York City, where life goes on in its usual messy and human-scale way. But in making the Convergence into a huge underground structure with an international cast of characters and international financing, DeLillo may be suggesting that the dreams of immortality brewing within it represent the hidden drive of our entire contemporary civilization, bent on mastering nature, which now also includes rebuilding the human being from our tiniest components. The 2020 Nobel Prize in Chemistry went to two women, Jennifer Doudna and Emmanuelle Charpentier, for their work on CRISPR-Cas9, a technique for editing DNA, which the Secretary General of the Royal Swedish Academy of Sciences characterized as "rewriting the code of life."[52] The fact that we do not perceive this rewriting of ourselves on the level of our daily reality does not make it any less massive, organizing our present and future hopes and possibilities. In this sense, the religion promoted by the Convergence remains secret, even if its proponents openly declare themselves to be transrational and faith-based. Its tentacles into our world are so interwoven with our institutions and with our imagination that we do not even notice. It is, to turn to Péguy's expression once again, the thought at the back of the mind.

Disorientation as a Religious Phenomenon

If an ordered world is one in which we distinguish below from above, the center from the periphery, Jeff's disorientation expresses the loss of that order. We see it graphically represented in the elevators of the Convergence that move not up and down but sideways, in the lack of windows which would separate outside from inside, in the homogeneity of the physical space, which prevents him from figuring out the significant markers distinguishing even one corridor from another. It is a world in

51. Dupuy, "Cybernetics," 241–3, discusses the goal of synthetic biology to create life from scratch, and the claims that contemporary science is erasing the boundary between inorganic and organic, artificial and natural, life and death.

52. Wu, Zimmer and Peltier, "Nobel Prize in Chemistry Awarded to 2 Scientists."

which he needs a guide, and even with the guide, he never really knows where he is. In that sense, the erasure of the correspondence between our categories and the world they help us to navigate is metaphorically represented in Jeff's inability to navigate the physical space in which he finds himself. Cosmos has turned to chaos, despite, or maybe because of, the mathematical proportions of all that surrounds him.

As the novel progresses, the religious dimension of Jeff's disorientation can also be understood as the confrontation with sheer power. "Technology has become a force of nature," lectures one of the spokespeople in the Convergence. "We can't control it. It comes blowing over the planet and there's nowhere for us to hide."[53] Jeff's bewilderment is comparable to that of the Hindu warrior Arjuna, when in Book XI of the *Bhagavadgita*, the god Vishnu reveals his true shape. Instead of seeing the charioteer with whom he had been talking, Arjuna beholds a form "with many mouths and eyes, appearing in many miraculous ways, with many divine ornaments, and divine unsheated weapons."[54] He expresses his fear to Vishnu, "When the worlds see your form of many mouths and eyes, of many arms, legs, feet/Many torsos, many terrible tusks/They tremble, as I do."[55] Fascinated and terrified, he ends up asking the god to take on his ordinary, four-armed representation.[56] It is as if Jeff, like Arjuna, is momentarily given a special eye to see the true reality beyond the technology he encounters in his daily life. He is relieved, when he leaves the Convergence, to find himself in the ordinary world of the blinking traffic lights and ATM machines of his native New York City.[57]

The overwhelming power of technology evokes not only emotions like fascination and dread but also physical consequences. It marks Jeff's very body. He had been watching one of the many screens that descend at unexpected places in all the corridors of the Convergence. As in all the others, this one depicts a catastrophe, in this case, people running away from a tsunami. Just as he concludes that the "images are computer-generated, none of it real," a group of men and women "spilled from the

53. DeLillo, *Zero K*, 245.

54. Bolle, *Bhagavadgita*, 127. Strangely enough, there is a reference to Arjuna in the novel, one of the names that Jeff imagines for a spokeswoman of the Convergence, DeLillo, *Zero K*, 72. It is too random to make my point, of course, but an interesting choice nonetheless.

55. Bolle, *Bhagavadgita*, 131.

56. Bolle, *Bhagavadgita*, 141.

57. DeLillo, *Zero K*, 151, 197.

screen," flattening him against the wall, nearly trampling him to death.[58] The stampede so overwhelms him that it is only when it passes that he realizes he is limping.[59] The erasure of the line between screen and reality has the ability to inflict real pain. We might think that a computer simulation may not affect us bodily, but here it is, spilling out into the street, into the daily world outside, just like the conspiracy theories on the internet produce people with guns, attacking pizza restaurants. The power of technology affects our very bodily existence.

Part 2: Heretical Countermoves

The Power and Powerlessness of Reason

Acknowledging the power of the Convergence does not mean that Jeff becomes completely submissive. Like a heretic who insists on doubting the claims of a triumphant Christianity, he parries and thrusts, continually wrestling with the premises that have led his father and stepmother to place their faith in science's promise of immortality. Like the biblical Jacob who wrestles with the angel, and to which the limp Jeff acquires may be a reference, he never vanquishes his opponent. That is to be expected. He does not even manage to fully convince himself of his own arguments. In part, his very reasonableness, his willingness to countenance the limits of his own logic, defeat him. When, for instance, his father announces that he will not wait until he is dying to undergo the cryonics process, Jeff screams in protest. "I think you have been brainwashed. You're a victim of these surroundings. You're a member of a cult. Don't you see it?"[60] But soon he begins to doubt his own judgment. "Were these people deranged or were they in the forefront of a new consciousness?"[61] In another instance, he reacts in disbelief when a spokesperson for the Convergence argues that impending planetary catastrophe opens new solutions for human survival. " . . . I didn't believe a word of it. it was a kind of wishful poetry. It didn't apply to real people, real fear." Yet he backtracks immediately. "Or was I being small-minded, too limited in perspective?"[62] Such doubt and counter-doubt dot the novel.

58. DeLillo, *Zero K*, 152–3.
59. DeLillo, *Zero K*, 154.
60. DeLillo, *Zero K*, 113.
61. DeLillo, *Zero K*, 120.
62. DeLillo, *Zero K*, 66.

If Jeff cannot fully land on one side or the other, it is also because he has internalized the claims to privileged knowledge of the science/technology edifice. When Artis, his stepmother, an archeologist by profession, explains to him that she will reawaken to a new perception of reality, after being reassembled atom by atom, and that she "will be reborn into a deeper and truer reality,"[63] Jeff does not know how to respond because he respects her expertise. "Artis knew the rigors of science."[64] She knows exactly, she tells him, the procedures she will be undergoing, the details involved. His father, not a scientist, leans on the authority of science by citing all the branches of knowledge involved in making future immortality a reality. "What's happening in this community is not just the creation of medical science. There are social theorists involved, and biologists, and futurists, and geneticists, and climatologists, and neuroscientists, and psychologists, and ethicists, if that's the right word."[65] What is Jeff's authority against this enormous pool of experts, which his father continues to name into the next paragraph? It is only his personal experience that living things die. His father urges him to "think beyond your experience."[66]

Yet, despite his reasonableness, which makes him see his father's point—one's own experience is not sufficient for the understanding of what is possible—and despite the authority of the scientific establishment, Jeff cannot entirely give up on his own experience. He insists that he needs his own window from which to look out.[67] Throughout much of his time at the Convergence, he creates such a window by imposing names on the many nameless people he encounters.[68] ". . . I understood that origins were not the point here and that categories in general were not intended to be narrowed or even named."[69] From the point of view of the Convergence, every person is reduced to his or her function, interchangeable with anyone else. Naming becomes Jeff's way of resisting interchangeability, a form of self-defense against the erasure of his own window on the world.[70] But even here, his doubt as to the viability of this

63. DeLillo, *Zero K*, 47.
64. DeLillo, *Zero K*, 47.
65. DeLillo, *Zero K*, 33.
66. DeLillo, *Zero K*, 35.
67. DeLillo, *Zero K*, 35, 115.
68. DeLillo, *Zero K*, 66–67, 71, 72, 238, 242.
69. DeLillo, *Zero K*, 231.
70. DeLillo, *Zero K*, 129.

technique reemerges. "Here I was, in a sealed compartment, inventing names, noting accents, improvising histories and nationalities. These were shallow responses to an environment that required abandonment of such distinctions."[71] He does not stop naming, despite his doubt, but his doubt keeps on shadowing the naming. In hearing one of the proponents speak, he reflects: "I didn't want to forget that she needed a surname. I owed her this. Isn't that why I was here, to subvert the dance of transcendence with my tricks and games?"[72] It is very unlikely that tricks and games do much to buttress even one's own arguments, let alone change the course of the Convergence.

If Jeff fails to surmount the claims of the Convergence, although he keeps on trying, it may also be because he has no God to pit against its God. He lacks a metaphysical grounding of his own that might truly challenge the materialist premises of the science/technology edifice. He relates that as a teenager, he stood on line at a local church on Ash Wednesday in order to have the priest rub ash on his forehead, just to see what it might feel like to walk around with such a spot. Growing up he says of himself and his family, "I was not a Catholic, my parents were not Catholic. I didn't know what we were. We were Eat and Sleep. We were Take Daddy's Suit to the Dry Cleaner."[73] This lack of grounding in anything beyond the daily evokes neither pride or regret. It is simply the way it is, inculcating in him a curiosity and respect at a distance for people who are grounded in an absolute point, outside what he himself can see. He pauses to observe the cabdriver in New York City who gets out of his car to prostrate himself in the direction of Mecca for one of his daily prayers.[74] When a person he meets in the Convergence whom he names The Monk describes to him the long and arduous pilgrimage he made climbing up a holy mountain, Jeff responds that such activities were "so far outside my own fragmented visions, a thing for others."[75] His reaction to his stepmother, Artis, is similar. When seeing her body encased in one of the many pods, toward the very end of his second stay at the Convergence, he sees her utter commitment to the project as giving the entire complex some measure of respect,[76] without abandoning

71. DeLillo, *Zero K*, 72.
72. DeLillo, *Zero K*, 242.
73. DeLillo, *Zero K*, 15.
74. DeLillo, *Zero K*, 265.
75. DeLillo, *Zero K*, 89.
76. DeLillo, *Zero K*, 258.

his sense that this was science awash in irrepressible fantasy, itself evoking admiration.[77]

What are we to make of Jeff's wrestling with the angel? His doubts, and his doubting of his doubts are, of course, a sign of his impotence. He cannot even convince himself, always seeing both sides of the issue. But looked at from a different angle, his wrestling might be the only sign that we do not coincide with the power that dominates us. In 1999, when DeLillo, was awarded the prestigious Jerusalem Prize for Literature, a commentator understood the committee to have selected the novelist because "[his] fiction creates the possibility of wresting a bit of freedom from necessity by so thoroughly diagnosing what constrains us."[78] Constraining us is not only the power of the science/technology complex and its dreams of immortality but also our own reasonableness, our willingness to weigh claims. That very reasonableness, however, also gives us warning signs that our humanity might be in danger. At one point in his visit to the area of the Convergence where people are waiting in cubicles for their turn to undergo the cryonics process, Jeff fears that he is witnessing a total centralized command, reducing human beings to headless and faceless bodies through a process of canning and curing.[79] In typical fashion, he takes back this judgment. "Was [calling cryonics totalitarian] a facile idea . . . Was there a hollowness to this notion?"[80] No matter Jeff's many doubts, the question he raises about totalitarianism in a new form remains and continues to haunt.

One can read Jeff's inconclusive wrestling with the premises of the Convergence in yet another way. Reason, reasonableness, argument, while integral to our struggle, cannot by themselves counter the weight of the Convergence. Only something as massively present and penetrating as the Convergence, but in an altogether different mode, has a chance to make us escape to a realm beyond its control, without even being aware of it. In the case of DeLillo's *Zero K*, that something is language. The novel is a song of praise to its ceaseless flow, the unfathomable depths from which it comes, and its playfulness, a playfulness that can turn very serious, as I hope to indicate by and by.

77. DeLillo, *Zero K*, 257.
78. Duval, "Introduction," 3.
79. DeLillo, *Zero K*, 142, 146.
80. DeLillo, *Zero K*, 146–7.

Language

New Forms

Language, by its very nature, produces unexpected patterns and shapes. We make up new words, as when Jeff refers to his younger self as "a boy in his neo-pubescence, his budhood."[81] Unexpected also is the sudden appearance of a rare word, or the unusual placement of an ordinary one. Referring to the quirks we all exhibit, Artis speaks of divots of personality,[82] as if the relative rarity of the word divot matches the idiosyncratic behavior it describes. Elsewhere, Jeff refers to his dimpled history.[83] What is the word "dimpled," usually associated with an indentation of the flesh, as in the dimples of a smile, doing here? It suggests a softness and fleshiness, an openness to impression, characteristic of life, missing from the glacial bodies preserved in the Convergence. Dimple's unusual placement, not on the flesh where it usually belongs, suggest the living quality of language itself, always moving and rearranging what is already there.

The play of language also becomes visible in the lists of strange technical vocabulary that punctuate the novel, bringing the odd inventiveness of bureaucrats, their ability to obfuscate, to displace our attention. Jeff applies for a job whose description is "cross-stream pricing consultant. Implementation analyst—clustered and nonclustered environments."[84] Each word is more impenetrable than the next, revealing the hermetic nature of high finance. Words such as biomedical redaction and brain-edit[85] work in a similar fashion, this time screens for bioengineering processes. The title of the novel, Zero K, is a case in point, the code word for the temperature at which people's bodies or their heads are preserved while they await immortality, and also the special unit for people who choose cryonics before their health deteriorates.[86] The process carefully avoids the term "death," which, is of course, what it either induces or confirms. It is sometimes difficult to disentangle the language of fiction from the language of the bureaucrats

81. DeLillo, *Zero K*, 248.
82. DeLillo, *Zero K*, 19.
83. DeLillo, *Zero K*, 15.
84. DeLillo, *Zero K*, 54.
85. DeLillo, *Zero K*, 238.
86. DeLillo, *Zero K*, 142–3, 112, 237–8.

and engineers it mimics. Is the term Zero K already in circulation, or did DeLillo make it up? Either way it is an invention.

Nonetheless, even if individual inventiveness is part of our daily speech, of speech itself, language is, of course, never purely an individual matter. We live in already established language fields. One is never the first on the language scene. Awareness of language fields, and the ability to name them and consciously play within them is the task of artists. It signals a specific inquiry into reality, a specific way of framing it. It would be very difficult, for instance, to miss DeLillo's reference to Franz Kafka in the first part of *Zero K*. Jeff, wishing to explore the immense underground complex to which his father has summoned him, takes walks down hallways with doors of many colors on either side.[87] He begins to wonder whether they are really doors or merely paintings of doors, knocking on them as he passes them to see if any would open. Just as he is about to give up, a door does open. "I must have the wrong door," Jeff tells the person facing him. "They're all the wrong door," the man answers.[88] The wink to "The Parable of the Law," in which a man from the countryside stands before a door guarded by a watchman who warns him against crossing its threshold, is there for the reader to catch.[89] Who else better than Kafka has captured the sense of being trapped in an immense system, whose machinations we can hope neither to decipher nor escape?

Other authors such as St. Augustine, Martin Heidegger, and Witold Gombrowicz are named outright.[90] Has not the whole edifice of the Convergence, and the techno-capitalist dream of immortality it represents been built on a vocabulary forged by Augustine, about the first death (physical death), the period before Judgment Day, and the second death, when the soul either attains heaven or is damned forever,[91] deployed in the Convergence in a radically different context? Who would not have Heidegger's analyses of technology in mind, as well as his view of art and of language, when discussing the view of the human as material to be reshaped expressed by the Convergence's spokespeople?[92] Who might not find the Polish playwright, novelist and essayist Gombrowicz

87. DeLillo, *Zero K*, 23–24.

88. DeLillo, *Zero K*, 25.

89. Kafka, *Kafka*, 3–4.

90. DeLillo, *Zero K*, 240, 214, 105.

91. Saint Augustine, *City of God*, 500–546.

92. Heidegger, "The Question Concerning Technology," 287–317; Heidegger, "The Origin of the Work of Art," 149–87.

helpful in an effort to resist a totalizing ideology, even if it is no longer communism or nationalism?[93]

When these authors' names appear, Jeff or some other character often partially dismisses their importance, as if cautioning us not to tarry on them. A sentence about death in St. Augustine's work was supposedly just an exercise in Latin grammar, according to a spokesperson of the Convergence.[94] Heidegger's Nazi affiliations, Jeff realizes, cast a shadow on his thought.[95] As to Gombrowicz, he tells us that when he was an adolescent he fell in love with the sound of his name, which he kept on repeating to himself rather than reading the works themselves.[96] Perhaps these qualifying remarks are meant to indicate that the vision in a given work of art, no matter how much it is in debt to other works, always comes out new, a play with its antecedents, but not a replica. We, as readers, are free to recognize the tradition in which the author situates himself, but that in no way diminishes the novelty and the particularity of the language that confronts us, if the new work really is a work of art.

Limits and Limitlessness

The play of language, both individual and within a tradition, that we have indicated thus far happens without commentary. It is simply the texture of *Zero K*. We cannot read the novel without being involved in the unexpected patterns that we create when we speak. But DeLillo not only deploys language but also invites reflection on it. One instance of such an invitation is Jeff's recurring need to define words, either by looking them up in a dictionary or by making the definition up himself. Looking up the word "fishwife," for instance, leads him to shrew, which leads him to mouse, which leads him to insect-eating animals, which leads him to eating and so on.[97] A word is situated in a web of other words, in a web of tangential meanings. To define is to contain the flow of associations, for one brief instant. At one point, Jeff asks an adolescent boy to define "rock." The boy complies: "It's hard, it's rock-hard, it's petrified, it

93. Although Witold Gombrowicz was also a novelist and a playwright, I am referring specifically to the three volumes of his autobiographical writings, translated into English under the title of *Diary v. 1–3*.

94. DeLillo, *Zero K*, 240–41.

95. DeLillo, *Zero K*, 214.

96. DeLillo, *Zero K*, 105.

97. DeLillo, *Zero K*, 25.

has major mineral content or it's all mineral with the long dead remains of plants and animals fossilized inside it."[98] Would not a rock, as a condensation of so many things, be a metaphor for what a word is? Both are condensations that hold within them a multiplicity. This, in turn, suggests that metaphor, also a condensation that holds a multitude of meanings, is the very essence of language, that perpetual contraction into a rock, and expansion as in rock-hard, which can refer to so many things. Nowhere, does DeLillo have Jeff or any other character make the observations I just made. But whether they hold up or not, the repeated desire to define calls for interpretation, calls for a reflection on how words behave.

To illustrate the contraction and expansion characteristic of language, I would like to turn to several of the metaphors DeLillo deploys in the novel. Metaphor, in my reading, is the stealth weapon against the Convergence, whose goal is to create a language devoid of it. "We will approximate the logic and beauty of pure mathematics in everyday speech. No similes, metaphors, analogies," pronounces one of its spokespeople.[99] What do we eliminate when we eliminate metaphor? *Zero K*, even if not explicitly answering this question, allows us to meditate on it through the very metaphors DeLillo uses. I have chosen ones that draw attention, either through their repetition in the course of the novel, or through their emphatic placement, as in the very conclusion.

In the first metaphor, Jeff remembers his mother on her deathbed.

> When my mother died, at home, I was seated next to the bed and there was a friend of hers, a woman with a cane, standing in the doorway. That's how I would picture the moment, narrowed, now and always, to the woman in the bed, the woman in the doorway, the bed itself, the metal cane.[100]

In the second iteration, Jeff gives the cane a name; it is a quad cane with four little splayed legs.[101]

In its starkness, the scene is an image for the very features of human life that the Convergence promises to do away with—old age, infirmity, and death. These limits are not romanticized. Jeff does not conclude that his mother, dying in her own bed, experiences a better fate than his stepmother, whose death was chemically induced at the Convergence.

98. DeLillo, *Zero K*, 216.

99. DeLillo, *Zero K*, 130.

100. DeLillo, *Zero K*, 9.

101. DeLillo, *Zero K*, 49–50.

He does claim, however, in the next addition to the image, that the very confrontation with loss leads paradoxically to a kind of transcendence.

> I'd never felt more human than I did when my mother lay in bed, dying. This was not the frailty of a man who is said to be 'only human,' subject to a weakness or a vulnerability. This was a wave of sadness and loss that made me understand that I was a man expanded by grief. There were memories, everywhere, unsummoned. There were images, visions, voices and how a woman's last breath gives expression to her son's constrained humanity.[102]

At moments of greatest loss, we experience an unprecedented depth, something seemingly bottomless, parts of which comes into consciousness, but not as a result of our control. In the passage above, the depth arises out of Jeff's connection to his mother. Endless memories and emotions rise to the surface. This expansion is not some beautiful feeling that erases suffering. It is not something that can be willed into existence. It is simply what happens as a result of the limits of human life, the fact that we do not live in splendid independence but that we are inevitably intertwined with others, an intertwining that makes us vulnerable. We experience our own depth most intensely at the moment our limits are made most evident.

The second metaphor also involved Jeff's mother, adding yet another dimension to the theme of limits and limitlessness. It comes in the context of his musings about the internet. All sorts of information rushes to our fingertips, "where it remains for a shaky instant before disappearing forever."[103] In contrast, he recalls a daily ritual of his life at home that fascinated him as a child. "My mother had a roller that picked up lint."[104] Upon coming home from work, she would take a hanger, twist the bent part of it so that it would hook over the open closet door, and vigorously pass the lint roller over the coat on the hanger.[105] This activity slowly turns into a metaphor for memory, "these occasions stick and hold, among other bent relics of adolescence."[106] Later in the novel, Jeff peels yet other layers of meaning from the event of watching his mother pass the lint roller over her coat.

102. DeLillo, *Zero K*, 248.
103. DeLillo, *Zero K*, 55.
104. DeLillo, *Zero K*, 55.
105. DeLillo, *Zero K*, 58–59.
106. DeLillo, *Zero K*, 59.

> Ordinary moments make the life. This is what she [his mother] knew to be trustworthy and this is what I learned, eventually, from those years we spent together. No leaps or falls. I inhale the little drizzly details of the past and know who I am. What I failed to know before is clearer now, filtered up through time, an experience belonging to no one else, not remotely, no one, anyone, ever. I watch her use the roller to remove the lint from her cloth coat. Define *coat*, I tell myself. Define *time*, define *space*.[107]

So much is compressed in so little here. The ritual of passing the roller becomes an image for ordinary life, with its mundane and repetitive details. It is precisely those details which leave an imprint in memory, "sticking and holding." We cannot command what rises to the surface of our memory as we command our screens to get information, for only the filter of time will reveal what has actually stuck. Unlike information, memory is not a one-dimensional answer to a question. It releases multiple layers of meaning over time, as the roller picks up yet more bits. But if the lint, the roller, the coat and the hanger are an image for memory, they are simultaneously an image for the fluid and utterly unique self that we all are. Those drizzly details of daily life that turn into memory belong "to no one else, not remotely, no one, anyone, ever." We are who we are because of our particular memories. Information gleaned from the Internet, insofar as it leaves no imprint, stands opposed to the slow lint roller of memory and self.

As it is used here, metaphor is not an artificial literary device invented to embellish a point. It arises spontaneously from the life lived, from the depths of one's unique experience. By repeating the same images, with slight modifications, at different points in the novel, DeLillo underscores the way events and the metaphors that express them accumulate meaning in the course of time, the lint roller adding one more layer as it moves along. It is very difficult to separate those meanings out completely in expository prose, however. The meanings within a given metaphor are very tightly bound together, a unity in multiplicity that our expository language cannot fully duplicate, although it also provokes us into expository language in the first place. Define coat, define space, define time.

The third metaphor is the one with which the book concludes, again a possible addition to our reflections on metaphor itself. It describes a spectacular sunset, or rather, it describes a spectacular sunset as seen

107. DeLillo, *Zero K*, 109.

through the cries of wonder of a little boy. Jeff is sitting in a crosstown bus in New York City, when he hears the boy wailing in the back. He turns around and sees through the window a phenomenon that occurs only once or twice a year. At sunset, the sun gets caught precisely within the grids of city streets, illuminating the glass of the buildings on either side. He briefly entertains the notion that the boy is wailing out of fear, seeing in the red glow everywhere the end of the world, but then refuses this option. " . . . I told myself that the boy was not seeing the sky collapse upon us but was finding the purest astonishment in the intimate touch of earth and sun."[108] The spectacular sunset becomes a metaphor for intimacy, the collapse of the great distance between two separate beings, as in the sun and the earth. But doesn't metaphor also collapse the distance between utterly different realms, bringing sunset and intimacy together? If so, intimacy, and not only the sunset remains the great wonder.

What follows seems to support this reading. Throughout his description of the sunset, Jeff focuses on the boy's imperfections. His head is a little too big; he has a thickset body; his wails sound like prelinguistic grunts. He even suspects that the boy might be mentally damaged.[109] Instead of shutting out these discomforting details, allowing in only the beauty of the view, Jeff does the opposite. He chooses the boy's cries over the unearthly glow of the sunset. "I went back to my seat and faced forward. I didn't need heaven's light. I had the boy's cries of wonder."[110] Language, even inarticulate, despite all the imperfections of the individual speaker or because of them, brings us heaven's light and not the other way around. It brings us the intimate contact for which the sunset is a metaphor.

What do we lose, then, when we lose metaphor, as the Convergence plans to do? Since the contraction and expansion of metaphor, its ability to touch at a distance reflect the many dimensions of our own humanity, we lose nothing short of that. But what is the big deal, people in the Convergence would reply. We promise something better, that human beings have always wanted, freedom from sickness, disease and death. Away with all this glorification of imperfection and limit. We can make you immortal, all-knowing, plan a language from above that will create unity among human beings.[111] *Zero K* cannot dismiss this

108. DeLillo, *Zero K*, 274.

109. DeLillo, *Zero K*, 274.

110. DeLillo, *Zero K*, 274.

111. DeLillo, *Zero K*, 33.

argument. But it can remind its readers of the taste of freedom that emanates from our very tongue. As long as we remain creatures whose speech arises from the mess of daily life, "from the free play of step-by step and word-for-word,"[112] we may remember the difference between the promise of total control and the taste of spontaneity, so present we do not even notice it most of the time, at the very tips of our tongue. Novels like *Zero K*, in the sheer delight they take in language, reminds us of the immense flow of which we are a part, and, which, at privileged moments, we recognize as our own depth.

Part 3: DeLillo and Péguy

It would not be a great leap to recognize in DeLillo's deployment of metaphor an analogy to Péguy's emphasis on intuition. We recall that intuition, just like metaphor, arises out of the slow build-up of memory. Language for DeLillo, just like intuition for Péguy, bespeaks of something unplanned, "the free play of step-by-step and word-for-word" characteristic of our ordinary experience, filled with routines, to be sure, but not following a tight script dictated in advance.[113] Both authors foreground, be it either through intuition or metaphor, a vast reality upon which we draw without even being aware of it, and which exceeds our grasp. That vast reality is both "'the thought at the back of the mind" emerging from the sciences and something equally vast and unreachable at the source of their skepticism. Neither pretends that he has the solution that will beat back the religion of science. Embodying what it dismisses is a worthy enough task.

It would be astonishing, however, if the hundred years that separate Péguy's writings from those of DeLillo had left no mark upon the latter's work. In DeLillo, we find a religion of science bathed in apocalyptic visions and in global capitalism in a way it does not appear in Péguy. This statement needs to be qualified if we recall the philosopher's fear of a world covered in ash, the consequence of the urge to duplicate creation. Neither did Péguy ignore the link between the religion of science and modern capitalism, insofar as he drew attention to a shared emphasis on interchangeability, and endless accumulation. But even if the links between science, capitalism and apocalypse have antecedents,

112. DeLillo, *Zero K*, 247.

113. DeLillo, *Zero K*, 247.

they appear in DeLillo's work with an unprecedented force, reflecting our contemporary reality.

In the first place, the end of the world is no longer a remote possibility, as it is for Péguy. On the contrary, in *Zero K*, DeLillo paints a world in which the end of life on earth is imminent, permeating his characters' concerns. The novel begins with a reference to it. "*Everyone wants to own the end of the world,*" Ross, Jeff's father pronounces.[114] At the very end of the novel, the thought does cross Jeff's mind that the spectacular sunset he sees through the bus window signals the sky crashing into the earth, although he makes an effort to move away from this interpretation.[115] The two main sections of the novel, labeled "Chelyabinsk" and "Constantine," respectively, both evoke apocalyptic fears. Chelyabinsk is the city in which a meteor fell to earth in 2013, a possible prelude to such an incident on a much wider scale, and Constantine is the site in Eastern Ukraine of a war between Ukraine and Russia, also a possible prelude to a much more ominous global conflict, as is only too clear ten years later.

Within the novel, while Jeff is roaming the halls of the Convergence, he is always bumping into screens, depicting natural catastrophes and wars—wildfires, tsunamis, ravaged landscapes.[116] The spokespeople in the seminars he is allowed to attend mention almost nothing else. "If our planet remains a self-sustaining environment, how nice for everyone and how bloody unlikely," one of them pronounces.[117] "Apocalypse is inherent in the structure of time," pontificates another.[118] Yet a third authority lists all the catastrophic events happening or likely to happen: "The loss of forests, the spread of drought, the massive die-offs of birds and ocean-life, the levels of carbon dioxide, the lack of drinking water, the waves of virus that envelop broad geographies."[119]

These visions of the imminent demise of life on earth are the underside of the search for immortality, what fuels it, as it were. In the first place, the Convergence, immense underground structure that it is, is built to be impervious to world catastrophe. Ross describes the care taken to make it so. "We have what is needed. Durable energy sources

114. DeLillo, *Zero K*, 3.

115. DeLillo, *Zero K*, 274.

116. DeLillo, *Zero K*, 36–37, 120–21, 259–61.

117. DeLillo, *Zero K*, 238.

118. DeLillo, *Zero K*, 243.

119. DeLillo, *Zero K*, 126.

and strong mechanized systems. Blast walls and fortified floors. Structural redundancy. Fire safety. Security patrols, land and air. Elaborate cyber-defense and so on."[120] It would not do to undergo the cryonics process and then be destroyed by a nuclear blast, or to have the scientists working on immortality be destroyed. In another way, however, immortality, rather than being the way out of the apocalypse, coincides with it. When the apocalypse comes, it will signal the end of humanity as we know it. The destruction of life on earth is a necessary prelude to a transcendent future. We will die as humans in order to be reborn as enhanced machines. "We are here to reconsider everything about life's end. And we will emerge in cyberhuman form into a universe that will speak to us in a very different way."[121]

As is the case for the immortality promised in Christianity, not everyone will be worthy of it. The spokespeople at the Convergence are not bashful about pointing out that immortality will be the gateway for the chosen few. "Life everlasting belongs to those of breathtaking wealth," one of them tells a group of mogul donors.[122] Their money has made them rise above everyone else, a sign of their difference. They can continue to affirm their transcendence of ordinary human beings by refusing the common fate, death. "Think of money and immortality," they are told, as if the two naturally go together.[123] Jeff speculates that the desire to buy immortality is the last realm people like his father can conquer.[124] They already own everything else. From the perspective of the Convergence, the privileged status of the wealthy is deserved. After all, it is people like Ross, a "godhead of world finance," who fuel, through their vast donations, the scientific work making immortality a possibility.

But in case immortality itself tarries, the fabulously rich can at least increase their wealth in the meantime. The apocalypse/immortality combination is profitable. "Everyone wants to own the end of the world," we recall Ross had said in his first conversation with his son about cryonics. Whatever he might have meant by the expression "owning the apocalypse," it also means making yet more money from attempts to escape it. One of the sources of his wealth had in fact been the profits to be made

120. DeLillo, *Zero K*, 30.
121. DeLillo, *Zero K*, 67.
122. DeLillo, *Zero K*, 76.
123. DeLillo, *Zero K*, 76.
124. DeLillo, *Zero K*, 117.

from natural disasters.[125] While preparing for immortality, tech centers all over the world are innovating, getting ahead, trying to reverse aging and the biochemistry of progressive diseases.[126] Surely, the fact that immortality is a good investment does not prevent Jeff's father from also being a faithful believer in the end result. One is saved either way.

Like so much of *Zero K*, the link between apocalypse, immortality through science, and enormous wealth has its counterpart in the world outside the novel. The research into reversing or slowing aging conducted both in American universities and in private corporations, mentioned at the beginning of this essay, is very expensive. The scientists often ask billionaires for the money, promising their potential investors what could be "their ticket to immortality."[127] The parallel between *Zero K* and the world outside it also extends to the "structural redundancy" that Ross claimed made the Convergence safe against catastrophe. A good number of centi-millionaires and billionaires, it turns out, plan to escape the coming apocalypse by buying properties in remote places, studied for their imperviousness to tsunamis, for instance, New Zealand being a favorite destination.[128] Some also invest in underground bunkers, one of which, called the Survival Condo Project, is a fifteen-story construction. Its main investor bought an underground Missile silo abandoned by the U.S. government.[129] Meant to withstand nuclear attack, it is a good location. The underground complex has been outfitted for the long haul: entertainment centers, LED screens to duplicate favorite natural scenes, a food growing area, a dentist's office, even a prison-like room, (no cemeteries, as far as I could tell). All thirty apartments have been sold, at prices ranging from three million dollars to half that amount, depending on the size. At the time of the writing of the article, the investor had plans to build four more such underground structures.[130]

For at least a portion of these very wealthy survivalists, imminent catastrophe and search for immortality are two sides of the same coin. In a lengthy essay about a Silicon Valley mogul, "Sam Altman's Manifest Destiny," the journalist reveals that Altman, on the one hand, has bought property in Big Sur, and that he has stashed "guns, gold, potassium

125. DeLillo, *Zero K*, 13–14.

126. DeLillo, *Zero K*, 126.

127. Regalado, "Google's Long Strange Life-Span Trip," 11.

128. Osnos, "Doomsday Prep," 1–29.

129. Osnos, "Doomsday Prep," 12–13.

130. Osnos, "Doomsday Prep," 13–14, 20–22.

iodide, antibiotics, batteries, water, gas masks from the Israeli Defense Force" in case of catastrophe. On the other hand, Altman speculates that "we need to level up humans because our descendants will either conquer the galaxy or extinguish consciousness in the universe forever. What a time to be alive!"[131] With this goal in mind, "he is thinking of establishing a group to prepare for our eventual successor, whether it be an A.I. or an enhanced version of Homo sapiens."[132] As already mentioned, Altman cofounded, with several others, among whom Elon Musk, the research center, OpenAI, now almost a household name, thanks to ChatGPT, whose goal is to duplicate human intelligence. The sums of money invested in this project are in the billions of dollars.

In the meantime, anti-aging solutions are also on the table. In the article painting his portrait, Altman is quoted as saying that he is "hoping to fund a parabiosis company,[133] to place the rejuvenating elixir of youthful blood into an injection."[134] In a recent *Washington Post* editorial, the author mentions rumors about billionaires who "undergo regular blood transfusions from the young, in hopes of improving their own health."[135] The reference to the rejuvenating elixir of youthful blood, also an idea of Peter Thiel, the venture capitalist who helped start PayPal and Palantir, brings to mind the conspiracy theories of QAnon, the internet group convinced that a group of powerful elites are capturing children to abuse them sexually. One version of this conspiracy is that the elites also drink the blood of their young victims in order to stay perpetually young. My point is not to provide evidence for the QAnon conspiracy but to show that in its grotesque way it reflects a world in which the very rich are thinking of some synthetic derivation of the blood of children in order to achieve immortality. QAnon members would then be expressing Nietzschian *ressentiment*. They too would want the opportunities of the unimaginably rich to live forever but since they cannot, they condemn it as evil. In the distortions of QAnon, the dream of immortality achieves another one of

131. Friend, "Sam Altman's Manifest Destiny," 7, 17.

132. Friend, "Sam Altman's Manifest Destiny," 17.

133. Parabiosis originally refers to "joining a young mouse to an old mouse so that they share blood—to see what would happen to the heart and skeletal muscle tissue." Zimmerman, "Biotech Start-Up." The concept, the author goes on to say, is now being developed so that it can be applied to humans.

134. Friend, "Manifest Destiny," 17.

135. Olen, "As basic health care grows unaffordable."

its permutations, devoid of science, to be sure, but grasping the desire that drives the science of the very rich nonetheless.

It would be a mistake to read *Zero K* as a wagging of the finger at global capitalism. It simply describes how much we are in its grasp. Jeff can as little escape the world of global capitalism as he can defeat the scientific dreams of the Convergence. He spends his whole life attempting to run away from his father's wealth, taking on all sorts of numbing temporary jobs, refusing to profit from his position as the son. His refusal is complicated by the fact that his father abandoned him and his mother when he was still a boy. But whatever his motivation, all the jobs for which he applies are on some echelon of the system in which his father has gained so much power—"systems administrator at a networking site. Human resource planner—global mobility . . . solutions research manager—simulation models."[136]

Of course, Jeff's situation cannot be made universal in any direct way. Most of us do not have a billionaire father. But his inability to shake himself loose of his father's world may indicate that we too cannot really refuse to live in the world global capitalism has created. We can at best, minimize our participation. This does not make us heroes. Jeff is adrift, without solid mooring in either a profession or a relationship. Yet, Jeff, adrift as he is, praises his mother for giving him the one lesson with which he navigates: "Ordinary moments make the life. This is what she knew to be trustworthy and this is what I learned, eventually, from all those years we spent together. No leaps or falls.[137] It may be that choosing to live within certain financial limits is also a prophylactic against the leap into dreams of transcending our humanity.

For Péguy, we recall, only works within the humanities, past and present, give us, through artfully choosing a part, the whole in which we live. DeLillo, in choosing to describe contemporary dreams of scientific resurrection, puts his finger on the religion of science in which we live, even if individually we do not subscribe to these dreams. They shape our world nonetheless. The light *Zero K* casts on our reality is not exactly the light Péguy's own work casts. We live with the catastrophes portrayed on the screens of the Convergence in a way that Péguy and his contemporaries could not. There were as yet no screens, and the catastrophes themselves did not portend a global disaster, or at least not with the same sense

136. DeLillo, *Zero K*, 57.

137. DeLillo, *Zero K*, 109.

of imminence. In these and so many other ways, the twenty-first century is very different from the early twentieth. But the narratives Péguy noticed in the nineteenth-century historians Renan and Taine already included a claim to a knowledge of the source of life itself, made possible by the natural sciences. These narratives were already so powerful that one could only oppose them indirectly, through finding a way of embodying an alternative rather than merely arguing about it. I do not present Péguy and DeLillo as isolated figures but as representative of a tradition as modern as the new narratives about the natural sciences, the tradition of identifying these narratives as religious, and the tradition, call it a new secularism, of trying to expose their metaphysical claims.

CHAPTER 3

The Humanist Scientist

Bernard d'Espagnat's *On Physics and Philosophy*

Preface

We may recall that Charles Péguy turned every which way the status that the natural sciences had acquired in our culture, pointing to the narratives of omniscience and omnipotence attached to them, and to their salvific role as the only guides to what is real and true. Péguy feared the consequences of these narratives for our world, the repeated attempts to replace the given and organic with the artificial, on the scale of replacing reality itself. He claimed that scientists, or at least some of them, might be among those who help us dispel these narratives. What he meant is best explained by his references to the scientists he found helpful. He turned to the writings of Henri Poincaré, the mathematician, and Pierre Duclaux, the biologist, for references to how intuition, and not merely analysis, operates in their respective fields.[1] He turned to the essays of Pierre Duhem, the physicist, chemist and mathematician, for the sober limits he places on what the natural sciences could tell us

1. Péguy, *Œuvres II*, 1179, 1190–93. For a clarification of how Péguy understands Poincaré, see Péguy, *Œuvres II, 1554*. For Duclaux, see Péguy, *Œuvres II*, 1134–69.

about metaphysics.[2] He turned to an article by Georges Sorel, an engineer by training, for an explication of the distance between the as-if of experiment and reality, and what scientists habitually do to compensate for that distance.[3] None of these thinkers had Péguy's broad critique of the "religion of science" in mind. They nonetheless provided a practitioner's look into the actual operations of a scientist, at some remove from the aggrandizing narratives around them. I see Bernard d'Espagnat as one of those scientists in our own time. Most significant for us, he does have an interest in metaphysics, in a way that implicates physics, but that also challenges the widely-held assumption that it is the royal, if not exclusive road to truth about our world. His enormous book, *On Physics and Philosophy*, might help us to think about the natural sciences in conjunction with the way of knowing characterizing the arts, and the humanities. As I indicate in the conclusion, questions remain about this conjunction. How could it be otherwise?

Introduction

Given the huge number of volumes on the philosophical implications of quantum physics, d'Espagnat's book might not appear a natural place to turn for anyone wishing to dip a toe into this topic.[4] A huge tome, systematic to a fault in any given section, it remains stubbornly nonlinear as a whole, the straight line of the exposition deflected as he responds to this or that possible objection to his argument, or this or that topic relevant to it. His central themes do appear frequently but always with additions and qualifications, and references to points made in another section, cited by chapter and paragraph number. Cross references such

2. Péguy, *Œuvres II*, 652–3. See also Burac, "Notes," in Péguy, *Œuvres I*, 1459.

3. Sorel, "Les Préoccupations métaphysiques des physiciens modernes," 859–89.

4. Many people might be familiar with Fritjof Capra's *The Tao of Physics (1975)*, a classic in the genre, or, more contemporary with us, the writings of Carlo Rovelli, the latest of which, *Helgoland (2021)*, is about Werner Heisenberg, who himself wrote a book entitled *Physics and Philosophy* (1958). This is only to mention three authors in this area whose works are generally well known, but, as Henderson, "The Quantum Mechanic," points out, "a veritable zoo of conjectures for what quantum mechanics might really imply about the world has been floated by physicists and philosophers over the years." Henderson's article evoked over eight hundred comments, revealing the broad interest in quantum mechanics in our culture at large. D'Espagnat makes his own conjectures, of course, different from the three authors mentioned above, but in addition he also makes the very fact of thinking philosophically about physics its own central topic.

as indicating section 2–3, and then referring to section 13–2, and then returning to section 2–3 multiply as the book progresses.[5] This practically ensures that the reader will leave out an important distinction, especially since d'Espagnat is inordinately fond of them. "World" has only two possible definitions. "Realism," however, has twelve sub-categories, and even what it means to describe can be spliced three ways.[6] One is always dropping something in the process of catching something else. If the interpreter of d'Espagnat's work is neither a professional philosopher nor a physicist, the task of reading his exacting prose is even more daunting. If even physicists found quantum physics incomprehensible, what is a lay person to say?[7]

If I persisted with *On Physics and Philosophy* nonetheless, it is not only because this is a book of philosophy, not physics, and most of it is intended for the general, educated reader.[8] This in itself is not a sufficient reason since many other books on the nexus between philosophy and physics share this feature, even if they are usually much less thorough. If I have persisted, it is also because d'Espagnat's book touches, in some ways, on the humanities. He is not content to show the philosophical implications of quantum mechanics, but, in addition, argues vigorously for the central importance of philosophy to the physicist's work. The door between physics and other disciplines opens yet wider. Tucked away here and there in d'Espagnat's voluminous writings, and yet of central importance, is the room he makes for the arts and religion. Physics, he says, authorizes us to validate a form of knowledge associated with poets, composers, painters and mystics that physics and the natural sciences in general are not capable of producing. It is this loop between physics and other methods of investigating the world—philosophy but also the arts

5. Espagnat, *On Physics and Philosophy*, 365.

6. Espagnat, *On Physics and Philosophy*, 379, 24–31, 455.

7. I refer here to the oft-quoted sentence of Richard Feynman, "I think I can safely say that nobody understands quantum mechanics." Polkinghorne, *Quantum Theory*, uses this sentence as an epigraph to his book. He also echoes this sentiment within it: "To be frank, we do not have as tight a grasp of quantum theory as we would like to have. We can do the sums, and in that sense, explain the phenomena, but we do not really *understand* what is going on," Polkinghorne, *Quantum Theory*, 56.

8. Espagnat, *On Physics and Philosophy*, 7. This is d'Espagnat's stated intention, but he also knows that some aspects of quantum physics can only be made clear in mathematical language. He reserved several chapters to those more mathematically inclined readers, warning the general reader to avoid them until they have read the rest of the book.

and religion—that is of central interest. Some questions remain about this loop, which I will leave to the end.

Part 1: Physics and Philosophy

D'Espagnat does not engage in his quest to understand the philosophical implications of quantum physics as an amateur. In 1954, he was appointed the first theoretical physicist at CERN. That is where he met John Stewart Bell, whose theorem he was instrumental in recommending for experimental verification to Alain Aspect, a graduate student in physics at the time. D'Espagnat later directed the theoretical physics laboratory in the Physics Department of the University of Paris, where Alain Aspect, at an earlier moment, had ended up verifying Bell's theorem.[9] Bell and Aspect are very big names in the later twentieth-century study of subatomic particles. D'Espagnat himself trained and worked with some of the great physicists of the first half of the twentieth century—Louis de Broglie, Enrico Fermi, Niels Bohr, among others. He also taught philosophy of science, and his knowledge of philosophy is prodigious, as indicated by his many discussions throughout the book with a wealth of philosophers whose work he studies in detail. They range from the classical Greeks to contemporaries, passing through many others in between. From each thinker he solicits an answer regarding the notion of reality. Can we know the Real and if so, in what way? His attempt is to understand a little better how information stemming from contemporary physics might shed light on this question.[10]

But before he can get to the great theme of his book—the philosophical implications of quantum physics—he wants to establish that the philosophical question regarding the notion of the real is not an aside to physics but central to it. In the most preliminary way, physicists need philosophy because it is inseparable from the very way they understand their task. D'Espagnat argues against understanding science

9. For an explanation of both Bell's theorem and of Aspect's experiments, see Espagnat, "The Quantum Theory and Reality," 158–81. Although Bell published his influential theorem in 1964, it took nearly two decades before it penetrated into the mainstream of physics. Aspect concluded his experimental verification in 1982. Both Bell and Aspect had been in the running for Nobel Prizes. Aspect finally won the Nobel Prize in 2022, together with Anton Zeilinger and John Clauser, for their confirmation of entanglement. One source for describing how Bell's theorem eventually took center stage is Kaiser, *How the Hippies Saved Physics*.

10. Espagnat, *On Physics and Philosophy*, 9.

as merely "a technology focalized on the long term."[11] Even if, as he says again and again, physics does not yield "the ground of things," it does reveal, in an indirect way "some form of the absolute."[12] It takes him the whole book to unpack what he means, but to get a little ahead of ourselves, he is saying that even if physics cannot tell us anything directly about reality, it bumps into its own limitations in such a way that it gives rise, indirectly, to reflections on the Real.

D'Espagnat is quite aware that many physicists would disagree with him. On the one hand, there are those convinced that science does provide access to reality directly, something that d'Espagnat will not concede. On the other hand, many physicists dispense with the need for thinking about reality at all. They feel a much closer affinity with technology than with philosophy. In a recent book, the physicist author argues that "there can be no sharp distinction between science and engineering."[13] He contends that "in recent decades the greatest portion of physics has drifted closer to techne, in the sense that the theoretical foundations are secure and the crucial matter is putting them to use."[14] Fundamental physics [the one that deals with subatomic particles], on the other hand, has drifted away from physics and become "a form of ancient philosophy in modern clothes," something the author clearly disapproves of.[15] The difference between a view like this and d'Espagnat's own position does not come from the practice of science, argues d'Espagnat. It is embedded in a philosophical choice as to what the scientific method can or should tell us about Nature to begin with.[16]

Physics relies on philosophy not only in determining its goals but also within its very practice. In an earlier time, d'Espagnat says, one argued that science was not interested in what something was, the realm of the philosopher, but only in how something behaved. But nonetheless physicists did name entities the reality of which most of them took for granted.[17] Without necessarily seeing it as a philosophical choice, the scientist relied on a metaphysics, that of materialism. D'Espagnat argues again and again that this philosophical outlook no longer fits the findings of post-classical

11. Espagnat, *On Physics and Philosophy,* 5.
12. Espagnat, *On Physics and Philosophy,* 5.
13. Lindley, *Dream Universe,* 135.
14. Lindley, *Dream Universe,* 143.
15. Lindley, *Dream Universe,* 143.
16. Espagnat, *On Physics and Philosophy,* 249–50.
17. Espagnat, *On Physics and Philosophy,* 249–50.

physics. The point is two-fold. Physics has always been intertwined with a metaphysics, even if individual physicists might remain unaware of that dimension of their work. Contemporary physics no longer allows for the reliance on the older metaphysics, however.

D'Espagnat is quite aware that materialism cannot be too narrowly defined. It is what he calls, following the philosopher of science Larry Laudan, a tradition of research.[18] "In Laudan's eyes, such traditions are neither research programs nor definite theories but rather tissues of theories and commitments of various kinds, both methodological and *ontological*."[19] "Materialism," he says at one point, is a "flag," "a banner expressing a visceral loyalty, "and nobody willingly gives up his flag."[20] He suggests several features that its many branches nonetheless have in common. It is "a conception of Nature in which basic Reality—matter, as it was called—was constituted by myriad simple elements—essentially localized "atoms" or "particles"—embedded in fields, and hence interacting by means of forces decreasing when distance increased." He calls this the "*multitudinist* world-view."[21] Later, he adds a new emphasis to his definition of materialism. "As a rule, the whole world—our brain included—is . . . taken to be composed of such 'atoms,' and the phenomena taking place in it—including thought—are considered to merely follow from the existence of the atoms and the forces that connect them."[22] The mind has no special status which would exclude it from the methods of scientific analysis. It can be broken down into component parts of the brain, parts that interact in a causal way with each other and with outside stimuli. There are no exceptions to the determinism regulating the universe. He calls this "the monist framework in which any materialism is by definition situated."[23] The flag d'Espagnat is talking about often centers on a taken-for-granted determinism, which, most emphatically includes human thought and emotion.

The problem that, at the moment, necessitates the active entry of philosophy into physics is that the sub-atomic stuff that quantum physics deals with makes materialism highly implausible. "Not only is it true that, in it [quantum field theory], the particles no longer play the role of

18. See Larry Laudan, *Progress and Its Problems*, 79, 82.

19. Espagnat, *On Physics and Philosophy*, 269.

20. Espagnat, *On Physics and Philosophy*, 281.

21. Espagnat, *On Physics and Philosophy*, 17.

22. Espagnat, *On Physics and Philosophy*, 267.

23. Espagnat, *On Physics and Philosophy*, 276.

the constitutive material of the Universe. What is more, the only 'entity' that, in it, might conceivably be thought to constitute basic Reality is the 'Something,' of which we saw that it is fundamentally the only one of its species."[24] The mathematical formalism synonymous with quantum mechanics makes it impossible to think of the particles as each having its own individuality. There are no longer separate units, to be discovered in a given space. The mathematics involved "implies giving up the very notion of a probability, for a particle, to *be* at such and such a place, and replacing it by the probability we have of *finding* the particle there."[25] He puts it even more strongly. "We know that an atomistic materialism reducing the whole world to a set of atoms, particles and so on, interacting through distance-decreasing forces, is an experimentally disproved notion . . . Such a materialism is simply false."[26] He adds that this does not necessarily negate the part of the materialist view that maintains an objective access to reality as such, as long as that reality has the characteristic of nonlocality.[27]

D'Espagnat is not making these pronouncements by fiat. Many chapters of his book are devoted to explaining the science behind the strange behavior of subatomic particles, which involve all the terms one can read about quantum mechanics—superposition, interference, entanglement, decoherence, Schrödinger's cat, Dirac's sea, Wigner's friends, and who knows what else.[28] The one phenomenon that D'Espagnat insists on the most is the one usually referred to as "nonlocality."[29] It is the fact that two elementary particles—electrons or photons—provided they were once together, will influence each other instantaneously, that is, at a speed greater than that of light, once they are split apart, no matter the distance between them. By contrast, locality by definition requires the decrease of influence the greater the distance between the entities involved.[30] In Bell theorem's, affirmed in Alain Aspect's experiments but also by subsequent ones, this decreased influence is no longer

24. Espagnat, *On Physics and Philosophy*, 17.

25. Espagnat, *On Physics and Philosophy*, 58.

26. Espagnat, *On Physics and Philosophy*, 268.

27. Espagnat, *On Physics and Philosophy*, 58.

28. This is especially the case in d'Espagnat, *On Physics* and Philosophy, 51–236.

29. This term intersects with Erwin Schrödinger's term "entanglement," and Albert Einstein's coinage, "spooky action at a distance."

30. Espagnat, *On Physics and Philosophy*, 57. Kumar, *Quantum*, 312, defines locality as follows: "What happens to A cannot simultaneously affect B."

the case. In several other books explaining quantum physics to the layman, it seems to be a settled matter among a majority of physicists that nonlocality is inexplicable through the classical vocabulary of physics, and that the image classical physics presents of the world as made up of separate entities, present before we measure them, and acted upon by forces we can measure no longer fits the data.[31] Of course, there are controversies as to what this not-fitting with classical vocabulary means. The point is not so much that d'Espagnat's view of subatomic physics is unanimously accepted, but that it lies within a tradition which sees the vocabulary of classical physics, referring to individual particles, as no longer adequate to the experimental data.

One might well ask, despite nonlocality, why physicists would need to actively engage in formulating a new philosophy, different from materialism, given that even without doing so, their calculations predict outcomes to a very high degree of accuracy. D'Espagnat characterizes their position: "We dispose of predictive rules that work well, and there is nothing more to ask for."[32] D'Espagnat's response is complex. On the one hand, he is sympathetic, not to materialism, but to the difficulty of moving away from this worldview. It seems intuitively correct to so many people, scientists and laymen alike. He attributes this partly to the time it takes for new discoveries to change our internalized image of the world.[33] In addition, the vocabulary of classical physics reflecting a materialist worldview—particles, forces etc.— is often necessary for physicists to picture what they are investigating. As a result, "those among them who feel unable to conceive that rationality can be exerted independently of

31. See, for instance, Polkinghorne, *Quantum Theory*, 80. "It had become clear that there is an irreducible amount of nonlocality present in the physical world." He calls this nonlocality ontological and not merely epistemological. That is, it is not merely a feature of what we do not know, but of the world the physicist examines. He gives an example of the inadequacy of classical vocabulary in his explanation of quantum logic. Classical logic works with the law of the excluded middle. Something is either in one place or in another. "In the 1930s, people began to realize that matters were different in the quantum world. An electron can not only be 'here' and 'not here,' but also in any number of other states that are superpositions of 'here' and 'not here,'" Polkinghorne, *Quantum Theory*, 37–38. Werner Heisenberg, in his *Physics and Philosophy*, 56, speaks of the paradox in physicists' use of language. "We describe our experiments in terms of classical physics and at the same time from the knowledge that these concepts do not fit nature accurately."

32. Espagnat, *On Physics and Philosophy*, 236.

33. Espagnat, *On Physics and Philosophy*, 3, 446.

a materialist world-view should keep the latter."[34] The only request that d'Espagnat makes is that "they [the scientists] refrain from converting their choices into an illegitimate doctrinal creed.[35] The concept of separate entities is a useful construction but no more than that. It does not express the way things really are. "[T]o raise a model to the level of a description of 'what really is' is scientifically illegitimate."[36]

But as sympathetic as d'Espagnat might be to those scientists who cannot part with the materialist paradigm, he does not give up on the necessity of rethinking it, and moving away from it. He agrees with the philosopher Whitehead's statement: "Each . . . science . . . stops at a halfway house. It finds a resting place amid notions which for its immediate purposes and for its immediate methods it need not analyze further."[37] That is, scientists usually stop at a set of concepts that work for what they need and do not go beyond that point. D'Espagnat argues, however, that a time comes when they need to go beyond that "halfway house." When, as is the case with post-classical physics, a whole range of notions—Euclidian space, universal time, precise location can no longer be taken "as basic elements of Reality,"[38] one needs to rethink the whole conceptual edifice anew, using as a necessary tool not only contemporary philosophy (it may be too closely allied with the old model) but also the whole history of Western philosophy.[39] This is the rethinking with which *On Physics and Philosophy* is involved, at once a very ambitious and a very tentative task. Before I turn, with much trepidation, to d'Espagnat's own alternative to materialism, I would first like to examine the other side of the argument, for he argues not only that physics needs philosophy but also that philosophy needs physics.

Here too, it is not at all obvious as to why philosophers need to consult physics in order to arrive at a worldview. Arguing against it is the well-known fact that scientific theories change through time. It is the natural sciences' source of pride, in fact, that their theories are not dogma, but

34. Espagnat, *On Physics and Philosophy,* 281.

35. Espagnat, *On Physics and Philosophy,* 281.

36. Espagnat, *On Physics and Philosophy,* 18.

37. Espagnat, *On Physics and Philosophy,* 282.

38. Espagnat, *On Physics and Philosophy,* 241, 287.

39. Espagnat, *On Physics and Philosophy,* 282. He does not exclude non-Western models, as he states in a brief section on Buddhism, Espagnat, *On Physics and Philosophy,* 440–41. But he clearly prefers staying within a historical tradition with which he is familiar, and which has given rise to modern science in the first place.

discarded if the evidence demands it. Quantum mechanics might triumph experimentally today but who is to say that a counter-tradition, associated most famously with Einstein, which predicts that we will eventually return to an observer-independent, precisely delineated object, will not one day be experimentally verified, dethroning the observer-dependent description associated with Niels Bohr?[40] As d'Espagnat himself concludes, "Consequently it is entirely conceivable that quantum mechanics should, one day . . . be replaced by some other theory based on different concepts and in which, therefore, the conceptual difficulties specific to quantum mechanics will not exist."[41] He thinks, however, that whatever else might change, nonlocality will survive. That is, the strange behavior of two subatomic particles, that, when separated, influence each other at a speed faster than light no matter how far apart they are has been corroborated in so many experiments that it is here to stay, and is independent of any theory. This is what remains philosophically noteworthy, challenging our notions of time and space, causality, and much else, claims d'Espagnat, even if his own conclusions about the metaphysical and epistemological implications, are not accepted.

D'Espagnat gives at least two other retorts as to why philosophers should engage with physics, despite the fact that scientific theories change. Theories do, yes, but the great mathematical laws, "the fundamental equations of mathematical physics have remained endowed with both a considerable heuristic and predictive value."[42] He will say frequently that even if these equations do not give us direct access to a human-independent Reality, reality as it really is in itself, these laws may be traces of it, in a highly distorted form.[43] His phrasing of this is cautious in the extreme, but he returns to it again and again. He ventures that these laws "*indirectly* furnish some *not altogether misleading* glimpses on the general structure of 'the Real,'" and adds that this conclusion "*seems not to be altogether unwarranted*."[44] [my underscoring]

But despite his caution, followed up with further limiting what mathematical formalism can tell us by emphasizing that *in its contents*

40. For a very clear description and analysis of the philosophical differences between Einstein and Bohr, see Kumar, *Quantum*. The entire book is on this topic.

41. Espagnat, *On Physics and Philosophy*, 58.

42. Espagnat, *On Physics and Philosophy*, 251.

43. Espagnat, *On Physics and Philosophy*, 438, footnote 8.

44. Espagnat, *On Physics and Philosophy*, 238.

it does not give us a direct description of the real,[45] he nonetheless insists that given their high level of predictability, the great mathematical laws remain important evidence for further reflection on metaphysics. In fact, he goes further to argue that they cannot be bypassed. In discussing Nicholas de Cusa's *Of Learned Ignorance*, he recognizes how close this fifteenth-century thinker comes to his own concept of Veiled Reality (more about which, shortly). But since the physics of de Cusa's time did not invite such a view, it "would be totally out of place."[46] It is a reasoning he repeats in regard to Plato and to medieval nominalist philosophers.[47] Parts of their metaphysics can be discarded because modern science provides evidence to the contrary. They assumed locality, individuated objects, when modern physics shows it to be an inadequate view. (Yet, as we shall see, at other times, he relegates the evidence coming from physics to being just one among other kinds, the others in some cases stronger than the data of physics. We shall return in our conclusions to this tension in d'Espagnat's thinking regarding the best evidence for thinking about "the Real.")

His second retort to the claim that science changes and is therefore an unreliable guide for philosophers' pursuit of a worldview is that many modern philosophers work within a tradition, materialism, closely associated with the natural sciences to begin with. "For example, some philosophers do still make unrestricted use of classical notions of quite a general nature, such as locality, distinguishability, etc., taken to be obvious since Galileo's and Newton's time."[48] In a later example of a philosopher who naively accepts "a world entirely composed of physical particles embedded in force fields," he points out that "such a conception is obviously obsolete."[49] The irony, as d'Espagnat sees it, is that a good number of philosophers who claim independence from science are nonetheless relying on an older version of it.

The only way to rectify this dependence is to consult contemporary science. Philosophers "tend to simply ignore recent scientific advances, which makes them miss the point that, by blocking some traditional perspectives, such findings may well open promising new ones."[50] Again,

45. Espagnat, *On Physics and Philosophy*, 239, footnote 8.

46. Espagnat, *On Physics and Philosophy*, 242.

47. Espagnat, *On Physics and Philosophy*, 1, 436, 444, 260, 459.

48. Espagnat, *On Physics and Philosophy*, 2.

49. Espagnat, *On Physics and Philosophy*, 267, footnote 1.

50. Espagnat, *On Physics and Philosophy*, 2.

quantum mechanics cannot tell us directly what the Real is. Nonetheless, the argument d'Espagnat is making is that science yields information of the negative sort, serving "to *limit* possible options, rather than put forward allegedly correct ones."[51] According to him, "we cannot build a trustworthy representation of the said Reality [a Reality independent of our concepts] that would be plural, merged in space-time, 'scattered' among a multitude of 'atoms,' etc."[52] Those mathematical formulations, so precise in their predictive capacity, guide us to what reality is not.

A summary of the relationship of physics to philosophy, as d'Espagnat sees it, may be in order here. They depend on each other, although each has its own task. Philosophy, or at least the branches that d'Espagnat finds relevant for his purposes, is the discipline that elaborates what is, ontology, and how we know, epistemology, our access or lack of access to reality in itself. Philosophers, at least in modern times, have done so in close conjunction with discoveries emanating from the sciences, but the sciences, whose role it is to investigate the behavior of the natural world, nonetheless work with received concepts that derive from the ambient philosophy. The only way for both disciplines to free themselves from received notions is if members of both consult the history of philosophy, on the one hand (since contemporary philosophy might not have sufficient distance from the sciences) and contemporary physics (to create distance toward philosophic concepts inadequate to account for confirmed findings in the sciences).

Taking this two-way street has nothing self-evident about it, since most physicists are not philosophers and most philosophers are not physicists. The difficulty goes beyond a matter of specialized training. Rather, it reflects a reluctance to give up jurisdiction over reality, in some cases, and a reluctance to venture into fields considered irrelevant to the performance of one's task. Yet, for d'Espagnat, the exchange between physics and philosophy is crucial. Beyond the intellectual broadening in both fields, it leads to practical consequences. ". . . the Aspect-like experiments, far from obstructing the path of research, are themselves elements of a fascinating scientific quest."[53] That is, thinking about the philosophical implications of nonlocality have opened new scientific paths. But the practical consequences of his philosophical inquiry into physics are also of existential

51. Espagnat, *On Physics and Philosophy*, 1.

52. Espagnat, *On Physics and Philosophy*, 380.

53. Espagnat, *On Physics and Philosophy*, 430.

importance, d'Espagnat tells us early on.[54] He never fully spells out what he means. We will return to this in our conclusion.

It would be a mistake to think that in promoting a philosophical reflection on physics d'Espagnat is urging all physicists to develop a philosophical interest or vice-versa. He is perfectly well aware that most physicists will continue to do their work without delving into philosophy and that there are branches of philosophy that do not need to deal directly with physics, not to mention that philosophers in all branches define reliable evidence according to their own disciplinary standard. His huge tome, however, speaks to the desirability of a physicist/humanist. This does not mean a physicist who can cite Shakespeare or who listens to Beethoven, in addition to his work in the laboratory, but a physicist who reflects on the meaning of the enterprise of physics within the larger world of inquiry within which physics fits. At that point, the point of thinking about the Real, the physicist must abandon mathematical language and resort to ordinary language, commonly in use,[55] forged in a long tradition that is not that of the natural sciences. That language includes interpreting what scientific findings tell us about reality. These interpretations are neither verifiable nor falsifiable in laboratory experiments. They can only claim greater plausibility than other such interpretations.

Of great interest is that d'Espagnat increasingly makes an appeal not only to philosophy but also to the arts and to religious traditions, or at least their most classical expressions. The findings of physics need to be placed within the whole range of human expressions, not in order to subordinate the latter to physics but to help understand physics' portents. Understanding the relation between physics and the arts/humanities correctly requires a new metaphysics, at the center of which, for d'Espagnat, is a concept he calls "Veiled Reality."

Part 2: Veiled Reality, Science, and the Arts

The first thing to stress about the concept of Veiled Reality is that it results from d'Espagnat's experience as a scientist. In every endeavor to know it, Nature says "no" to a great number of our concepts, rarely yielding results. "There 'is something' that tempers the imaginative impulses of our creativity . . . In other words, the physical laws do not totally

54. Espagnat, *On Physics and Philosophy*, 9.

55. Espagnat, *On Physics and Philosophy*, 7.

depend on us, which means that they also depend on something else."[56] In the case of quantum physics, however, Nature says "no" not to this or that concept, but to our conceptual understanding altogether. Although quantum physicists can predict the statistical probability that a particle will be found in such and such a place, they do not know why it gets there rather than elsewhere, and what it is that appears and to which we give the name of particle. It appears only as a result of the instruments put in place to measure it. "Certainly . . . it is nowadays impossible to claim with full confidence, concerning any physical measurement correctly performed by some well-trained team, that it discloses 'what, in itself, the investigated object really is, quite independently of the human aptitudes at apprehending.'"[57] These and other features of quantum mechanics suggest to d'Espagnat that our intellects run up against a wall, not just provisionally, but permanently. It is a most significant fact for him. Contrary to the many scientists who think we have a conceptual key, at least theoretically, that opens an access to knowledge of "'all that is' . . . in the situation we are actually at present things appear in an altogether different light since we know that in fact we are not in possession of the key—which, moreover, seems not to even exist."[58]

For him, it does not mean as, in his reading it does for Kant, a simple limit to our ability to know reality in itself, with no consequence for our world, a position in which reality is a "pure X." If we can't know what reality is, d'Espagnat insists, we can at least know what it is not. Because of the way quantum particles appear, we know that it is not local, not multitudinous, not contained in space-time etc. The only positive thing we might be able to say, as mentioned earlier, is that Reality is a Something, which is the only one of its kind. That is, the scientist's experience of the very way the stuff he or she investigates eludes definition and measurement as an individual object *may* lead him to conclude that there is an indivisible Whole, a Something prior to the measuring instruments that the physicist sets in place. But this, in the end, also amounts to a negative statement, a statement about what we can't know, for the only thing that can be said about that Something is that it eludes us. At one point, d'Espagnat refers to the neo-Platonic thinker Damascius to clarify what he means. "To the name 'the One,' Damascius preferred the expression *pantè aporeton* which,

56. Espagnat, On *Physics and Philosophy*, 118. For a similar sentiment, see also Espagnat, *On Physics and Philosophy* 240, 391.

57. Espagnat, *On Physics and Philosophy*, 450.

58. Espagnat, *On Physics and Philosophy*, 431.

roughly speaking, means something like 'the absolutely inexpressible.'"[59] This helps d'Espagnat explain that when he had previously spoken of the Something that is the only one of its kind, he did not mean "one" in the numerical sense. One here is not a number distinguished from other numbers, or unity as opposed to multiplicity. What he means, rather, is that 'the One' cannot be grasped through our concepts, which necessarily separate, distinguish and compare.[60] Whatever that Something may be, we cannot define it, break it down into components parts. It is beyond our categories altogether, ineffable.

Yet because it is a Something and not a pure X, that is, a pure mental blank, an experience of its ungraspability exists. To be clear, d'Espagnat is not saying that quantum physicists experience that Something, but they do experience an absolute limit to what they can explain, all the while dealing with appearances arising from that Something that eludes them. One particle here can immediately influence a particle at huge distances from itself, once the two have been in contact. They remain a unit despite their separation into two. To characterize this defiance of categories in the very process of encountering the phenomena, d'Espagnat uses a metaphor, that of Veiled Reality. A veil is a sign that something we cannot penetrate is there. If there were no veil, there would be no sign at all. For d'Espagnat, quantum physics makes it possible to see that there is a veil, but we can say nothing about what is behind the veil.

I realize that in describing even this much of what d'Espagnat means by Veiled Reality, I have departed from his own vocabulary, and, in some ways, dangerously so. He does not speak of the *experience* of limits, stressing over and over again that Veiled Reality is a *concept*, a *conjecture* based on the way quantum particles appear to the observer. It does not arise spontaneously and inevitably from the work of the physicist. It is a way of interpreting the very odd behavior of subatomic particles. This is, of course, an essential point. The philosophical conclusions do not exist at the same level as the laboratory results, or the theories that account for them. They do not have the same authority. He often stresses this. "Now, concerning the said postulate [of Veiled Reality] I couldn't think, of course, of proving it (this is why I called it a postulate!)"[61] He goes on to add, however, that this conjecture is far from arbitrary and that he can

59. Espagnat, *On Physics and Philosophy*, 395.

60. Espagnat, *On Physics and Philosophy*, 395.

61. Espagnat, *On Physics and Philosophy*, 240.

show, through argument, that it is difficult to discard. The word "experience" that I have used can suggest something like a mystical insight, and d'Espagnat resolutely wants to place himself on the side of reason. It is rational, plausible to conclude, given quantum mechanics, that there is a ground of things from which the particles proceed, but to which we have no access conceptually. He is most definitely not appealing to a personal revelation of some sorts. Yet, as we shall see shortly, a full appreciation of Veiled Reality is indeed a matter of experience, even if it cannot be that of the scientist as scientist.

For now, I just want to stress again that if, for d'Espagnat, Veiled Reality is a philosophical option made plausible by current physics, materialism is also a philosophical option, made plausible by an earlier physics, but increasingly implausible today. Both are conjectures, not apodictic statements of what reality is. One of his major points against the materialist position is that what its proponents simply take as demonstrated by science—on the level of established fact—is a leap. There is no way of avoiding leaping, and thus there is no way to avoid metaphysics. We all operate with one metaphysics or another, materialism being one among other options. We cannot avoid such options. "[O]ur intuitive notion of reality is the hidden string that moves our everyday thinking."[62] In other words, even if we do not bother to think about what is real at all, we operate on the basis that some things are real and some things are not. It is an inevitable part of our make-up as humans, and we do it intuitively. But that does not mean that reality coincides with a given intuition. At times, new developments dislodge a given one, and a shift is required. "The point is that, since our common way of thinking proves not to be universally valid, the 'feeling of reality' on which it rests cannot be regarded as being in any way unalterable."[63]

In d'Espagnat's arguments on behalf of the notion of Veiled Reality, he spends much time distinguishing between empirical reality and Independent Reality. He disputes those philosophers—the empiricists—who deny we can get to Reality in itself, if it exists at all, and who limit us to phenomena, to what appears to us.[64] He also disputes those—the realists—who insist that our investigations do get us to the Real as such. He forges a path neither like that of the empiricists nor like that of the realists, all the while taking elements from both. He agrees with the empiricists

62. Espagnat, *On Physics and Philosophy*, 128.

63. Espagnat, *On Physics and Philosophy*, 128.

64. Espagnat, *On Physics and Philosophy*, 127–8.

that science reflects only our experience, not Reality itself. "[I]ndeed physics cannot be interpreted to be a faithful description of 'the Real' and this reduces it to merely be concerned with phenomena . . . a description of 'empirical reality.'"[65] But he also agrees with the realists, if only in a very qualified way. There is a reality in itself, but unlike the realists he strongly denies that it is intelligible, transparent to our concepts. He calls his position "open realism," which he defines as follows, "*there is something the existence of which does not hinge on thought.*"[66] If physicists do touch the Real at all, it is only in a negative way, by excluding possibilities, and also, through the great mathematical laws, which provide those "not altogether misleading glimpses on the general structure of 'the Real.'"[67] These glimpses, as we will see, do not make Reality intelligible.

D'Espagnat's weaving in and out of the empiricist and realist positions is tough going, his approach filled with nuances and qualifications. His point throughout is that we need to reconsider what it is that our concepts can get to, given the quandaries of quantum mechanics. It is, ultimately, an argument about the limits of our intellect, crucial to his argument against materialism. Put another way, he uses all manner of definitions and distinctions to show that, ultimately, those definitions and distinctions fail when it comes to describing what the pursuit of the most precise of all sciences, quantum mechanics, shows us we cannot know.

In d'Espagnat's way of describing Veiled Reality, two major points stand out. The first we have already mentioned. Although Veiled Reality is a concept suggested by quantum physics, it constitutes a leap, that is, something not proven by the evidence at hand. Scientists deal with empirical reality, not metaphysics, and yet they operate within a metaphysics, which was also, in its time, a leap. It is time to evaluate which leap is closer to the current evidence. But the second major point has consequences we have not yet discussed. Although d'Espagnat insists that the "ground of things" or "the Real" can only be described by what it is not, that is, negatively, he cannot but fall into a kind of positive description, as

65. Espagnat, *On Physics and Philosophy,* 238. In his relegation of science to our experience of nature and not to nature as it really is, d'Espagnat is consciously following Niels Bohr, whom he quotes on the limitations of science several times. As quoted in Kumar, *Quantum,* 262, Bohr's position was the following: "'It is wrong to think that the task of physics is to find out how nature really is,' Bohr would argue later. Physics concerns what we can say about nature. Science has but two goals, 'to extend the range of our experience and to reduce it to order.'"

66. Espagnat, *On Physics and Philosophy,* 28.

67. Espagnat, *On Physics and Philosophy,* 238.

the very metaphor of the veil indicates. A veil is the absence of access, a metaphor for a barrier, but, depending on the veil, one can at least make out some indefinable shape. Most of the time, d'Espagnat insists on the utter thickness of the veil, a symbol for what we cannot know, but at times he does suggest that we perceive, at the very least that there are shapes, or more in line with his vocabulary, structures, even if we cannot get conceptually to what they are. When he speaks of Veiled Reality as more than "pure X," he speaks of its "being endowed with *general* structures," which, he quickly claims, "are far from being knowable."[68]

This combination of something we cannot know but that has structure sounds downright contradictory. How can we know the Real has structure and not know it at all at the same time? We must remember, however, that knowing, for d'Espagnat always means conceptual knowledge. But there is another kind of knowledge, which he calls "grasping."

> Contrary, as it seems, to many scientists and philosophers, I consider (and people with literary tendencies will perhaps agree on this point more readily than others) that between the notion of discursively and precisely knowing something and that of being radically ignorant of the same an intermediate one exists. It may—imperfectly—be described as consisting in an intrinsically vague 'grasping.' Indeed, it seems clear, at least to thoughtful people, that there are things that can only be 'grasped' and that some of the most important ones are of such a nature.[69]

The general structures d'Espagnat speaks of, then, are accessible in that intermediate way.

A word that d'Espagnat uses frequently in reference to "grasping" is "glimpse." We have already come across this mode of apprehending when he referred to the mathematical formalism of physics, which, he says again later, is likely to "yield glimpses on some structures of 'the Real,' and I did stress in this connection that glimpses are nothing like pictures or descriptions."[70] But he uses the word at least as frequently, if not more frequently, in reference to the arts and to mystical insights. Already in the first reference to "grasping," he had mentioned literature. Within literature, he gives a special place to poets. He agrees with the French philosopher Ferdinand Alquié, whom he quotes. "'Poetry is meant to be a seizure

68. Espagnat, *On Physics and Philosophy*, 424.

69. Espagnat, *On Physics and Philosophy*, 384.

70. Espagnat, *On Physics and Philosophy*, 393.

of Being: if this it is not, it is but the most idle of games.'"[71] Poetry does not yield conceptual knowledge, of course. "Whatever we perceive through this window shows no contours."[72] But, quoting the French thinker Jean Onimus, d'Espagnat maintains that it puts us in relationship with that Veiled Reality, which is "'not a relationship based on knowledge.'"[73] Later, in defense of the idea that we can get "glimpses" of what human beings cannot conceptualize, he claims that while this may seem questionable to many, it gives no shock to the poets.[74] He has decided to agree with the poets. Beyond poetry, d'Espagnat gives at least equal standing to other arts and to religion, in the realm of glimpses. He proposes that ". . . poetry, music, painting etc. sometimes provide us with genuine vistas in the direction of 'the Real,' alias sorts of glimpses concerning it."[75] In a footnote, he mentions Shakespeare's *The Tempest*, Beethoven's *Ninth Symphony*, and Michelangelo's Sistine Chapel as instances of glimpses into the Real, distinguishing them from concepts.[76]

Interesting in this regard is the way he both does and does not align the great mathematical laws of physics alongside the arts and, elsewhere, mystical insights. He had spoken of the glimpses that mathematical laws also give, but, at times he changes the wording, speaking of traces instead.[77] Perhaps I can venture my own conjecture as to the difference between glimpse and trace. Artists and mystics would have direct "glimpses," a kind of intuitive grasp of the Real that those who then come in contact with their expressions can also experience. D'Espagnat speaks of "some approach to mystery," an access that is not conceptual, as not being in the least problematic for people like mystics and divines. He includes among others who would understand a grasping that is not conceptual, at least up to recent times, poets and composers, of course, but also "their interpreters, and—perhaps even more genuinely—their admirers."[78] Mathematical laws do not offer that kind of access to a general public. They are more remote, and, and as he says frequently, distorted

71. Espagnat, *On Physics and Philosophy*, 433.
72. Espagnat, *On Physics and Philosophy*, 433.
73. Espagnat, *On Physics and Philosophy*, 433, footnote 6.
74. Espagnat, *On Physics and Philosophy*, 456.
75. Espagnat, *On Physics and Philosophy*, 396.
76. Espagnat, *On Physics and Philosophy*, 456, footnote 24.
77. Espagnat, *On Physics and Philosophy*, 384, 396, 455.
78. Espagnat, *On Physics and Philosophy*, 431.

reflections.[79] (He never uses the word "distorted" when he speaks about the glimpses of artists and mystics.)

Perhaps he is suggesting that mathematical laws, not in their content, but in the intuition that brings them about, become equivalent to other grasps of Veiled Reality, some immediate take on an aspect of it, ineffable, yet producing a distant reflection of that take when put into mathematical form. If so, physics and science in general become "only one reference (though presumably the main one) in the quest for understanding."[80] In other words, when it comes to "grasping" the Real, physics stands next to other human expressions, perhaps central, but not alone. As a result, d'Espagnat speaks of a necessary referral to "our common cultural patrimony," by which he means the great philosophical and religious traditions, which "are kind of sesames, almost indispensable for opening the road that leads from knowing to understanding."[81] Physics provides us with analytical knowledge, but understanding, the broader view about the Real, requires placing the implications of nonlocality, for example, in a much broader context, the context of the humanities.[82] At the end of the book, he proposes a dialogue between the great religious and philosophical traditions, on the one hand, and the new metaphysics that modern physics suggests, on the other. It is beyond his expertise, he says, although he nonetheless suggests in a sketchy manner how this might be done.[83]

In stressing that the concept of Veiled Reality is not a pure X, in that it can be approached through glimpses, d'Espagnat frees human subjectivity from being a mere epiphenomenon, the result of something else. Here, again, I have departed from his vocabulary. D'Espagnat never uses terms such as "subjectivity" or "interiority." Rather he uses words such as consciousness or mind, as if erasing the particularity of the poet or composer. "It is," he says, "reasonable to conjecture that, concerning Being, affective consciousness sometimes provides us with genuine elements of information, which are not obtainable from other sources since science essentially informs us on nothing but phenomena."[84] Yet what are the glimpses of the poets and mystics, if not the glimpses of

79. Espagnat, *On Physics and Philosophy*, 438, footnote 8, 455.

80. Espagnat, *On Physics and Philosophy*, 401.

81. Espagnat, *On Physics and Philosophy*, 457.

82. Espagnat, *On Physics and Philosophy*, 457.

83. Espagnat, *On Physics and Philosophy*, 457.

84. Espagnat, *On Physics and Philosophy*, 433.

people who have particular, direct experiences of those structures of Veiled Reality d'Espagnat had mentioned earlier? In a sense, they constitute the best evidence for his notion of Veiled Reality, even if he has come to this notion because of quantum physics, and considers this the best reason to agree with the poets. It is a strange circularity, to which I shall return in the conclusion.

In any case, despite d'Espagnat's use of words such as consciousness and mind rather than interiority, his emphasis on interiority is nonetheless very visible in the last, very personal pages of the book. He refers to Einstein's understanding of the religious vocation of scientists, motivated as they are by love and faith in their desire to know the Real, despite obstacles.[85] But since the Real is not knowable, as is suggested by quantum mechanics, is that religious dimension gone, asks d'Espagnat? He insists that it is not. If scientists cannot make Reality transparent through their concepts, their minds nonetheless "*tend*, with confidence and perseverance toward something that it [the mind] will never reach, and that, therefore, same as a horizon, partakes of transcendence."[86] The very longing and persistence scientists exhibit in their search may be hidden marks of the Veiled Reality in the human mind,[87] perhaps in the sense that it pulls us toward itself. He calls this the spiritual impetus that has always moved mankind, now including the scientist as a prime example of *homo religiosus*, but only one example among others.[88] Immediately, after this affirmation of our interiority as offering us a glimpse into Veiled Reality, the book concludes with Bell's theorem, the one that established nonlocality, complete with some mathematical formulas, followed by his explanation of its relation to the Broglie-Bohm model, even more replete with formula. It is as if interiority is validated by those formulas, while being engaged in an altogether different kind of knowing, which precedes and accompanies the intelligibility scientists are pursuing.

In going directly to d'Espagnat's affirmation of interiority, I have neglected some of the laborious paths he takes to free consciousness from a materialist interpretation. I cannot hope to do it justice, but the contrast he wants to establish is clear. In the materialist view, the brain, broken down into myriad parts, is either identical to mind or is the cause of mind. That is, thought and feeling can ultimately be explained by looking at physical

85. Espagnat, *On Physics and Philosophy*, 461.

86. Espagnat, *On Physics and Philosophy*, 463.

87. Espagnat, *On Physics and Philosophy*, 463.

88. Espagnat, *On Physics and Philosophy*, 463–64.

components and how they interact with each other. Once we know how all of this works, we can reproduce or manipulate thought and feeling, or at least duplicate a semblance of them. Like some others, d'Espagnat argues against this position along the lines of "the hard problem," a term associated with the philosopher David Chalmers.[89] An ability to duplicate certain functions—calculation, recognition of faces etc.— is not the same thing as consciousness because consciousness is an internal awareness, a qualitative feeling of existing, and not only information processing at very high volume.[90] He argues strongly, on several different fronts, that this internal awareness is not an epiphenomenon.

For instance, some of the most recent findings of neuroscience show the mind working, not as separate parts, but as one whole.

> For indeed mind is today considered by neurologists to be, at the neuronal level, an essentially collective phenomenon, involving brain states of considerable complexity, that are not separable, not even theoretically, into individual neuron (or groups of neurons) states. The similarity with quantum entanglement is obvious.[91]

He knows these neurological findings are not probative. "Their nature is that of mere plausibility arguments."[92] Yet the data thus far suggests that neurologists have come up against a whole not separable into parts, when it comes to thought, consciousness itself.

The analogy between neuroscience and quantum physics would go further. Quantum physics leads us to conclude that the conceptual apparatus with which we probe the world does not get at the Real. Particles etc. are merely convenient terms physicists use to describe their observations but physicists actually do not know what they are measuring and how it behaves before the moment of measurement or whether whatever they were measuring was ever a separate something to begin with.

> . . . [T]he notions that make up the conceptual basis of materialism, those of atoms, particles etc. can be . . . but elements of a

89. Espagnat, *On Physics and Philosophy*, 412–3.

90. Espagnat, *On Physics and Philosophy*, 412–3.

91. Espagnat, *On Physics and Philosophy*, 417. Raymond Tallis, himself a neuroscientist, makes a similar point. "The allocation of human faculties and sentiments to different parts of the brain is also being increasingly undermined by evidence that even the simplest tasks . . . require the brain to function as an integrated unit." Tallis, *Aping Mankind*, 81.

92. Espagnat, *On Physics and Philosophy*, 417.

> 'carving up' of reality that *we* operate, according to *our* mind structure. But then the thesis that the mind is a mere 'epiphenomenon'—that thoughts emanate from brains that are themselves composed of atoms—obviously becomes inconsistent. Within it, the objects that are supposed to explain thought turn out to only exist relatively to thought.[93]

Neurons and genes, similarly, are terms we have come up with to describe the world we can observe, the empirical world, not reality in itself.[94] They serve us well as ways of cutting up that world, and manipulating it, but that world also says "no" when it comes to the origin of awareness, consciousness itself. Our concepts, which cut wholes into parts, do not get to that whole. D'Espagnat is not saying that our minds are independent of material influences, but that those influences did not give rise to mind. Neither is he saying that the observable world is completely the product of our concepts. Both mind and what we call the material world, he speculates, arise from Veiled Reality, each influencing the other, but not being the cause of the other. In the Notion of Veiled Reality, "mind [is conceived] as emerging (but atemporally) from a *Something*, (thereby making empirical reality also emerge from the latter.) This *Something* . . . is thus conceptually prior to the mind-matter scission."[95]

In hinting at some of d'Espagnat's main arguments, I have excluded his elaborate reasoning for how he gets to each point. It probably would not help because what he says sounds so outlandish to ears long wary of the mind/matter split (which he denies making at least in any classic sense of the term "dualism"),[96] and to minds long wary of claiming that something might be impervious to the scientific method, that is, to being reduced to identifiable parts or processes whose operations can be known.[97] D'Espagnat is merely proposing that we contemplate a different

93. Espagnat, *On Physics and Philosophy,* 268.

94. Espagnat, *On Physics and Philosophy,* 280; D'Espagnat, *On Physics and Philosophy*, 415, 426.

95. Espagnat, *On Physics and Philosophy,* 378.

96. Espagnat, *On Physics and Philosophy,* 378.

97. Tallis, *Aping Mankind*, 182, mentions how difficult it is to speak of consciousness as irreducible to a materialist explanation, claiming that this is "because neuro-evolutionary ideas are now woven into the very language in which we are invited to think about ourselves." One might also mention the negative reception of the philosopher Thomas Nagel's book, *Mind and Cosmos,* 42. Nagel argued that "the physical sciences will not enable us to understand the irreducibly subjective centers of consciousness." Rovelli, *Hegoland,* 190, shows his contempt for Nagel's thesis. "On a careful reading, I find that it [Nagel's book] doesn't offer any convincing argument to sustain its thesis,

possibility, which would not contradict scientific findings, although it cannot be established by them. He feels, given both quantum physics and, to a lesser degree, neuroscience, that it is no longer implausible to draw those different conclusions. That is, one can affirm that poets and mystics occasionally have "glimpses" into the Real, and that scientists in love with their work exhibit an interiority marked by the Real, without shutting one's eyes to science, and, in fact, being more in harmony with some of its findings than those who maintained the equally speculative position that those glimpses and that interiority can be explained away. It is no longer absurd to suggest that poets and mystics give us glimpses of the Real, rather than mere illusions to be dispelled by scientists.[98]

Conclusion: Picking Up the Threads

Glimpses

In the course of our exposition of d'Espagnat's ideas about physics and philosophy, we have left several threads hanging. The first involves the subject of "glimpses," the non-discursive, non-conceptual knowledge of the Real that he also refers to as "grasping." It is in this context that d'Espagnat mentions artists and mystics. At their height, they inhabit that realm that is neither knowledge nor ignorance, which he claims is the realm of the most important matters.[99] But it is also on the topic of glimpses that d'Espagnat seems to be saying several things at once, potentially in contradiction with each other. These contradictions are not always resolvable, and are an interesting indication of the power of the assumption that only the natural sciences provide a path to the truth. Even people like d'Espagnat, who wants to question it, remain beholden to it.

I detect at least three different positions on glimpses in *On Physics and Philosophy*. At times d'Espagnat maintains that they are the exclusive province of great artists and mystics, *excluding* scientists, who always by necessity work conceptually and, in physics, quantitatively. "[A] scientist as scientist must aim at discursive knowledge only. This implies "an ever-increasing limitation to relative knowledge" [as opposed to a knowledge

---

but rather declares ignorance, incomprehension and, especially, explicitly lack of interest in the natural sciences."

98. Espagnat, *On Physics and Philosophy*, 431.

99. Espagnat, On Physics and Philosophy, 384.

of reality independent of our discursive categories].[100] The same point is made slightly differently elsewhere, ". . . concerning Being, affective consciousness sometimes provides us with genuine elements of information—which are not obtainable from other sources *since science essentially informs us on nothing but phenomena* [not Reality in itself or Being]."[101] Where do we find this knowledge about Being? He points to mysticism, poetry and music (without barring other arts).[102] He reiterates his point: ". . . I do not rule out the possibility that poetry, art and mysticism might yield rare and precious glimpses [about the Real], but that still is, for us human beings, basically nonconceptualizable."[103]

In all these statements, d'Espagnat argues that great art—literature, painting, music—as well as the writings of mystics, have long provided us with glimpses, from many different angles, of that something that cannot be divided into parts, and which d'Espagnat calls at several points the source of both consciousness and the phenomenal world. The concept of Veiled Reality would then align the sciences with what the highest arts and religious traditions have always known. "The conjecture in question [Veiled Reality] takes place (with appropriate changes) within the continuity of an 'intuition,' that of the existence of some reality outside us, that all men, all civilizations, always had."[104] He qualifies this by saying that it is not a one-way movement at all, since quantum physics requires not merely aligning with an older metaphysics but reinterpreting that metaphysics anew.[105] Still, he seems to be saying that the arts and humanities at their best have a mode of access to the Real, if only in glimpses, that the sciences do not have.

At other times, as we have seen, d'Espagnat includes the great mathematical laws as possible glimpses or traces of the Real. He insists that he is not, in contrast to Einstein and others, a mathematical realist. For one thing, the same mathematical formalism can be explained by several different theories. He mentions "the theory of the Dirac sea," "Feynman graph theory," and "quantum field theory," as three theoretical explanations, widely different from each other, but all grounded on the

100. Espagnat, *On Physics and Philosophy,* 401.
101. Espagnat, *On Physics and Philosophy*, 433. My italics.
102. Espagnat, *On Physics and Philosophy,* 433.
103. Espagnat, *On Physics and Philosophy,* 455.
104. Espagnat, *On Physics and Philosophy,* 399.
105. Espagnat, *On Physics and Philosophy,* 456–57.

same quantum rules.[106] In addition, in quantum physics, "mathematics does not incite us to build ontological or even just empirical objects. It essentially serves to express the general observational predictive rules and calculate the detailed predictions following from applying the rules under specified circumstances."[107] But if mathematical formalism does not lead us to the real in itself, but only to rules to be followed in limited circumstances, in what way does it provide glimpses of the real nonetheless? This is none too clear. I had suggested that, for d'Espagnat, the physicist "grasps" the universal law through an intuition of an undivided whole, seen from one aspect, that is then translated into mathematical language. One might also go back to his insistence that Nature says "no" to so many of our concepts. In the rare instances that it says "yes," we can see that the Real is structured, although not in such a way that the Veil is lifted. One cannot assume that even our more successful mathematical laws, dealing with space and time, can get at what is beyond space and time, and it is precisely physics that suggest this dimension beyond space and time. Whatever d'Espagnat might mean by the glimpses mathematical laws provide into the Real, it is clear that he places those glimpses and traces *alongside* the glimpses provided through the arts and religions. They all connect us to a reality that is veiled. The result of their probing is the same, glimpses, even if the language in which they are communicated is different. Read this way, d'Espagnat is claiming that no discipline or field of inquiry has pride of place, even if the poets and the mystics understand much better than scientists the central importance of glimpses. A non-conceptual "grasping" "gives no shock to the poets. My own conjecture is that, on this point, poets are in the right."[108]

There is a third way, however, that d'Espagnat speaks of glimpses, especially prominent in his short discussion of Nicholas de Cusa, although it reemerges elsewhere, when he talks about the Platonic forms, and about medieval nominalists.[109] We recall his claim that a metaphysical position such as de Cusa's, even if it now conforms to quantum physics, was illegitimate in his own time because it did not conform to the physics of the fifteenth century.[110] Only the kind of evidence provided by the latest science is authoritative. But why would evidence from the sciences

106. Espagnat, *On Physics and Philosophy*, 16.

107. Espagnat, *On Physics and Philosophy*, 360.

108. Espagnat, *On Physics and Philosophy*, 456.

109. Espagnat, *On Physics and Philosophy*, 242, 444.

110. Espagnat, *On Physics and Philosophy*, 242.

be so determinative if, as d'Espagnat insists so often, the sciences cannot get at the real in itself, but only to phenomena, what appears as a result of our perceptual and conceptual apparatus? His way out is to claim that the sciences have the power of negation. They can reject certain claims about the Real, even if they cannot tell us what the Real is in a positive way. But if the science of the time suggests a deterministic metaphysics, does that mean that the artists and mystics who give us a glimpse of a Reality beyond local cause and effect are inevitably wrong? Would de Cusa not be ahead of the science of his time, rather than merely wrong? D'Espagnat's position would, in this instance, mean that natural science is always dictating which metaphysics is admissible. This seems in stark contradiction with what d'Espagnat says elsewhere about the centrality of poets and mystics, when it comes to the Real. It would also contradict his statement about the *equal but not superior* access of mathematical glimpses, relative to that of the artists and mystics.

I would argue here that the contradiction in d'Espagnat's work regarding the authority of the sciences—not authoritative regarding the Real, and yet as a kind of gatekeeper nonetheless—is a mark of our times. We are not yet two hundred years from now, the time he estimates necessary to internalize the new metaphysics. "In fact, we live in an age in which, due to the findings in question, the picture of the world entertained by the general public has entered a process of extensive evolution—not to say 'revolution.' But such great moves take much time (one or two centuries in general.)"[111] I do not know what will happen in two hundred years, but, if I am right that d'Espagnat wavers about the authority of science, it is a sign that even the opponents of science's ability to give us a direct, and exclusive path to the Real, are still in the grip of that authority. It is a testimony to the "religious" nature of that authority, inhabiting even those who oppose it, functioning as the thought at the back of the mind.

In another sense, however, d'Espagnat might be right about the authority of science to validate a metaphysics, at least in our world. When that authority is so often taken for granted, it is impossible to pretend it is not there, to bypass it by fiat. Even those who want to limit that authority have to speak in its name. This is why, in my estimation, d'Espagnat's work is so important. He opens a door to a metaphysics, which he sees as aligned with the sciences, but which does not relegate to irrelevance

111. Espagnat, *On Physics and Philosophy*, 3.

or to mere entertainment or self-expression the insights of the arts and humanities, broadly speaking. On the contrary, he raises their status, at least at points in his book, to a privileged position regarding access to the Real, or at least to a position equal to the scientist. In making his claims, he is continually deemphasizing his authority as a scientist. After all, the notion of a Veiled Reality, he tells us, is a plausible conjecture about the meaning of experimental results, not the experimental results themselves. Yet in our world, the voice of a quantum physicist who argues against the viability of a materialist metaphysics on the basis of the latest science, has a weight that an artist or a scholar in the humanities arguing the same position does not have.

One might argue that artists and mystics do not need this authority. In fact, it might be dangerous to rely on it, since it only confirms the hegemony of the sciences over what constitutes the Real. There is much merit to this point. One can hardly imagine a mystic or a poet accepting his or her visionary experience or insight only if it is mediated by contemporary physics or biology. It is also possible, however, that, like the rest of us, many artists and mystics live within the taken-for-granted metaphysics of their time, which does shape their expression. If they live in modern times, they resonate with materialism, whether they want to or not, revealing multitudinous and deterministic reality from ever new angles. But even if some great artists and mystics reach beyond the metaphysics of their times, those of us who are neither artists or mystics, but who chafe at the explaining away of consciousness, and the attendant brushing aside of the human, cannot help but appreciate the support that a work like d'Espagnat's provides to ways of knowing that are not quantitative or analytical.

Another objection, evident from the start, is the lone voice that d'Espagnat represents among scientists, many of whom would dismiss his complicated reasonings about the limits of science. D'Espagnat himself is very aware of going against the grain of both his intellectual communities, that of the scientists and that of the philosophers. Beyond disagreeing about the place of philosophy and the limits of the scientific method, many quantum physicists in particular would also disagree about the implications he draws from quantum physics, a fact he is quite aware of as well.[112] Many other scientists would disagree about the central role he gives to quantum physics within the sciences, an argument

112. Espagnat, *On Physics and Philosophy*, 20.

he answers. Still, the careful way this particular quantum physicist separates physics from metaphysics, and the careful way he shows their implication in one another remain. We may not need d'Espagnat to affirm Veiled Reality, a notion that he himself admits has a long precedent. But we do need d'Espagnat to show us that in rejecting materialism, we are not necessarily opposing the sciences, but merely engaging in a common quest for the Real.

The Existential Significance of Veiled Reality

As we mentioned earlier, d'Espagnat attributes existential significance to his search for the philosophical implications of modern physics. "[M]y dearest hope is that this book should help some . . . readers to carry somewhat further still their inner reflections on the truly basic existential issues."[113] It is not easy, in a book that runs to nearly five hundred pages, to get a glimpse into what these existential issues are. Towards the very end, we do get a clue, but I wonder if d'Espagnat's reticence is a function of the form which he has chosen for himself, whose strengths and virtues I want to examine briefly before proposing what he might mean by existential issues he wishes his readers to consider.

In our introduction, I had mentioned the highly analytical nature of d'Espagnat's style. No distinction is left unmade. This is, of course, the result of his training in the natural sciences, and his commitment to precision. Despite a rigor that might discourage the faint-hearted, and even the courageous, this form has several distinct advantages, given his goals. Ultimately, he is arguing for the existence of mystery, which he defines as that which is "not accessible to discursive knowledge."[114] He is quite aware, not least because he is one of them, of the distrust of the word "mystery" among scientists.[115] They often see it as a fig leaf for mystification, making deliberately vague what with time and effort can be made intelligible. Invoking mystery is a sign of sloppy thinking. "True, in any field in which it proves possible, the quest for clarity—implying rejection of what is vague and mysterious—should be eagerly carried on. Indeed, we might almost claim that the right of invoking the notion 'mystery' should be saved for the persons who did long and earnest efforts of such a

113. Espagnat, *On Physics and Philosophy*, 9.

114. Espagnat, *On Physics and Philosophy*, 430.

115. Espagnat, *On Physics and Philosophy*, 430.

kind."[116] D'Espagnat's many conceptual distinctions, on this reading, earn him the right to claim that the Real is beyond them.

The other advantage of this style of thinking is that it affirms his commitment to reason at the same time as he is showing its limits. Commitment to reason manifests itself not only in following the rules of logic but also in acknowledging the valid points made by philosophical opponents, the proponents of materialism, say, or the empiricists and realists whose positions he qualifies. These acknowledgments make for the length of his book. He could have simply stated his thesis and responded to a few objections. He insists instead on situating his voice within a large chorus, distinguishing himself from others but also responding to valid criticism.[117] It is the only way to show the plausibility of his argument. Reason is what limits reason. It gives his voice a uniquely calm, dispassionate quality. By contrast, when someone today questions the validity of the materialist metaphysics, he or she will use irony, humor or a heated polemical tone, immediately revealing a personal stake that seems for the most part to be missing in d'Espagnat's exposition. Let us not get too excited, his style seems to be communicating. Reason will sort things out in the end. It makes his notion of Veiled Reality something to argue about, a proposition like any other, as if to dismiss one of the pillars of the modern natural sciences, materialism, while affirming science, is simply an ordinary part of the conversation.

But d'Espagnat's commitment to analytical distinctions and his even-handed arguments has an underside, his aversion to metaphor. Even if he is forced to make one central to his argument—Veiled Reality involves a veil—he is quick to correct any ambiguity this might suggest. "[T]he metaphor was in no way aimed at suggesting some vague similarity between 'the Real' and our everyday experience."[118] Yes, there are veils in daily life but the reality to which he is referring does not appear in space and time, and thus the metaphor is deceptive. Later, he also corrects a false impression which he claims he himself created inadvertently (and which I have perpetuated), that the veil lies between the subject and the empirical world. It lies, rather, between consciousness and what is at its source, also the source of the empirical world.[119] "[A]ccording to the Veiled Reality conception, the Real is prior to mind-matter splitting . . . Here indeed it is

116. Espagnat, *On Physics and Philosophy,* 430.

117. Espagnat, *On Physics and Philosophy,* 376.

118. Espagnat, *On Physics and Philosophy,* 239.

119. Espagnat, *On Physics and Philosophy,* 378.

not on a matter taken to be lying 'in front' of it that mind gathers the said glimpses. It is on what lies at its very source."[120]

Even when he speaks favorably of poets, he takes pains to agree with the philosopher Ferdinand Alquié that poetry is in no way metaphorical but, rather, yields genuine information about Being.[121] It is very difficult to understand how a poetry that eschews concepts could also eschew metaphor, but metaphor here seems to be what operates only on the aesthetic level, telling us nothing about the Real. A similar mistrust of anything but analytical language may account for the dearth of concrete examples as to what a poetic glimpse might be. When, in one instance, he does give examples, in a footnote (!), he merely cites authors and some of their works—Shakespeare, Beethoven and Michelangelo—but how *The Tempest*, or the *Ninth Symphony* or the Sistine Chapel might be pointing to a Veiled Reality, in some sort of concrete seizing upon a detail remains unexplained.[122]

I wonder whether this mistrust of metaphor, image, concrete example from daily life, all associated with vagueness, is not another sign of the influence of the natural sciences, even on people who want to limit that influence. Only logic, d'Espagnat tells us, is a universal language, structuring all particular natural languages.[123] The distrust of the thick associations of metaphor, indivisible into parts, makes him take back with one hand what he has given with the other. Do not metaphors have their own precision, the only way of apprehending a multi-dimensional reality? The lack of such images in the book might, in fact, contribute to the reader's difficulty in figuring out the existential issues to which d'Espagnat refers. Existential issues, if one means ideas that penetrate and affect daily life, touch the heart as well as reason, as he himself suggests.[124] They require an inner appropriation, something that functions not only at the conscious level but also reaches "the thought at the back of the mind," the secret center from which we perceive the world. D'Espagnat's argument is that we are not yet at a time when a position taken to be self-evident can be toppled to the extent that it affects the heart and reason at once. Without denying that, one can also conclude that when it comes to that inner appropriation, a physicist/philosopher

120. Espagnat, *On Physics and Philosophy*, 454.

121. Espagnat, *On Physics and Philosophy*, 433.

122. Espagnat, *On Physics and Philosophy*, 456, footnote 24.

123. Espagnat, *On Physics and Philosophy*, 260–61.

124. Espagnat, *On Physics and Philosophy*, 446.

using an exclusively analytical language falls short in any time period. Arguably, only those who work with images, metaphors, humor and irony, might penetrate into that realm where the heart meets the mind, a claim d'Espagnat is perhaps himself making when he speaks of the unique role of artists and mystics.

By existential issue, however, d'Espagnat, might not mean the penetration of a metaphysics such as Veiled Reality into daily life, its appropriation as more than idea. Rather, as the last pages of his book indicate, the existential issues would refer to the question of the meaningfulness or absurdity of human life, a philosophical debate that modern science itself helped to initiate. Because the natural sciences work within a materialist metaphysics, the monism integral to it reduces everything, including consciousness, to tiny components whose behavior is determined by quantifiable forces. In doing so, it seems to make illusory the love or responsibility or whatever other good upon which human beings base the meaningfulness of their lives. From the materialist point of view, these goods are comforting illusions at best, instruments for the survival of the species, but with no essential reality of their own. Materialism makes human beings strangers in the world, says d'Espagnat, or it makes the world absurd, which is the same thing.[125]

Twentieth-century physics makes it possible to challenge this meaninglessness. In his view, it "largely liberates us from such blocking conceptions as materialism."[126] Consequently, we no longer need to see our consciousness as reducible to myriad component parts to be understand through scientific experiments.[127] We no longer have to abandon the felt reality of our own consciousness in order to be in conformity with the latest science.[128] The latest science, even if it does not prove it, d'Espagnat had argued, makes plausible that our minds function as an indivisible something. It is not even implausible that this something reflects Veiled Reality.[129] This Veiled Reality is not passively in the mind, but must be recalled, tended toward. This, I surmise, is what d'Espagnat means by "the spiritual impetus, that has always moved mankind," "to *tend* with confidence and perseverance, towards something that it [the mind] will never reach, and that therefore, same as a horizon, partakes

125. Espagnat, *On Physics and Philosophy*, 464.
126. Espagnat, *On Physics and Philosophy*, 458.
127. Espagnat, *On Physics and Philosophy*, 463.
128. Espagnat, *On Physics and Philosophy*, 464.
129. Espagnat, *On Physics and Philosophy*, 463.

of transcendence."[130] Of course, physics does not establish that love or desire—that "tending toward" d'Espagnat speaks of—are marks or traces of the Real in us. But neither does it negate such possibilities any longer. We no longer have to live a bifurcated existence, taking our subjectivity and that of others seriously in our daily life and negating its reality on the intellectual plane. This might be what he means when he claims that his and other philosophers' refutation of "physical realism," the claim that physics gives us direct access to how things really are, is essential "for attaining a well-balanced relationship between human beings and the World."[131] At the very end of his book, he expands on this point. "Indeed, anyone aspiring to a well-balanced, that is, broad and consistent inner life would appreciate the possibility of linking the world view knowledge suggests [that of the natural sciences] to such or such great philosophical or religious tradition."[132]

In the end, in this essay on d'Espagnat's work, I do not pretend to judge whether the concept of Veiled Reality is a plausible interpretation of post-classical physics. This essay is not meant to argue on behalf of that notion. I can, however, judge the importance of the task that d'Espagnat sets for himself in his enormous tome: to place the findings of quantum physics, which defy the concepts that physicists have traditionally used to explain the natural world, within the larger sphere of the reflections of philosophers, artists and religious thinkers, claiming a common, and even interrelated search. He does not complete this gargantuan task. Nobody could. When it comes to the arts and religions, he remains in the antechamber of such investigations. But the very fact that he suggests this integration, and pursues some aspect of it, despite the enormous difficulties standing in the way in our time, make me hopeful for a rethinking of our intellectual life along less hegemonic lines. That is, according to my reading of d'Espagnat, the natural sciences, rather than dictating the terms of valid knowledge, stand in some ways ahead, in some ways behind, and is some ways side by side with other human gropings into the nature of reality. This goes a long way toward deflecting some of the omniscience/omnipotence in many narratives around the natural sciences. As an illustration of this very point, when it comes to thinking about the impact of either a materialist or Veiled

130. Espagnat, *On Physics and Philosophy*, 463.

131. Espagnat, *On Physics and Philosophy*, 239–40

132. Espagnat, *On Physics and Philosophy*, 457.

Reality metaphysics upon daily life, we had best, as I think d'Espagnat 's work suggests if only indirectly, leave this crucial work to the artists and mystics, and, possibly, their interpreters.

Brief Reflections on d'Espagnat and Péguy

We have in d'Espagnat's work an analytic defense of intuition, for what else are the glimpses the philosopher refers to but a mode of knowing that Péguy referred to by that name? Striking to me is that both authors have the same or at least a similar difficulty in delineating the place of intuition in the sciences. It is implicit in the great mathematical laws, D'Espagnat repeatedly tells us, without being able to say how, other than to specify it is not in the content of those laws. How that intuition relates to that of the mystics and the artists and their interpreters is not clear either, other than that the latter take for granted this way of knowing, whereas the former do not. But there is also the different language d'Espagnat uses when describing each kind of intuition, distorted reflections when it comes to mathematical laws, glimpses when it comes to the arts and religion. It is not the same or is it?

It may be that the difficulty of spelling out how intuition works in the sciences results from the barrier erected between them and the humanities through the dominance of the scientific method in the modern imagination. Reflecting on intuition is precisely to lift that barrier, in places where it can be lifted. It does not imply a departure from the scientific method in the natural sciences. Rather, it is to insist on something prior to scientific method, which needs to be there for anything truly creative to enter the world, and which may require an immersion in the human sciences to come to fruition.

For neither d'Espagnat nor Péguy is the time ripe for the overturning of the metaphysics associated with the modern sciences. D'Espagnat speculates, as we recall, that it might take another two hundred years before the implications of the current physics really lodge into the hearts of people. Péguy had been more hopeful, thinking that it might take just another generation to dispel that metaphysics. The hundred years that separate them seem to have increased the sense of the omnipresence of the narratives associated with the sciences, which for neither author is merely a matter of ideas but of penetration into one's most intimate reality. If that is the case, it is also true that the tradition of resisting the narratives continues, even if the resistance takes on very different forms. It is surprising, for instance, that the note of catastrophe is missing from d'Espagnat altogether. There is no ash covering the whole world as a result of what he calls the flag of materialism, associated with the sciences. One would think that d'Espagnat, living in the age of environmental disaster, and nuclear threat, would have been more vocal than Péguy regarding this aspect.

An explanation might lie in the fact that d'Espagnat's task was much more a "geographic" one than Péguy's. He preferred to stay at the level of ideas and arguments severed from an exploration of the daily world in which we live. Perhaps, in addition, as a practicing scientist himself, his emphasis naturally fell elsewhere than on catastrophe. Rather, his is an affirmation of the work of the scientist as a quest for transcendence inseparable from being human, a quest for transcendence that requires a metaphysics adequate to it, which he felt was currently missing. We need to keep his affirmation in mind. In opposing the narratives around the natural sciences that dismiss human interiority as a source of knowledge about the real, we cannot forget the full dimension of the human—that is, the thirst for transcendence—present in the quest of the scientist. How to honor that human quest and yet remain clear-eyed about some of the profoundly dangerous implications of the narratives that accompany it remains our challenge.

CHAPTER 4

"To See Things from All Six Sides"

Wisława Szymborska's Dialogue with the Natural Sciences

Preface

Wisława Szymborska is, from one perspective, an unlikely candidate for inclusion in this volume. In her poems, she accepts the narratives around the natural sciences, works within them, rather than attempts to free herself from them. Reading her, however, points to one of Péguy's chief emphases. The natural sciences have spawned not just a method but a metaphysics. That is, a particular sense of what is real and true has lodged in most of us as "the thought at the back of the mind," a secret center spawning many manifestations. Poets such as Szymborska, who explore daily life and the larger questions it raises against the background of this secret center, show us the endless and varied dimensions of the images drawn from the natural sciences. The fascinating consequence, as regards Szymborska, is that she ends up affirming the centrality of ethics and of interiority in a way that the metaphysics within which she works denies. Fully aware of this dichotomy, she often makes it the subject of her poetry. We can read her as an honest witness to the bewilderment we face about ourselves in our times. It is a bewilderment laced with humor, embodying the very subjectivity that has become so problematic.

Introduction

The Polish poet and Nobel laureate, Wisława Szymborska, is renowned for the great variety of her themes. She herself, in one of her rare interviews, stated:

> In the beginning, poetry could be anything. Crafted speech was used to express both feelings and the most basic information, ranging from prayers, through codes of savoir-vivre and historical chronicles, to the rules of the art of writing . . . Poetry then began shrinking more and more, and as the most extreme consequence of this process there only remains writing poems about writing poems . . . I do not accept this . . . It would be good to recapture some of those territories from which poetry withdrew or was pushed out.[1]

One of those territories, it turns out, is the natural sciences. That is, a good number of her poems engage with the images we receive of ourselves from biology, chemistry or physics, among others. Characteristic of Szymborska is that she does not strike a defensive pose against those images. On the contrary, she seems to take the materialist view they suggest for granted, or, to put it more precisely, she takes for granted the insignificance of the human being in a universe governed by physical laws utterly indifferent to our particular existence. We are a chance collection of matter, soon to disappear.

Our insignificance flits in and out of her poetry. In "A Speech at the Lost and Found," we are but a blip in evolutionary history, "one first-person sing., temporarily declined in human form."[2] In "Life while You Wait," our lives occur on a stage lit up by "the farthest galaxies."[3] Who is

1. Bojanowska, " Szymborska," 200.

2. Szymborska, *Map*, 176. All the poems cited in this essay are from this collection, in the Cavanagh and Barańczak translation. I have consulted other translations, notably Krynski and Maguire, *Sounds*. I have also consulted the Polish original of every poem I analyze. There are, of course, departures from the literal in Cavanagh and Barańczak's versions but I thought they stayed faithful to the larger meaning of the poems in question. For a less favorable view of their translations, see Pióro, "Rampa Pampa Pam," 213–6; For an overview of the Cavanagh/Barańczak translation process, see Barańczak, "The Americanization of Wisława," 229–42.

3. Szymborska, *Map*, 229.

watching us, one might ask, as we fumble about trying to get our lines right? In the other direction, at the microscopic level, entities we have no way of understanding, that defy our concepts of time and space, "still . . . decide our life and death."[4] Given this situation, can we even speak of a meaning to life, a reason for which we have come into being? In "Possibilities," it becomes a very fragile proposition. "I prefer," the speaker writes, "keeping in mind even the possibility that existence has its own reason for being."[5] Since this is the last sentence in a poem that lists the author's other preferences—she prefers dogs with tails; she prefers cats (presumably to dogs either with or without tails)—the possibility that life has a meaning appears as arbitrary as all the other items on the list, a personal whim.

Szymborska's acceptance of our insignificance, and the taken-for-granted images of a cosmos devoid of any kind of supernatural revelation, identify her as a poet who reflects "the scientific lessons of thinkers from Copernicus to Darwin," as American poet Billy Collins put it.[6] In this he echoes Szymborska's fellow Polish poet, Czesław Miłosz, who characterizes her poetry as "coming after—after Darwin, after Einstein—after so many others."[7] We all live in that world, more or less, and so it is not surprising that a poet would give expression to it, give us a language to perceive our human situation. Miłosz, however, rebels against the image of ourselves that the natural sciences yield. He worries about the political consequences of reducing us to such insignificance,[8] and he worries about the limits placed on imagination, whose nature is precisely to see beyond the physical to the final meaning of things.[9] He criticizes Szymborska for undermining poetry itself, not because she does not see beyond the physical, but because she does not draw on a metaphysics, like Christianity, for instance, or even humanism, that affirms the significance of the individual voice, of the centrality of the human being.[10]

4. Szymborska, *Map*, 397.

5. Szymborska, *Map*, 273.

6. Szymborska, *Monologue*, xiii.

7. Miłosz, "On Szymborska," 17.

8. Miłosz, *Witness*, 50–52.

9. Miłosz, 37. The book in which Miłosz explores these themes most fully is his *Land of Ulro*.

10. Miłosz's criticism mentioned here is not of Szymborska alone but of twentieth-century poets in general, who have grown up under the shadow of biology. See Miłosz, *Witness*, 41–57. The section especially on Szymborska, Miłosz, *Witness*, 44–49, centers most specifically on the first poem I discuss below, "Autotomy." Miłosz considers this

I have never been at ease with Miłosz's reading of Szymborska. He himself expresses some unease, noticing how light her touch is, and how heavy-handed it is to pin her down to something like a "scientific world view."[11] Nonetheless, she remains for him representative of an imagination under the reign of the natural sciences.[12] In response to Miłosz, I would like to suggest that Szymborska's poems, even as they offer us vistas of galaxies and subatomic realms, affirm what these images are denying. If we are specks, we are specks endowed with a sense of humor, and a sense of wonder, standing outside looking in, retaining our independence somehow.[13] The best way to get at this double dimension—insignificance and yet not— is to read the poems themselves. The interpreter is in the unenviable situation of prying apart what Szymborska so skillfully weaves together.[14] The best solution would be to compose another poem in response, as thick with associations as hers, but unfortunately this is not given to everyone.

I take comfort from the fact that, as the poet puts it herself, the best fate of a poem is to be "read attentively, discussed, remembered."[15]

---

poem "a good example of the influence exerted by the lessons of biology," Miłosz, *Witness*, 44.

11. Miłosz, "On Szymborska," 17.

12. Miłosz occasionally qualified his views on Szymborska's poetry, but retained his unease throughout. For a review of his attitude toward her, see Grądziel-Wójcik, "Lekcje Biologii," 99–112. His unease is well expressed in the second edition of his anthology of postwar Polish poetry, which he assembled in translation. In the first edition, he had only included one of Szymborska's poems, considering her "too dependent on intellectual fashions" and encouraging "preciosity." In the second edition, he includes a few more, praising her maturation as a poet. But his lack of personal enthusiasm is palpable. Miłosz, *Postwar Polish Poetry*, 109.

13. In one of his later evaluations of Szymborska's poetry, Miłosz acknowledges she does this. " . . . Szymborska offers us a world in which we can breathe. I think this happens primarily because the objectification is so far-fetched that the 'I,' with its own sadness, is completely excluded, so we have a game that gives us a sense of the enormous multiplicity of forms and, after all, magnificence of human existence." Miłosz, "Poetry as Consciousness," 17. In that very same paragraph he compares Szymborska to Philip Larkin and Samuel Beckett, claiming all three share a "hopeless vision."

14. A similar sentiment was expressed by another one of Szymborska's interpreters. "The analytic language of literary criticism often seems powerless and inadequate when dealing with these deceptively transparent poems; it is heavy-handed and clumsy in comparison with the lightness and agility of the poetic lines." The author of these lines then goes on to speak of "the necessity to go back to the poems themselves, to let the poet speak in her own voice and defend herself against the awkward approximations of the critic." See Carpenter, "Wisława Szymborska," 7.

15. Szymborska, *Map*, 431.

Better an unpoetic reading than no reading at all. Still, a discussion is just that, a dialogue with the poet, along with others. In this dialogue, the voices do not coincide. The poet continues to respond from within the poems themselves. If readers of this chapter wish to experience the difference in the voices fully and yet the back and forth between them, they should consult the relevant poems in their entirety, either before or after my own discussion.[16]

In what follows, I will trace four themes in Szymborska's work, each of which shows "the scientific worldview" and something juxtaposed to it, seemingly escaping its grip. These four themes appear together, my division into four more a convenient framework for interpretation than an absolute dividing line in the poetry itself. Still, the divisions are not altogether arbitrary. A given poem does give prominence to one or another of these emphases. The first set of poems focus on what I call the ethical demand, the term to be unpacked as I interpret the poems in question. Similarly, I will wait until I read the specific poems on interiority to reveal what is encompassed by this term. In a third set, a subset of the second, I draw attention to the double vision characteristic of our interiority, as Szymborska presents it, split between denying and affirming itself. The final set of poems tackles poetry itself. All the poems already discussed touch on the subject, to different degrees, but more remains to be said concerning poetry's place in our time, and perhaps in all times.

In the conclusion I want to return to Miłosz's criticism of Szymborska. He does not deny that she makes room for, and at times even celebrates, the particularity of the human voice.[17] Still, without a metaphysics, either Christian or otherwise, which would account for the reality of our "I," of our internal world as we experience it, poets like Szymborska, he suggests, are unable to resist the erasure of the human, even if they themselves do not practice it. Is Miłosz right or can we consider her playful creations to be a sufficient defense of something that eludes the gaze of the natural scientist? It is one of the chief questions Szymborska's poetry raises, despite its fabled lightness of touch.

16. The translation I cite in these pages is Szymborska, *Map*.

17. He recognizes, for instance, that even though she is influenced by the natural sciences, she does not head in the direction of reductionism, Grądziel-Wojcik, "'Lekcje Biologii,'" 105.

The Sciences and What Eludes Them

Part 1—The Ethical Demand

Autotomy[18]

In this first example, the poem begins with a description of the biological process that gives the poem its title. Autotomy occurs when a small sea animal, the holothurian, for instance (also known as a sea cucumber), splits itself in two. It sheds a part of its body to its predator while the remaining part escapes and can even regrow the part it shed. In Szymborska's hands, the holothurian's division into two becomes a metaphor for the human being's attempt to escape mortality.

> We too, can divide ourselves, it's true.
> But only into flesh and a broken whisper.
> Into flesh and poetry.

In a subsequent stanza, to expand on what human autotomy consists of, Szymborska quotes the Latin poet Horace who famously proclaimed "*Non omnis moriar*," not all of me will die (Ode XXX). Our bodies die but through poetry something of us survives our death.

Splitting into body and poetry need not be understood as restricted solely to poets, however. That split occurs in metaphor, which everyone uses every day. Here is the very physical split of the holothurian, and there is all the very unphysical meaning we see in that physical split—doom and salvation, two shores, "Life on one shore, death on the other. Here hope and there despair." The very nature of metaphor is to rise above the physical to find in it an unphysical meaning. If that is so, all of us split ourselves into flesh and poetry on a continual basis, as if positing a realm beyond the physical. It does not work.

> The throat on one side, laughter on the other,
> quiet, quickly dying out.
>
> Here the heavy heart, there *non omnis moriar*—
> Just three little words, like a flight's three feathers.

Feathers do not stay in the air very long, just as the laughter in our throats quickly dies out. The transcendence over the physical momentarily acquired through metaphor is a strategy that does not afford us access to

18. Szymborska, *Map*, 183.

immortality of any kind. "The abyss doesn't divide us/The abyss surrounds us." Is this a materialist view? It certainly accords with one. According to Miłosz, it is the direct result of the influence of the biological sciences. It certainly accords with the view attributed to Szymborska that "any claims about the essence of humanity or man's place in the universe must be rooted in the physical, tangible repository of information that only a materialist and biological conception of nature can provide."[19]

Yet the great poignancy of the poem is hardly captured by placing it within a materialist point of view. If we pay attention to the epitaph that immediately accompanies the poem, "In memoriam Halina Poświatowska," is it not better to understand "Autotomy" as a poem of mourning? Poświatowska was a beloved Polish poet who died at the age of thirty-two, after years of struggle with a debilitating heart ailment. On this reading, the poem is not so much a metaphysical statement about the utter lack of transcendence in a world regulated by physical laws as simply an expression of the void everyone feels when a beloved person dies, the inability to reach beyond that void.

I am not satisfied by this interpretation, however, although it may constitute a dimension of the poem. This is not primarily a poem about one's subjective experience but about the way things are. But, if we take it at the metaphysical level, which, in the end, I think we must, why then write in memory of a person, when the poem clearly refuses the immortality that poetry supposedly bestows? It is here that we can address the ethical dimension of this poem, understood as obligation to another person. We are obligated to keep those feathers in the air as long as we can. That is, we must keep in the air whatever traces of the person that once was, attempt to save them from oblivion, protect them from utter dissolution. Where does this ethical obligation come from? No doubt an evolutionary theorist could reduce it to some sort of biological mechanism. The significant thing is that Szymborska doesn't. The ethical obligation is simply there, giving rise to the poem. Poetry cannot vanquish death, and yet the poet is obligated to try.

In the poem "Possibilities," Szymborska says that she prefers the absurdity of writing poems to the absurdity of not writing them.[20] It might be absurd to try to save someone else from inevitable oblivion. But it is also absurd to resist a call so basic that it defines our very

19. Bojanowska, "Wisława Szymborska," 200.

20. Szymborska, *Map*, 272.

humanity. "*Et le malheur veut que qui veut faire l'ange fait la bête,*" Pascal famously said. "It is unfortunately the case that anyone trying to act the angel acts the beast."[21] To refuse to split ourselves in two, to refuse that gesture of obligation in order to be logically consistent is not to heighten ourselves but simply to reduce ourselves to animals, who do not attempt to save others. Yes, one might retort, but Horace was talking about his own immortality, and Szymborska, in writing the poem is also sending her own words into the future, like feathers into the air. The poem nonetheless is dedicated to the memory of someone else. It ties one's own future fate to that other person.

If the ethical obligation in "Autotomy" lies in the relation of the poem to the epitaph, in the two poems cited below, published about thirty years apart, it is fully present as a theme in the body itself. In each case, the human is juxtaposed to the animal.

In Praise of Feeling Bad About Yourself[22]

The buzzard never says it is to blame.
The panther wouldn't know what scruples mean.
When the piranha strikes, it feels no shame.
If snakes had hands, they'd claim their hands were clean.

A jackal doesn't understand remorse.
Lions and lice don't waver in their course.
Why should they, when they know they're right?

Though hearts of killer whales may weigh a ton,
In every other way they're light.

On this third planet of the sun
among the signs of bestiality
a clear conscience is number one.

The playfulness of this poem gives it the appearance of a fable, in which animals stand in for human traits. It sounds as if the animals should be apologizing for their behavior but somehow it does not occur to them,

21. Pascal, *Pensées,* 215.

22. Szymborska, *Map,* 227.

introducing a note of humor since predatory behavior is in the order of things, the very sign that an animal is just that, an animal. To expect otherwise is absurd. The last stanza provides the moral we expect from a fable. It is not as simple as it appears, however. What does it mean to say that a clear conscience is the number one sign of bestiality? Bestiality is an accusatory term. Animals can't be accused of bestiality since they are beasts to begin with. The verse is referring to human beings, of course. But, wait a minute, are we not animals, killing in order to survive, just like the others? Why use the term "bestiality," if our behavior does not differ from that of other predators? Bestiality seems to refer, then, not to killing itself, but to the lack of a notion of good and evil, to instincts unrestrained by a moral sensibility.

Where does this notion of good and evil come from? Szymborska positions us on the third planet of the sun, in a space empty of a god who might have revealed his commandments to us. Neither does she provide another explanation for the fact that ethics defines us. It just does. We are animals that refuse bestiality, at least in principle, since it seems that people with a clean conscience do exist, creating the need to praise those who know their conscience is not clean. Perhaps what defines us is not our moral standard but that we fall perpetually short. Animals just are. Insofar as we behave like the buzzard and the jackal, with a totally clean conscience, the fable animals are us. In this poem, an obligation to restrain our predatory instincts defines the human, but the line between human and animal nonetheless remains thin, given our failures to recognize this obligation.

The contrast between "the way things are," and an ethical demand imposed exclusively on human beings reoccurs in a later poem. The line between humans and animals is at once clear and blurred.

The poem begins with a description of the beauty of a landscape, filled with color, peaceful.

An Occurrence[23]

Sky, earth, morning,
The time is eight fifteen.
Peace and quiet
in the savannah's yellowed grass.

23. Szymborska, Map, 360–61

An ebony tree in the distance
with evergreen leaves
and spreading roots.[24]

That beauty will soon be filled with violence, the death of an antelope, caught and eaten by a lioness. Once again, as in the previous poem, a predator devours her prey. The human being is missing from the scene but reappears in the last stanza, as the observer of it all, as the one "who watches through binoculars."[25] The presence of the human immediately introduces the question of guilt and innocence.

On the question of guilt,
nothing, only silence.
. . .
The antelope, *gazella dorcas*, is innocent.
The lioness, *leo massaicus*, is innocent.
The ebony tree, *diospyros mespilformis*, is innocent
And the observer who watches through binoculars
is, in such instances,
innocent.[26]

We can't accuse the lioness for wanting to live, we can't accuse the tree for having roots that become obstacles to the life of the antelope. This is simply the way things are. And yet, the notions of guilt and innocence haunt the poem. Their silence is very loud. It is broken in the human realm, but in a problematic way. The last lines of the poem suggest that our innocence is limited to instances of seeking knowledge. Insofar as we classify and name, we are *homo sapiens innocens*. Presumably, in other situations, we lose our innocence, although those situations are not specified. All that the poem tells us is that we are not innocent in the way that the other actors in the drama are innocent.

Maybe even acquiescing to nature's ways is already a dubious enterprise. Of course, we have no choice in the matter. It would be absurd to interfere, and try to change the way nature is organized. But is not merely accepting "the way things are" a path to justifying the greatest crimes? The two poems that follow pursue that question. In these

24. Szymborska, Map, 360.
25. Szymborska, *Map*, 361.
26. Szymborska, *Map*, 361.

poems, we are in the human world and not in the world of the savannah. In the human world, is it possible to be *homo sapiens innocens,* simply reporting on the way things are?

Tortures[27]

The great refrain of "Tortures" is "Nothing has changed," repeated at the beginning of each of its five stanzas. Every time, it refers to the perennial practice of torture. Each stanza not only repeats that first line but adds a description of the tortured body.

> Nothing has changed.
> Except perhaps the manners, ceremonies, dances.
> The gesture of the hands shielding the head
> has nonetheless remained the same.
> The body writhes, jerks, and tugs,
> falls to the ground when shoved, pulls up its knees,
> bruises, swells, drools, and bleeds.[28]

The reasons given for inflicting torture might have changed, and we might be more aware of it as a global phenomenon, but the act of inflicting unbearable physical pain on another human being has not gone away. Is the speaker in this poem, in reporting on the universality of torture, its law-like nature, not an instance of *homo sapiens innocens*? We are wearing our binoculars when we notice "nothing has changed."

Yet the voice in the poem is not merely observing. The refrain "Nothing has changed" is a cry of frustration. The insistent description in just about every stanza of bodies writhing, jerking, the hands raised to protect the face, the teeth and fingernails waiting to be taken off, vividly evokes the violation that torture is. What is being violated in this description? Our bodies, to be sure. But why would violating bodies, an example of the law of the powerful taking advantage of the weak, be wrong? Where would our moral repulsion come from, if this is indeed a law to which we cannot but submit? We could posit the existence of something beyond our bodies—the soul—the putative source in us of the concepts of good and evil. But Szymborska makes short shrift of the soul.

27. Szymborska, *Map*, 260–61.

28. Szymborska, *Map*, 260.

The little soul roams among those landscapes,
disappears, returns, draws near, moves away,
evasive and a stranger to itself,
now sure, now uncertain of its own existence.[29]

The soul has nothing like the self-evidence of the body, "which is and is and is/and has nowhere to go."[30] Might not the lack of evidence for the soul lie in that it cannot turn "what is" into "what should be?" Twenty centuries of Christianity, the poet says in another stanza, have made no dent in our willingness to inflict torture.

It is crucial, it seems to me, that although the soul is a small, idle creature with no firm ground to stand on in the face of the immense vistas of nature and its laws, Szymborska does not deny its existence. Perhaps, in this poem, the ethical demand is its preeminent sign. It cannot undo the laws of nature but the soul appears whenever those laws are not accepted as the final word about human beings. The poem, seemingly so intent on describing "the way things are," embodies our refusal to give up on an ethical demand. The knowledge of the ubiquity of torture does not stifle our protest against it. On the contrary, it brings it out, in all its weakness, and in all its counter-natural reality.

Discovery[31]

In this poem, the question regarding the innocence of *homo sapiens*, the human who seeks knowledge, becomes more pointed yet, and the ethical obligation distinguishing us as humans seems even more problematic than in the previous ones. Every one of its ten stanzas proclaims the speaker's belief in the responsibility of the scientist. The researcher will burn his notes, destroy the work of his hands, when he realizes the harm his invention will cause, risking his all for the sake of human beings.

I believe in the great discovery.
I believe in the man who will make the discovery.
I believe in the fear of the man who will make the discovery.
. . .
I believe in the refusal to take part.

29. Szymborska, *Map*, 261.
30. Szymborska, *Map*, 261.
31. Szymborska, *Map*, 170–71.

I believe in the ruined career.
I believe in the wasted years of work.
I believe in the secret taken to the grave.[32]

If we did not sense the irony of the poem, it becomes crystal clear in the last stanza, turning on its head what the narrator is proclaiming.

These words soar for me beyond all rules
without seeking support from actual examples.
My faith is strong, blind, and without foundations.[33]

There is not a shred of evidence, the voice in the poem concludes, that any scientist has ever given up fame or livelihood to avoid the great harm which would result from the knowledge he has obtained. How very naive, or perhaps better put, how stubborn. To cling to the idea that the good of the human race will prevail over the self-interest of the scientist, or even over the thirst for knowledge, is to behave like a religious believer, for whose object of worship there is no corroborating evidence. On second thought, however, the irony of the poet might not be so unidirectional. In the process of appearing to mock our naive trust in the good, it also deconstructs the innocence of the scientist merely observing with his binoculars. The researcher who continues his research in the face of the catastrophe his very work is causing is not *homo sapiens innocens*.

What, then, are we supposed to do, given the ungrounded nature of ethics, the lack of evidence for it? Reason would require us to give up on a good that is never enacted. Just as likely, however, reason would require us to give up our naive ideas about the pursuit of knowledge as a good in itself. This is not a condemnation of the pursuit of knowledge but a questioning of the ethical pass given to the scientist. That is, knowledge is not its own end. The categories of good and evil still apply to its processes and consequences. "Discovery" preserves the tension between ethics and "the way things are." It does not dissolve it.

One last confrontation with *homo sapiens innocens* occurs in a poem whose setting is the aftermath of the horrors the Germans perpetrated in the Second World War. We seem far removed from the question of nature and counter-natural ethics, but, from a different angle, this is the central issue here as well.

32. Szymborska, *Map*, 170–71.

33. Szymborska, *Map*, 171.

Innocence[34]

This poem describes the generation of young German women born during or right after the war. Maybe they know about Nazi war crimes in general. But they do not know about the mattresses filled with human hair upon which they were conceived. They are unaware of the intimate penetration of the crimes into their own families. Their parents never transmitted it, as if to transmit it would be to introduce impurity into what is otherwise clean.

> Conceived on a mattress made of human hair.
> Gerda. Erika. Maybe Margarete.
> She doesn't know, no, not a thing about it.
> This kind of knowledge isn't suited
> to being passed on or absorbed.
> The Greek Furies were too righteous.
> Their birdy excess would rub us the wrong way.

As the irony marking the poem indicates, the carefree lives of the young women disturb the poet. What is there to be disturbed about, one might ask. What reproach can be made to young women for learning "'the three languages that all travelers need," for being good at business, for reveling in their own young bodies, in their long hair, in the beaches of Europe?[35] They were not the ones who committed the crimes. They were not even the ones who looked the other way, buying mattresses stuffed with human hair, as their parents did. Besides, their parents did not tell them anything. Berta and Ulrike are indeed irreproachable, innocent, exporting "the finest mattresses, synthetic fabric only."[36] Yet the poet acutely feels the injustice of it all. These young women have individual names, which she repeats insistently throughout the poem. They have young healthy bodies, they have a future. They have everything that their parents brutally crushed in millions of others, over and over and over. Is Szymborska insisting that children are, after all, responsible for what their parents did? What an unbecoming desire for revenge.

I think that Szymborska is indeed insisting that children are responsible, if not for the crime of their parents, then at least for

34. Szymborska, *Map*, 132.
35. Szymborska, *Map*, 132.
36. Szymborska, *Map*, 132.

acknowledging the burden it imposes on them. These young women behave as if they have no past. "She does not know, no, not a thing about it," as if these young women are answering an accuser. This denial makes them akin to animals, who also have no past. To have a past, in the case of Ulrika and Hildegard, and no doubt in all cases, is to become aware of the evil that lurks in the most ordinary activities, within the very mattresses upon which the girls were born, within all those good intentions to spare them difficult dilemmas. The poet, in yelling out in the last stanza that an unimaginable evil occurred, *tausend- und tausendmal,*[37] refuses to reduce human beings to the cycle of nature, to the perpetual round of births and deaths and births again, as if all ethical concerns disappear and we are left only with biology.

This poem, like the previous ones, confronts what seems to be a law of nature—the inexorable cycle of birth and death oblivious to good and evil—with an ethical demand. Life, of course, goes on, but past crimes should leave a trace in the conscience of the living. Yet is not the ethical, here as in all her poems, powerless? It will not make those young women more conscious of evil, it will not make scientists give up their careers to fend off the effects of a dangerous discovery, it will not stop torture, it will not save human beings from oblivion. The ethical demand nonetheless persists, illogically, insistently, in defiance of nature, aware of its own lack of ground, its own lack of justification. I will return to this groundlessness at a later point. For now, it is enough to notice how central this theme is in Szymborska's poetry, appearing in many different contexts. Her poems reflect a universe devoid of consolations, ruled by implacable laws. At the same time, they express her refusal to give up on a good not explicable in terms of those laws. Although different facets of the good appear in the poems, in each case, they involve the demand to protect another human being from suffering and death, and perhaps equally so, the responsibility for becoming aware of how short we fall of that responsibility, as a means of keeping it alive. In each case, also, good and evil are anti-natural categories. Nothing in "the way things are" supports a commitment to ethics.

37. Szymborska, *Map*, 132.

Part 2—Interiority

In the next series of poems, the ethical demand is not missing but I would like to stress a different strand, the exploration of interiority. I will allow the poems to define what I mean by this term, but it too is something that a purely biological or physical gaze on the human denies. Still, because the term interiority is not Szymborska's own, as opposed to good and evil, guilt and innocence, which are very much present in many of the ones I have discussed to date, more needs to be said from the start. Our discussion is complicated by the fact that the term "interiority," with its suggestion of an invisible realm not transparent to the eye of the observer with binoculars, seems hopelessly outdated. Scientists are working on locating thoughts and emotions in various parts of the brain. We are told we have a gene for everything, including belief in God, which implies that our feelings and beliefs are localizable in space, like objects. Other scholars, without objectifying our inner life to the same extent, nonetheless show how our most intimate thoughts are the result of complex social factors, from which we cannot escape. Once those social factors are known, we can be seen in our totality. In such a world, using a word that implies something inviolate and ours only is as if to be blind to the reality in which we live.

Szymborska is aware of the tendency to see right through us, even if she does not always address it directly. In a poem such as "Confessions of a Reading Machine," she imagines a robot who has taken the place of the "I am" of humans, "discontinued long ago." The robot can reconstruct everything humans have done or said but cannot understand the expression "I am." There is only another computer to ask for clues.[38] In the poems below, the poet mulls this threat to our "I," our immediate inner world, from many different angles. She is not so much bent on defending our "I" as an essential conduit to reality as in showing the oddity of wanting to eliminate it. It is, after all, so self-evident that it remains an inescapable part of our humanity. Only a computer would think of it as a secondary phenomenon that one can learn about from the outside, by asking another computer. Still, this is where we are, and so she writes both about the self-evidence of the "I," with its attendant "interiority," opacity, if one wishes, and about the threat of its disappearance.

38. Szymborska, *Map*, 419–20.

Experiment[39]

The poem describes a short film introduced before the main attraction in a movie theater. It features a scientific experiment in which a dog's head, cut off from its body, is attached to tubes, themselves attached to a machine. The head responds to signals from the outside, its sense of sight, smell, taste, and touch unaffected by the fact that it is no longer a living whole. It has been reduced to mechanical inputs and outputs, "salivating its salute to physiology."[40] The poet's response to this image appears most directly in the last stanza. More indirectly, her reaction is already present in the very structure of the poem, which leaves us in suspense as to whose head this is. Only in the fourth stanza is it identified as the head of a dog.

> A dog's faithful head,
> a dog's friendly head
> squinted its eyes when stroked,
> convinced that it was still part of a whole
> that crooks its back if patted
> and wags its tail.[41]

If the poet waited this long to let the reader know whose head is thus attached to tubes, is this not because the experiment could just as well have been on a human being? That is, it reveals something about us, and not just about dogs. According to the image in the short film, we are nerve endings that respond to stimuli, completely open to external manipulation. After all, the main attraction that the poet is about to see is meant to evoke her tears and her laughter, as if she too were a set of neurons, "salivating its salute to physiology." The experiment dissipates any sense of an interiority, an "I am," not transparent to an external eye. We can be manipulated because we are known, with no remainder. The poet's brief meditation on happiness in the last stanza reinforces the point that the tubes and machine pertain to humans.

> I thought about happiness and was frightened.
> For if that is all life is about,
> the head was happy.[42]

39. Szymborska, *Map*, 207–8.
40. Szymborska, *Map*, 207.
41. Szymborska, *Map*, 207.
42. Szymborska, *Map*, 208.

If this is all we are, we might as well be a dog's head, that is, dead.

In those last lines, the poet does not deny the possibility that the experiment reveals the truth about ourselves. It frightens her, which is not the same thing. Yet, even if the poem is not an argument against the findings of the experiment, it nonetheless posits a contrast between our *experience* of a living dog and the dog's head of the *experiment*. In the penultimate stanza, just cited, "A dog's head/a dog's friendly head," Szymborska invokes a living dog, faithful, friendly, responsive to the affection of a human being. Do this living dog and the dog's head really coincide? In the experiment, the mechanical reactions don't require relationships, just the stimulation of the right nerve endings. In our experience, by contrast, relationship is central, a relationship manifest in the very compassion that the poet feels for a dog no longer alive, deprived of the whole that made it itself. In our experience, faithfulness is not just the response to a pet on the head. It is a way of staying in relation over time. Are we making that interior life up or is it real? Even if the poet does not dismiss the findings of the experiment, neither does she cede the reality of experience. In the latter, even if all our physiological needs were to be fulfilled, we require an interior world, always in relationship to other interior worlds, in order to be happy.

In the following poem, interiority is in danger again, but from a different angle than in "Experiment." It is not dismissed out of hand, but as if absentmindedly ignored at the very moment that it is being investigated.

Archeology[43]

The poem operates on a comical reversal. Archeology is personified, speaks about her accomplishments, while human beings are de-personified, insofar as they have no voice. No individual scientist appears in these verses for archeology speaks monolithically. More to the point, the people that archeology studies have no voice. Archeology boasts of this as a success. It no longer needs human expression—art and writing—in order to understand human beings. She can reconstruct entire external and internal worlds based on detritus alone, of which she needs just a tiny trace.

> Show me whatever
> and I'll tell you who you were.

43. Szymborska, *Map*, 241–2.

Something's bottom,
something's top.
A scrap of engine. A picture tube's neck.
An inch of cable. Fingers turned to dust.
Or even less than that, or even less.[44]

Some of the material remains the poet mentions might strike us as strange. A scrap of engine, a cable? Aren't these contemporary with us? Why should archeology be looking at such evidence when we are still alive and can speak for ourselves? From the point of view of archeology, however, we are already matter to be analyzed, not expressions to be interpreted. In the last two stanzas of the poem, archeology is not interested in a human expression that speaks back.

Oh no, you've got me wrong.
Keep your funny piece of paper
with its scribbles.[45]

It sticks to what doesn't speak back—pieces of earth and physical traces of large-scale catastrophes.

The poem presents the claims of archeology ironically. While expounding on its achievements, archeology draws attention unwittingly to the lack of distinction it makes between reconstructing a forest or a highway, difficult enough to do, and the reconstruction of human emotions or values.

Show me your nothing
that you left behind
and I'll build from it a forest and a highway,
an airport, baseness, tenderness,
a missing home.[46]

It begs the question of whether tenderness can be found in an eye socket, in a piece of dirt, in a scrap of engine. Can you reconstruct doubts and intentions, without interpreting actual human expression, as archeology so confidently maintains in the following stanza? Can archeology really "peer down the throat of your silence" and turn it into sound, as it

44. Szymborska, *Map*, 241.
45. Szymborska, *Map*, 242.
46. Szymborska, *Map*, 242.

intimates? We sense, although it is never said overtly, that violence lurks in the vaunted modern methods of this old science. It forces something out of the matter it is examining, or rather from a human voice that has been turned into dead matter, even when it is still alive.

The irony of the poem lies precisely in that archeology's utter assurance hides the improbability of archeology's claims. It is precisely the depth hidden by a surface meaning that the poem is about. Can archeology, the science of digging beneath the surface, see an inner life, which requires another inner life to detect it? We cannot pretend to know with certainty anything involving our interior lives, past or present. Interpreting even one poem, as I have just done, is a risky business. I might have overemphasized, underemphasized, missed the boat. The poem remains, speaking back. No doubt archeologists will take exception to this depiction of their craft. Whether Szymborska has provided a full picture of archeology is not the point as much as her critique of techniques, supposedly advanced, that claim to reconstruct inner worlds without going to the trouble of interpreting the only evidence there really is for it—human language, either verbal or plastic.

If "Experiment," places our interiority on trial, and "Archeology" simply ignores it while reconstructing it, the following poem, "Onion," light and playful, celebrates our "innards," as she calls them, messy and vulnerable, and imperfect as they are.

The Onion[47]

As the poem presents it, one of the chief characteristics of the onion is that "its innards don't exist." What you see on the outside is what you see straight through to the core. The onion is all of a piece, with no contradictions, no internal infernos. To have innards, on the other hand, means to have a skin, an exterior, that hides an interior, and that interior is blocked to external access.

> Our skin is just a cover-up
> for the land where none dare go,
> an internal inferno,
> the anathema of anatomy.
> In an onion there is only onion

47. Szymborska, Map, 223–4.

from its top to its toe,
onionymous monomania
unanimous omninudity.[48]

Our interior also defies anatomy since an inferno, a blazing fire, does not really lend itself to being sub-divided into parts. In the verses that follow, the theme of something that cannot be cut up without destroying it can be read into the description of our innards as "all those veins, nerves and fat, "secretions' secret sections."[49] Once cut open, these innards give up their secret, the life within. The image of veins, nerves and fat also makes our inner life synonymous with vulnerability, with a relationship to an outside world—a potentially dangerous one—that the onion does not have. The latter is completely self-contained, and, in contrast to humans, it does not cry, "it follows its own daimonion without our human tears."[50]

If we look at the linguistic play of the poem as a whole, our innards are synonymous with imperfection, not unconnected to our unpredictability, unlike the onion. Each layer of the onion reproduces the layer below it, echoing the same initial voice throughout. The human being—because of all that infernal internal stuff, and all those fragile, oozing things—has the capacity to express something new, not in the same voice as all previous expressions. Onionhood, daemonion, onionesque, omninudity, onionymous[51] are all variations on the word "onion," of course, but they are not identical to each other in meaning. Even when the human being tries to capture sameness, as in this poem, what comes out is variety.

Part of the humor of the poem is in the very comparison of human beings to onions. To compare ourselves to the great apes, even to whales, that we know, but to onions? Why not, after all, since both onions and human beings are products of nature. Who are we to despise the onion as unworthy of comparison with us? From a less anthropocentric point of view, the regularity, the homogeneity, the self-containment of the onion is indeed a great achievement of the evolutionary process, "Nature's greatest success story."[52] Even from our own point of view, do we not look for regularity and universality as that which rules nature? Yet we are also

48. Szymborska, *Map*, 223.
49. Szymborska, *Map*, 224.
50. Szymborska, *Map*, 223.
51. Szymborska, *Map*, 223.
52. Szymborska, *Map*, 224.

beings who are not regular and homogeneous. We are the products of a nature that by creating us with innards also made us recalcitrant to being measured by the standards the onion embodies.

One might dispute my claim that all three of these poems, so different from each other, belong together. What does the dog who is shown to be just input and output have to do with the lack of innards of an onion and what does archeology's preoccupation with dead matter in order to reconstruct human worldviews have to do with either? Phrasing their content this way already reveals the link. Something is missing in the wired head of the dog, in the onion, in archeology's methods. Each poem hints at that missing something, inviting reflection on what it is. I have called that missing something interiority, "a first person sing.," as Szymborska calls it in "A Speech at the Lost and Found." That singularity expresses itself, although it always keeps its secret, no expression revealing it fully. Szymborska's poems juxtapose that secret to a world intent on making everything, including humans, share in the onion's omninudity. She does not always overtly choose between the two possible ways of looking at the human—on the one hand, the transparency, and the other hand, the opaqueness of the "I am." But the play with words and the irony so frequent in her poems are themselves barriers to direct entry into an inner realm.

In all these poems, Szymborska recognizes, as we already saw in the experiment about the dog, and in the brash assurance of archeology, that we live in a world that challenges our own internal sense of ourselves as anything but an illusion. We may be fooling ourselves that there is something like love or faithfulness distinct from our biological needs and urges. We may be fooling ourselves that our own expressions are the royal path to understanding us. That challenge becomes part of our very image of ourselves. We see ourselves from the inside and the outside simultaneously. The following poems examine more closely what I would like to call the double vision. From one angle, we are the center of everything, the measure of what is real. From another, we are but a temporary passageway for entities of which we are not even aware, which run the show.

Part 3—Double Vision

Motion[53]

You're crying here, but there they're dancing,
there they're dancing in your tear.
There they are happy, making merry,
they don't know a blessed thing.
Almost the glimmering of mirrors.
Almost candles flickering.
Nearly staircases and hallways.
Gestures, lace cuffs, so it seems.
Hydrogen, oxygen, those rascals.
Chlorine, sodium, a pair of rogues.
The fop nitrogen parading
up and down, around, about
beneath the vault, inside the dome.
Your crying's music to their ears.
Yes, *eine kleine Nachtmusik*.
Who are you, lovely masquerader?

In this poem, we coincide with entities that we do not experience directly. When a person cries, she or he sheds a tear, feels sorrow. That tear and that sorrow, however, are not wholes but many tiny particles at play. When we do see these chemicals, presumably under a microscope, we notice the beauty of their movements and their structure. That beauty is completely divorced from what we feel inside when we shed a tear. It is as if we were inhabited by masked dancers at an eighteenth-century ball, a ball to which we have not been invited. They are alien to us and yet they are us. "Your crying's music to their ears." This double vision we have of ourselves—the feeler of emotions experienced from the inside and the knower of the physical structure of these emotions, altogether indifferent to us—is expressed as a dissonance. You cry; they (the particles) are making merry. You are conscious; they are not. What we feel so intently is not felt by the very elements that express it.

The question remains as to whom the last line is referring to. "Who are you, lovely masquerader?" If the lovely masquerader is the "you" who

53. Szymborska, *Map*, 149.

cries, the poet questions our self-understanding. What we call our "I" is just a mask for forces that elude our experience of ourselves. Presumably, those elements would explain better what our crying amounts to than our own reasons for our sorrow. Or, much more plausibly, given the beauty of the patterns the poet evokes, the lovely masquerader addressed in the last line is nitrogen, and all the other elements, so puzzling, not in their mechanism, but in their relation to our self-consciousness. If that is so, the poem expresses our wonder that we have a self-consciousness made up of unconscious elements. That does not eliminate our self-consciousness. It merely intensifies our awareness of its strangeness.

A much later poem, picks up on the double vision we have of ourselves. The theme of wonder reoccurs, but marked by a concern to express the role of the poet vis-a-vis scientific discoveries.

Microcosmos[54]

In this poem, as in the preceding one, we are determined by something absolutely alien to us. The contrast, as in "Motion," is also between consciousness and the utter lack of it. "They," whatever we see at the microscopic level, do not have what Szymborska calls "decent innards."[55] In the very last stanza, also as in the previous poem, the poet expresses the sense of amazement that our world should be constructed this way, made up of entities, "them," "foreign to a fault."[56] Szymborska speaks of this amazement, as "perhaps worthy of a better poet/even more stunned by the world than I."[57] Yet, in this poem, this sense of wonder is not unalloyed.

In the first place, the poet articulates our dread before these new discoveries, a dread which started with the invention of the microscope centuries earlier but which has by no means disappeared. The poem begins with it. "When they first started looking through microscopes/a cold fear blew and it is still blowing."[58] The poet suggests where that sense of dread comes from. The microscope revealed an entire universe beneath the one we see with our naked eye. Even before the microscope, life was

54. Szymborska, *Map*, 397–8.
55. Szymborska, *Map*, 397.
56. Szymborska, *Map*, 397.
57. Szymborska, *Map*, 398.
58. Szymborska, *Map*, 397.

difficult enough to encompass. There was so much variety and so many different scales of beings. But at least we thought that what we saw corresponded to reality. The microscope shattered that correspondence. Our experience of everyday reality was suddenly dethroned.

One might well ask why the correspondence of our thoughts with reality was not restored, once we accepted the findings of the microscope. Now we see how things are again, if on a different scale. The problem is that at the subatomic level what we see defies our very intelligence, our ability to make sense of the world. Our concepts of time, space, and number do not fit "them" at all. Szymborska does not even call "them" particles, since particles would denote they can be counted and that they occupy a definite area. Whatever contemporary microscopes reveal, "they" multiply in such a way that we cannot see them as units. We can't say they occupy space. We can't say they have duration. "They don't know gender, childhood, age."[59] The very tools we have invented to pierce through to what is real put a limit on our ability to do so. Our cold fear of the microscope is the fear of no longer being able to trust that we have any handle on reality at all. What and who we are is dictated to us from the outside, by those unnamed "petite" entities, who gather in "mute parades," composing "blind iliads and upanishads,"[60] invisible to us, existing at a level of tininess that strain metaphor. Yet they write us through their epics, deciding our life and death.

Despite this characterization, "Microcosmos" can hardly be read as a poem about dread, or about dread alone. The poet delights in describing the behavior of these "particles," in finding a language that evokes their strangeness, their incomprehensibility. In the process, the poem makes their "mute parades, their blind iliads and upanishads," not purely a matter of the natural sciences. Since they radically challenge our sense of reality, they have metaphysical implications which address us all. It is her task as a poet, Szymborska says outright, to convey this challenge. "I've wanted to write about them for a long while/but it's a tricky subject/always put off for later."[61]

Conveying this is tricky perhaps because the poet's very restoration of our interiority, through the writing of a poem about physics, remains in tension with physics itself, which eliminates "I" from the scene. In the last line of her poem, Szymborska implies that the task is urgent. If she

59. Szymborska, *Map*, 397.

60. Szymborska, *Map*, 398.

61. Szymborska, *Map*, 398.

has always put off writing on this subject, she says, now "Time is short. I write."[62] Of course, this is a reference to her age. But why should she take up this particular theme in her old age? Perhaps it is urgent because the poet cannot leave the writing of iliads and upanishads to "them" alone. If the world eludes our understanding in a new way, in a poet's hands, this becomes another, fascinating aspect of our interiority.

If the two preceding poems present us with a microcosm, composing our consciousness and yet not itself conscious, the next two present us within the macrocosm, evolutionary, and geological time and the vast expanse of space. Once again, we have double vision, and a new meditation on the word "I."

A Speech at the Lost and Found[63]

I lost a few goddesses while moving from south to north,
and also some gods while moving from east to west.
I let several stars go out for good, they can't be traced.
An island or two sank on me, they're lost at sea.
I'm not even sure exactly where I left my claws,
who's got my fur coat, who's living in my shell.
My siblings died the day I left for dry land
and only one small bone recalls the anniversary in me.
I've shed my skin, squandered vertebrae and legs,
taken leave of my senses time and again.
I've long since closed my third eye to all that,
washed my fins of it, and shrugged my branches.

Gone, lost, scattered to the four winds. It still surprises me
how little now remains, one first person sing., temporarily
declined in human form, just now making such a fuss
about a blue umbrella left yesterday on a bus.

The "I" in the poem—the universe, perhaps—is making a speech at the cosmic Lost and Found, contrasting its losses with the losses of a human being. What are they, compared to what the cosmic "I" has lost? In the last

62. Szymborska, *Map*, 398.
63. Szymborska, *Map*, 176.

stanza, a human being is concerned about a lost umbrella, but in geological time, entire bodies of land disappeared; in evolutionary time, all kinds of creatures vanished, making room for others; even human historical time, so much shorter, has caused the loss of a divine being or two. There is not even a scale in which a comparison can be made between those losses and the loss of an umbrella. It is too insignificant to count. The issue is not only a blue umbrella, of course. The human being complaining about the blue umbrella is like a blue umbrella himself, insignificant, a momentary passage way for the cosmic process, destined to be replaced by something else. From the cosmic perspective, not only do our losses not register at the Lost and Found, but also neither do we.

The "I" in the poem is nonetheless odd. Since when does the cosmos or the life force, should there be one, have an "I"? Can the cosmos complain, feel loss, be surprised? These are features of the human being, whose first-person singular perspective endows her with an imagination that experiences loss, significance and insignificance. Only the human "I" can understand its position vis-a-vis all there is, and be surprised by it. Contrary to what we might conclude upon a first reading of the poem, we are not merely the person making a fuss about a blue umbrella left yesterday on the bus, but also the person who sees from the point of view of the cosmos, which does not have a point of view. The "I" sees double but it is the "I" who sees.

The double vision in the poem, like the double vision in the microcosm poems, undoubtedly reflects the findings of the natural sciences. From the perspective of the time and space with which scientists operate, we are insignificant. The poem can be read as proclaiming that insignificance. But the incongruity of an "I," "washing its fins of its third eye, and shrugging its branches," brings up the whole question of the uniqueness of the human "I." Can a being with fins ever express itself as an "I"? Can it invent the concept of a third eye, and then lose it? We are not done with human interiority. It reappears even when it reports on its utter insignificance.

Before A Journey[64]

Sticking to the human scale at the same time as we see beyond it is even more emphatically the theme of this poem. It begins with a meditation

64. Szymborska, *Map*, 400.

on a word, space. We have a grasp on it when we do not think about it, but when we try to unpack its meaning, we instantly run into conundrums. The images Szymborska brings up are our modern scientific ones. This is not a world with above and below, a sky and an earth, for example, or, going back further, a hierarchy of perfections, distinguishing the sub-lunar from what is above it. It is an enormity whose limits we do not know. We do not even know whether we can speak of limits at all. Space is not like a closed box, in which everything is contained, and yet we cannot speak of anything without locating it in space. The world that our language names transcends our intellectual grasp.

This reflection arises for the narrator on the eve of taking a flight. What exactly will she be traveling through, she seems to be asking. She abruptly drops this reflection.

> Well, all fine and good. But go to sleep now.
> It's night, tomorrow you've got more pressing matters
> made to measure for you:
> touching objects placed close at hand,
> casting glances at the intended distance,
> Listening to voices within earshot.

Even if space has no fixed points, no center, no direction, we must live in a world in which all these features are present. We must live at the scale that corresponds to our own bodies, on the basis of which we measure distance and closeness. That is how we establish points of departure and arrival. Only for us is there a point A and a point B, a local time, "departure at 12:40 and flight above the puffs of local clouds." This is quite arbitrary from the perspective of the wide expanse, but we have to live this way. Otherwise, we will miss our plane. As she says in another poem, "Sky," she needs fixed points such as the sky above and the earth below, so that "I can be reached promptly if I'm sought."[65]

Yet, even if we are beings limited to perceptions relative to our own body, we also recognize these limits and want to transcend them. We cannot live our daily lives in the space of the scientist but, even in the space made to our own measure, we already sense something beyond it, that "infinitely fleeing strip of sky," above the puff of local clouds. How strange, we might conclude after reading this poem, that our very local perceptions lead us to what is beyond them. In whatever way we choose

65. Szymborska, *Map*, 282.

to interpret this apparently so simple little poem, the poet dismisses neither the scientific view of a space, utterly independent of us, nor our own experience, in which space is always relative to us. Do these perspectives meet when we take a flight or do they remain separate even then? In any case, we have both.

In this section on the double vision, as in the other sections, the poems vary in mood and emphasis, and have very different starting points. In all of them, the poet reflects on the implication of the images taken from the natural sciences for our understanding of ourselves. In the time and space revealed by the scientist, we cannot take our selves to be central to the larger scheme of things, should there be such a scheme to begin with. That would be absurd. But it would also be absurd to ignore the inescapability of our own consciousness, even as it becomes aware, in a new way, of being an epiphenomenon. It would be, to return to the loss of a blue umbrella on the bus, as if we should deny our losses because they pale in comparison to the loss of claws and fins in our pre-human ancestors. That would be as absurd as taking the loss of that umbrella to be significant, from a cosmic point of view. Who is noticing those clashing absurdities to begin with? We cannot take ourselves out of the picture without making ourselves ridiculous.

Part 4—Poetry

In this section of our perusal of Szymborska's poems, we will stop at some poems that address the place of poetry itself. All the poems we have already presented touch on poetry to varying degrees, but here it will be the central emphasis. I will limit myself primarily to two additional ones, "Into the Ark," and "Plato, or Why." Together, they reflect the double vision from yet another angle, the first expressing the fear of extinction of what Szymborska calls the "solo voice," and the other affirming the indestructability of poetry, always hinting at the glimpses of the Silence up on high that only the poet can properly suggest. These two poems do not address the natural sciences, but the two moods they reflect are the two moods also found in the poems more directly in conversation with the scientific worldview.

Into the Ark[66]

In this poem, a catastrophe has already started, spelling the end of a great number of things. First among them are poems for a single voice.

> An endless rain is just beginning.
> Into the ark, for where else can you go,
> you poems for a single voice,
> private exultations,
> unnecessary talents,
> surplus curiosity, short-range sorrows and fears,
> eagerness to see things from all six sides.[67]

The single voice suggests a range of meanings. In a musical performance, for instance, it suggests a quality unlike anyone else's. A single voice, distinct, rising above the instruments, or heard distinctly among them, also brings to mind its contrast with the voices of a crowd, blending into each other. It might also mean something not grand. It is not a whole orchestra, just one instrument, and thus not intended to convey the whole, just one tonality.

In the description of that voice, Szymborska mentions some elements that don't seem to fit the serious themes we have discussed above. Poems for a single voice, she says, include "private exultations," "short-range sorrows and fears."[68] It is good to be reminded that her poems do not all immediately jump into metaphysical realms—she has a poem expressing gratitude that her sister does not write poetry, another about being Polish on a visit abroad, yet others on love and childhood, jealousy, among many other down-to-earth subjects—"the lambs, cauliflowers, diapers" of the last stanza of "Into the Ark."[69] Even the metaphysical poems, however (and the ones I have chosen are only a small sample), retain a personal element, expressed in the humor of the voice, in the playfulness of the language. They remain idiosyncratic, expressing a solo voice. In the two stanzas that follow the first, the list of endangered species that must enter the ark no longer refers to poetry directly, yet each quality has an affinity with the single voice. In the second stanza, it is nuance, and play for play's sake, and laughter to the point of tears. In the third stanza, there

66. Szymborska, *Map*, 270–71.

67. Szymborska, *Map*, 270.

68. Szymborska, *Map*, 270.

69. Szymborska, *Map*, 271.

are simply too many disparate traits to fit under one roof, and maybe that is the point, the celebration of not being able to fit things all into one category, to reflect on that, and to think that what does not fit our current sensibilities may yet be useful in ways we can't predict.

Poetry, in this poem, is not one among many other endangered things. It embodies what is endangered. If nuance and play for play's sake are qualities considered dangerous or useless in the world at large, there is no room for poetry, and if poetry is endangered, those qualities will not be tolerated in the world at large. They are symbiotic or in correspondence to each other. This poem underscores some themes more lightly treated in poems like "Experiment" and "Archeology," in which the note of catastrophe is missing but in which fear, bemusement or protest about the disappearance of the single voice is present.

The final stanza does not bring good tidings either for poetry or for the qualities associated with it.

> For the sake of the children
> that we still are,
> fairy tales have happy endings.
> That's the only finale that will do here, too.[70]

It would be too cruel to say that the ark will not find dry land, that these qualities will disappear permanently, the poet tells us. That is, we need a fairy tale ending telling us the threat to poetry is temporary, and the poem provides it, warning us all along about its fairy-tale nature. If we cannot help engaging in wishful thinking, let us face up to that fact. Poetry, as much about private exultation as it might be, is also in the business of confronting us with our illusions. The poet is not above them, as if she were unmasking the rest of the human race. "For the sake of the children that we still are," she says, including herself. She is as hopeful as the next person, but also entertains the possibility that we might be fooling ourselves.

I cannot help alluding at this point to a contemporary of Szymborska, the Polish writer, Stanisław Lem. In one of the fables in his famous collection *The Cyberiad*, a robot engineer, Trurl, invents on a whim (in order to show off in front of another robot engineer) a computer that can write poetry.[71] The story, under the title of "The First Sally (A), or Trurl's Electronic

70. Szymborska, *Map*, 271.

71. Lem, *Cyberiad*, 43–57. Is it a coincidence that Google originally named its A.I. system Bard? (It is now called Gemini.)

Bard," was first published in the late 1960s, at least sixty years before the existence of artificial intelligence programs like GPT-3, and now ChatGPT, and others. These artificial intelligence programs do indeed produce facsimiles of poems in response to prompts. In Lem's story, after a few false starts, Trurl's computer produces poems on command, the requests absurd in their specificity. "Let's have a love poem, lyrical, pastoral, and expressed in the language of pure mathematics. Tensor algebra mainly, with a little topology and higher calculus, if need be. But with feeling, you understand, and in the cybernetic spirit."[72] The machine executes the task perfectly, producing a rhymed eight-stanza poem.

The consequences of the invention of a robot bard are dire. The flesh and blood poets of the day become dejected, some of them to the point of suicide. The computer, they recognize, composes high quality poetry, and gets published so often that the human poets become obsolete. The computer bard causes other problems as well. It turns out to be very expensive to maintain, and, once it gets going, is impossible to stop, producing poetry endlessly, even without waiting for a prompt, and without need of an audience. Trurl cannot manage to silence his machine, and eventually hits upon the solution of sending it off to a small asteroid far away, after which, following further incidents, it becomes attached to a major galactic monarch who amplifies its sound, which now resounds throughout the universe. Trurl repents of ever having created the poetry robot, and vows "never again to make a cybernetic model of the Muse."[73]

Lem's story, summarized to the bare minimum here, is so playful and so multi-faceted that it fits exactly Szymborska's criteria for what will have to go into the ark. It is playful on a most disconcerting topic, however. In Lem's story there is no such thing as a poem for a single voice any more. We exist in a world in which the single voice can be artificially reproduced to the point that one cannot tell the difference between it and the voice of a flesh and blood poet. Is this the fear that Szymborska's poem is expressing, if not about artificial intelligence per se, then about the imminent erasure of all that emanates from an inimitable "I," or more precisely, the imminent erasure of the very idea of an inimitable "I"? If so, her only remedy is to keep writing poems, which may be the very ark in which the qualities she describes can be saved, for who knows how long.

72. Lem, *Cyberiad*, 51–52.

73. Lem, *Cyberiad*, 57.

But it may also be that the very proliferation of poetry perpetuates the fairy tale. Despite the fact that poetry is still alive and well among us, the computer bard is already here, as she indicates herself in one of her late poems, previously alluded to, "Confessions of a Reading Machine."[74] The machine in the poem, "I, Number Three Plus Four Divided by Seven," does not compose poetry. It merely produces reams of information about the human being, who has, in the meantime, disappeared.

> Everything that they recorded with their signs,
> even when crushed under layers of disasters,
> I extract, reconstruct
> in its original form.[75]

In another playful poem, "Nonreading," about the obstacles to reading Proust today, Szymborska wonders whether our contemporary predilection for speed makes it difficult to concentrate on any one thing long enough to remember it. It presages the "nonreading" of the title, since reading requires slowing down, internalizing meaning over time, and adapting to the idiosyncrasies of the writer. We do not seem to think we are any the worse for wear, our nonreading notwithstanding. On the contrary, as the last two verses verse proclaim, "But we're still going in fifth gear/and, knock on wood, never better."[76]

If in "Into the Ark," and in the two other poems briefly mentioned here, the prognosis about the future of poetry is not good, although one keeps writing poems anyway, in the following poem, Szymborska argues that poetry is not going anywhere, a companion and a foil to philosophy simultaneously, and perhaps, by extension, to any system.

Plato, or Why[77]

In the poem, Szymborska engages with what Plato himself called the perennial struggle between poets and philosophers. Plato, as is well known, built a metaphysical system, according to which the Ideal Form is the true reality. Roughly described, according to him, human beings, when they make things or act, can only imitate the Ideal from afar. Poets are in the worst situation of all, for they are at a third remove from the Real, imitating the imitators, since they take their models from the

74. Szymborska, *Map*, 419–20.
75. Szymborska, *Map*, 419.
76. Szymborska, *Map*, 405.
77. Szymborska, *Map*, 331.

world of things or events that others have made or done, but do not themselves know how to make or do them. They entrance us but derail us from the truth. In addition, Plato's opposition to poetry lies in that poets do not attempt to educate mankind. They do not present characters who control their passions through reason. Rather, they favor those whose passions dominate them. They even go so far as to exploit those passions, making them so dominant that they inflame them in others. Both on the political level and on the individual level such an unrestrained imitation of our emotions is dangerous, and thus Plato's reluctant ban of the poets from his city.[78]

Szymborska does not an attempt to argue against his philosophy by proposing another one. Rather she wants to show the incompleteness of philosophical systems, and the role of poetry in pointing this out. If we assume that the world is the way Plato describes it, why is it that way, she asks. Why would there be such imperfection alongside Perfect Being? To this, she claims, the philosophers, no matter how much they seek the Truth, do not provide an answer, or if they do, it is human made, made of earthly garments. Poets thus become the perennial reminders that the large questions remain unanswered, but not by attempting to answer them in turn. Rather, they simply present the world in all its messy reality, the thorns in the heels of wisdom, the entrails that mar beauty.[79] Poetry reaches for what is uncontainable in a whole. It eschews "everything," as she says in a poem by that name. "Everything—/a snug and bumptious word. /It should be written in quotes."[80] Paradoxically, the fragments, the litter that poetry embodies can give us a glimpse of what is on high—Silence.

> Not to mention, Plato, those appalling poets,
> litter scattered by the breeze from under statues
> Scraps from that great Silence up on high . . .[81]

It is possible to read "the Silence up on high" in at least two ways. On the one hand, it may refer to a Something that maintains its secrecy even when it communicates. This would be the Silence on the side of that interiority whose nature is so opaque. It is the subject of the poet, even when he or she does not know what this interiority amounts to, and even when the poem does not address it directly. It is that particular

78. Plato, *The Collected Dialogues*, 819–33.

79. Szymborska, Map, 331.

80. Szymborska, *Map*, 352.

81. Szymborska, *Map*, 331.

interiority, always expressing itself anew, that defies the closed "everything." On the other hand, the Silence up on high could also mean that there is no revelation, no final glimpsing of the Platonic Sun, or the God on Sinai, only the silence of those eternally empty spheres, the silence of the stone, of the plant, of the grain of sand, present in so many of Szymborska's poem, to which we shall return in our conclusion. The cosmos does not speak to us, and nothing beyond the cosmos, should something beyond it even exist, does either. Perhaps that last verse of "Plato, or Why" signals that the poet brings scraps, glimpses, of both kinds of Silence, the silence of the "I," that opacity that communicates, and the silence of no communication at all, the cosmos.

"Plato, or Why" expresses a very different view of poetry from the one in "Into the Ark," at least on the surface. In the first place, if my reading is correct, "Plato, or Why" is more hopeful. It says what Szymborska expressed in a different way in the last sentence of her Nobel lecture. "It looks as though poets will always have their work cut out for them."[82] After all, the litter beneath the statues is never going to disappear, and it is the poets who see it. In "Into the Ark," on the other hand, it looks as if poetry might not survive. Secondly, in "Plato," poetry shows its kinship with philosophy, its preoccupation with the large unanswerable questions, even if their approaches differ. Both are in pursuit of the real. By contrast, in "Into the Ark," poetry is a much more whimsical affair, the stress put on its personal dimension, on private sorrows and exultations. Of course, these private sorrows, if we read the two poems in tandem, manage to reach the Silence up on high in their own way. Nonetheless, the difference between these two poems should make clear that Szymborska does not enclose poetry within one view of its role, reinforcing the non-systematic nature of poetry through the very proliferation of the themes about it.

> Poetry—
> But what is poetry anyway?
> More than one rickety answer
> has tumbled since that question first was raised.
> But I just keep on not knowing, and I cling to that
> like to a redemptive handrail.[83]

As she also says in her Nobel lecture, "Poets if they are genuine, must also keep repeating, 'I don't know.' Each poem marks an effort to answer this statement, but as soon as the final period hits the page, the poet begins

82. Szymborska, *Poems*, xviii.

83. Szymborska, *Map*, 285.

to hesitate, starts to realize that this particular poem was pure makeshift, absolutely inadequate."[84] "I don't know" in her words means a willingness to start thinking on the basis of some new insight or reaction, never completely contained in a previous one. Does this mean that Szymborska does not have a unified view of poetry?[85] It is a capacious view but, as I hope all the poems above have shown, it is a quest for knowledge about our situation as humans, always. The solo voice remains the royal road into a view of ourselves, encompassing the findings of scientists, but operating on a level, which, by definition, cannot get rid of the "I."[86]

Conclusion

Miłosz and Szymborska, Again

I would like in these concluding remarks to understand more clearly what it is that Miłosz objected to in Szymborska's poetry. One could, of course, dismiss his reading of her as simply a misunderstanding, as one of her interpreters has done.[87] I myself, as all the preceding shows, was not comfortable with his judgment. Yet, I think that he was getting at something important, although I am not sure that I can do more than hint at it. Maybe this is already too much. In one of Szymborska's poems,[88] she describes an idea that comes to her, with which she proceeds to have a conversation. The idea tries to convince her to give it expression in a poem. Szymborska tells it that, although she has been thinking of this for a long time, she is not up to the task. The idea insists, until finally, when Szymborska has a cup of coffee instead of writing the poem, the idea finally retreats in defeat. What follows should be understood as my struggle with an idea, before I have given up and had a cup of coffee instead.

In all the previous discussions of her poems, I have stressed her affirmation of ethics and interiority. It is quite possible, however, to emphasize

84. Szymborska, *Poems*, xvii.

85. For an overview of Szymborska's comments on poetry, both within her poems and outside them, with some very apt examples of how her views translate into poetic forms, see Grądziel, "The World Trapped in a Poem," 83–96.

86. Cavanagh, "Poetry and Ideology," 183, characterizes Syzmborska's poetry as "an extended—if implicit—philosophical meditation on what it means to have an individual point of view, and what is lost or gained each time we take up this or that angle of vision."

87. Bojanowska, "Szymborska," 220, calls Miłosz "one of the least perceptive of Szymborska's readers."

88. Szymborska, *Map*, 391–2.

another facet of her poems: Szymborska lives in a world that does not speak. Better put, if it speaks at all, as it does in "Conversation with a Stone," it is to tell her that any kind of message from it is by nature impossible. The first line of many stanzas is "I knock at the stone's front door."[89] The poet wants to be let in, to go inside the stone, to understand it. In the course of the poem, as the speaker keeps on seeking entrance, and the stone keeps on refusing it, the stone tells her that the problem is that "You lack the sense of taking part. No other sense can make up for your missing sense of taking part."[90] The poet only has imagination, the stone tells her, which is not enough. Even though imagination makes us leave the narrow confines of our own experience, it does not merge us with something else. We retain our separate identity. There is no way of entering the stone and retaining our identity at the same time. "I don't have a door, says the stone,"[91] rebutting even the possibility of having an inside distinct from an outside. One would have, in order to understand the stone, to lose that distinction oneself, an impossibility.

A similar theme occurs in "The Silence of Plants." The poet would so like to communicate with her house plant, but it is always a monologue. All the plant ever lets her know is that she, the poet, is "a being so totally/a nobody to you" [to the plant].[92] The plant does not ask questions, does not listen. This does not deter the poet, who feels the one-sided conversation with the plant is urgent: "Talking with you is essential and impossible."[93] She continues to seek a knowledge of what it is like to be other than human. The human remains human precisely in that she seeks such a knowledge while other living beings do not. By not seeking it, they also do not reveal anything, do not speak, have no message, other than that there is no such message.

Impenetrability, at the cosmic scale, appears in the oft-quoted "View with a Grain of Sand." We name everything around us, but the things we name do not name themselves. We impose dimensions and colors on to the view outside the window, but the view "exists colorless, shapeless, soundless, odorless, and painless."[94] Language does not capture the world as it is. It merely reflects our experience. Nothing to be

89. Szymborska, *Map*, 103–5.
90. Szymborska, *Map*, 104.
91. Szymborska, *Map*, 105.
92. Szymbroska, *Map*, 330.
93. Szymborska, *Map*, 330.
94. Szymborska, *Map*, 243.

too upset about, one might say. Except that the news we think we hear about our own life, the flow of time that sends us messages as to what is urgent, is also of our own making.

> Time has passed like a courier with urgent news.
> But that's just our simile.
> The character is invented, his haste is make-believe,
> his news inhuman.[95]

If the news is inhuman, would this not mean that everything we think of as important, consequential—birth, death, all the events in between—is actually of no real concern to "the way things are." The world goes on, impenetrable and indifferent to us. This is certainly a common enough realization. Stones and plants and the cosmos as a whole are not concerned with us. But if there is nothing outside these material non-speaking entities, where do we find the meaning as to what we are and what we should be doing? Is it all a mere social convention or personal whim, or is there a real truth about ourselves which we need to decipher and to embody as best as possible? For Miłosz, Szymborka's poetry is too close to a descent into meaninglessness.[96] That meaninglessness, of course, encompasses the "I" itself. Is it like time, just our simile, to be broken into all those elements of a poem like "Motion," that dance while we cry? To see what an alternative might look like, I turn to a few religious thinkers.

Szymborska's poems about the impenetrability of the cosmos are reminiscent of Pascal's famous pensée, "the silence of these infinite spheres fills me with dread."[97] Nature gives us no sign as to why we are here, how we should live, what the purpose of it all is. Nonetheless, for Pascal we have not been left without an answer to these questions. God has revealed himself through Christ, and Christ has revealed himself to him, as is well known from what he recorded on a piece of paper and kept close to his heart until he died.

95. Szymborska, *Map*, 244.

96. Milłosz, *Witness*, 48.

97. Pascal, *Pensées*, 66. Szymborska may be referring to this pensée in her "Evaluation of an Unwritten Poem," when she mentions "The despair of a Pascal . . . How are we to live et cetera?/since 'we can't avoid the void,'" Szymborska, *Map*, 219.

Fire.
God of Abraham, God of Isaac, God of Jacob,
not of the philosophes and scholars.
Certainty, certainty, heartfelt, joy, peace.
God of Jesus Christ.
God of Jesus Christ.[98]

Nature might not speak, but beyond nature, a message comes. That message has to be appropriated and internalized individually in order to mean anything, but it is objectively there for the taking, the Scriptures and the liturgy giving access to that reality. As Pascal continues to record his experience, he emphasizes both the objective and subjective aspects of his revelation. "He [God]can only be found by the ways taught in the Gospels. Greatness of the human soul."[99]

When Miłosz says that Szymborska lives "after," "after Darwin, after Einstein etc.," he means that this absolute reference point for meaningfulness is gone, and with it, a notion of a self as recipient of a meaning not found in nature also disappears. In Miłosz's case, that meaning is most forcefully made available in Christianity, but we can point to thinkers from other religious traditions who have made a similar claim to a meaning communicated to human beings alone, making them unique in the cosmos. The eleventh-century Muslim philosopher and theologian Al-Ghazali, in his autobiographical account, *Deliverance from Error,* affirms a secret realm within the human being.

> Beyond the stage of the intellect there is another stage. In this, another eye is opened, by which man sees the hidden, and what will take place in the future, and other things, from which the intellect is as far removed as the power of discernment is from the perception of the intelligible.[100]

Coming into contact with this hidden realm beyond the intellect defines us as human, differentiating us from animals. "Man is formed by a body and a heart, and by the heart I mean the essence of a man's spirit which is the seat of the knowledge of God, not the flesh which man has in common with corpse and beast."[101] This hidden realm is made

98. Pascal, *Pensées*, 285.

99. Pascal, *Pensées*, 285.

100. Ghazzālī, *Al-Ghazali's Path*, 57.

101. Ghazzālī, *Al-Ghazali's Path*, 64.

accessible through a practice of meditation and prayer already present in the Islamic tradition.

Even if a neo-Confucian philosopher such as the twelfth-century Chou Hsi does not refer to a source of truth beyond nature common to the traditions deriving from the Bible, he posits that *li*, that which gives form to everything in nature, can only become accessible through a slow and repeated reading of classical Confucian texts. These texts make it possible to see into *li*, the essence of things. The key lies in individual internalization of a wisdom that is very different from acquiring knowledge about how the empirical world is structured. Reading in the correct manner retrains the self to "do for one's own sake," rather than "for the sake of others."[102] It frees one to become independent of external pressures, and aligns one with the real, hidden, structure of the cosmos.

These are two tiny fragments of quite different bodies of thought, but in both, there is revelation, not from nature understood as component particles, but from another source, usually, but not always, mediated by a tradition of literature and practice. This kind of metaphysics, in which the human is the only conduit of Truth, with a capital T, a truth which makes human life meaningful, cannot be found in Szymborska. It is what Miłosz means when he says that she comes after all the great scientific minds of the modern era. In a world in which the theory of evolution or physics is taken for granted, it is simply not on the horizon. There is, as in "Plato, or Why," only "Silence up on high."

From within the view derived from biology and physics, affirming something beyond nature, accessible to a particular human being, who, in this respect is also beyond nature, is to reflect an older worldview, doomed to disappear, like the third eye or the fins lost in the cosmic process in Szymborska's "Speech at the Lost and Found." The particular human voice is nothing other than the material constituted by composite entities. It lies completely within the natural realm and can be explained by the same methods we use to explain any other entity. This perspective makes understandable Miłosz's opposition. We need, not a consciousness split between its own insignificance and its centrality, as Szymborska's poetry reflects it, but a consciousness fully confident of its own significance as the sole recipient of a meaning revealed to human beings from a realm not accounted for by the methods of the natural sciences. We need

102. Chu Hsi, *Learning*, 13.

a metaphysics beyond the confines of what the natural sciences allow us to consider legitimate knowledge.

A counterargument to Miłosz might again be in order. When it comes to ethics, for instance, does it really matter which metaphysics is in place? In those metaphysical systems affirming the human as a privileged source of truth, have people necessarily treated each other better than they do now? A poem of Szymborska, "In the Park," indirectly addresses this issue. In it, a boy and his mother are walking in a park, past a dilapidated statue of a woman. The mother explains that it is a statue of Charity. To the boy's question as to why it is in such bad shape, she explains that it has always been this way. "Don't dawdle," she says to her son. No use spending too much time on this. Charity is always in bad shape but is never completely removed from view either. "The city should do something about it./Get rid of it, fix it."[103] But clearly, it is going to do neither. We can stretch the mother's "it has always been this way," to mean that whether we live in a world which affirms ethics as part of the very intention of the Creator, or one in which ethics is merely a useful survival mechanism, it will be in short supply in either case. The statue will remain in the park, neither fixed nor removed.

Szymborska and Levinas

Along those lines, and yet addressing the question from another angle, the French Jewish philosopher Emmanuel Levinas tells us that ethics is by nature groundless. That is, the responsibility for another human being does not arise on the basis of a prior worldview but as an unmediated response to the vulnerability of the human being facing me.

> The epiphany of the other person is *ipso facto* my responsibility toward him: seeing the other is already an obligation toward him. A direct optics—without the mediation of any idea—can only be accomplished as ethics.[104]

Levinas even claims that the discredit into which religious thinking has fallen in the modern world liberates us to focus on the ethical act as itself the source of transcendence rather than the other way around.[105] That is, belief in God is not the source of our responsibility. Rather it is

103. Szymborska, *Map*, 340.

104. Levinas, *Nine Talmudic Readings*, 67.

105. Levinas, *Proper Names*, 3–6.

the command to protect the other that suggests to us the idea of God in the first place. "It is in this ethical perspective that God must be thought, and not in the ontological perspective . . . of some supreme being or creator correlative to the world, as traditional metaphysics often holds."[106] God is our term for the source of a command whose beginning in time human beings can never retrieve, beyond us by definition, since we did not impose it on ourselves. That source of the command is always gone by the time we respond to it. But even if we did not give the source the name "God," the command would address us nonetheless. There can be Silence from on high because the transcendent message comes from the human face confronting me.

Responsibility to another is certainly not in conformity with nature either, in Levinas's understanding of it. "Ethics is, therefore, *against nature* because it forbids the murderousness of my natural will to put my existence first."[107] Nature would have us perpetuate ourselves, concern ourselves with our own survival. "The irruption of the human in being is the interruption of the being that perseveres in being—and of the violence that this notion of perseverance and *conatus essendi* (right to existence) connotes somewhat."[108] Responsibility, on the other hand, is turned not toward perpetuating the self but toward another. In our response to and for another person, says Levinas, the "I" arises. Only "I" can answer. In that answer, I become an integrated self. "Responsibility for the creature—a being for which the ego was not the author—which establishes the ego," Levinas writes.[109] From this perspective, the ungrounded, anti-natural ethics in Szymborska's poetry is simply the way the ethical manifests itself. "Ungrounded" here does not mean lack of evidence but the way the response to vulnerability is unmediated by a prior cultural perspective.

Like Szymborska, Levinas does not think that obeying the command is very frequent. Acts of responsibility, those that protect the vulnerability of the other in defiance of self-interest, are very few, and yet that command to protect the other orients us, making social life possible, even if we fail it most of the time. The dilapidated statue in the park, neither fixed nor removed, testified to the permanence of ethics and to our falling short simultaneously. A metaphysics embedded in a

106. Cohen, *Face to Face*, 20.

107. Cohen, *Face to Face*, 24.

108. Levinas, *Hors sujet*, 11.

109. Levinas, *Hors sujet*, 70.

given time or culture has nothing to do with it. If an act of responsibility happens, it happens at any time and place.

And yet, and in this Levinas differs considerably from Szymborska, for him that gesture of responsibility needs to be protected by a tradition which proclaims it. In his Talmudic readings especially, he claims that Jewish teaching is necessary to the world precisely because it brings to expression the nature of the responsibility all human beings always already have, before they have consciously chosen to be responsible.[110] Without a tradition that reflects on it, the little good that there is in the world stands to be even less visible. In other words, an articulated metaphysics—in his case, describing the transcendence inseparable from responsibility—is necessary to protect the very notion of responsibility, and, by extension, the irreplaceable "I," *even if* acts of responsibility arise quite independently of any tradition. This metaphysics does not establish the existence of God. It establishes the transcendent nature of the ethical itself.

In the end, I would like to think that Szymborska's poetry, even if it does not make a claim for the centrality of the human being as the conduit of truth, reminds us of a human frailty, made prominent in our times. This frailty no longer refers to our perennial vulnerability to death and disease, but to our awareness that our most intimate reality—our very self—may be utterly irrelevant in the larger scheme of things, and dispensable, to boot. In the process, Szymborska is also surprisingly feisty. Her poems are not an elegy for the human, even if the human is a transitory being in the evolutionary scheme, whose longings and sufferings are met with cosmic indifference. While on this third planet from the sun, the human wonders and laughs and doubts, and protests, and loves. We need to dance at the fireman's ball, as she says in one of her poems, even with the knowledge that we are parochial beings in an immense universe.[111] We need to celebrate our intimate reality, even if we cannot ground it in a larger scheme of things.

I do not think that Szymborska's double vision is the only resistance to our erasure. There may be better ones. But in a world in which the authority of the narratives around the sciences cannot be ignored, it may be one of the few available strategies to keep ourselves in view from the inside, and to point to the absurdity of doing otherwise. Her

110. He does not think it is the exclusive prerogative of what he calls, in some places, the Judeo-Christian tradition. That is, associating ethics with transcendence can be find in other religious and even philosophical systems. Cohen, *Face to Face*, 25.

111. Szymborska, *Map*, 348.

approach has as its advantage that it is so light, so devoid of confrontational arguments, allowing what we might dismiss on the intellectual level—the centrality of that pesky "first person sing."— to sneak in sideways, without our awareness. When it comes to the thought at the back of the mind, always partially hidden, and impervious to argument, it helps, if one wants to affect it, to operate at a similar depth. In this, we rejoin Péguy and his emphasis on the importance of style, understood as the peculiarities and accents of the particular person. It reminds us of a reality that we normally take for granted to the point of forgetting it. When we read great poetry, there it is again, in full force.

CHAPTER 5

Dark, Cool Sea

Inwardness, Metaphor, and Physics in Marilynne Robinson's *Gilead* (and Beyond)

Preface

In both Marilynne Robinson's novel, *Gilead*, and in her essays, we find multiple references to a whole not exhausted by its parts, characterizing both the cosmos and consciousness. John Ames, the protagonist in her novel, encounters this whole embedded in the events of his daily life, revealing itself now here, now there, when he pays attention. It is this inexhaustible whole that Robinson defends in her debates with the proponents of a scientific method who insist that, because they cannot seize it, it does not exist. We hear echoes here of one of Péguy's central themes. The issue, once again, is the affirmation of a reality independent of the findings of the natural sciences, which the narratives around the natural sciences either deny or relegate to insignificance. In both the writings of Robinson and those of Péguy, we nonetheless find bridges to the natural sciences.

Introduction

Marilynne Robinson, a contemporary American novelist and essayist of note, like our other authors, like anyone living today, is immersed in the world that the natural sciences have shaped, both in the images they suggest about our place in the cosmos, and in their practical consequences. If one reads a novel like *Gilead*, set in the mid-1950s in the Midwest, one would be hard put to corroborate this statement. Not a word about her polemics with the claims of neuroscientists and evolutionary psychologists, so frequent in her essays, appears there. Nor do we find any reference to modern physics, a source of wonder and praise in her nonfiction writings. My claim, however, is that *Gilead* forms a part of Robinson's larger conversation with the natural sciences. In intertwining these two facets of her oeuvre, I will make frequent use of two terms: mystery and materialism, which she often pits against one another.[1] Perhaps unexpectedly, she removes the material world from the materialism supposed to explain it, placing it on the side of mystery instead. Modern physics, in the very questions it raises about the nature of matter, in her reading, makes a valorization of mystery possible once again.

Illustrating what these terms mean, what is at stake in their opposition, and how physics fits in will be the goal of this chapter. A hint ahead of time might be helpful. In privileging "mystery," Robinson eschews the word "transcendence." For her, the latter connotes a world beyond nature, known only after death. She wants to stay squarely within the world we know, but one endowed with a hidden depth. "I think" she says, "the concept of transcendence is based on a misreading of creation. With all respect to heaven, the scene of miracle is here, among us."[2] That is why she prefers "mystery," since the word's original meaning is to a hidden or secret dimension. As to "materialism," in her essays she often uses other terms to mean the same thing—positivism, reductionism, parascience, and even modern thought, insofar as it is an amalgam of the other isms. Her main objection is to their common project as she sees it: the erasure of the human subject's own felt experience as a source of truth about the real.

1. Robinson, *Givenness*, 13–14.

2. Robinson, *Death of Adam*, 243. See also, Robinson, *Givenness*, 212. "What is often described as the sense of the transcendent might in some cases be the intuition of the actual."

> I propose that the core assumption that remains unchallenged and unquestioned through all the variations within the diverse traditions of 'modern' thought is that the experience and testimony of the individual mind is to be explained away, excluded from consideration when any rational account is made of the nature of human being and of being altogether.[3]

We can read Robinson's deployment of "mystery" against "materialism" as an attempt to restore the centrality of the human, the only entity capable of perceiving mystery. This is a tall order, given the view of the cosmos prevalent in our world, something of which Robinson is quite aware. "Our conception of the significance of humankind in and for the universe has shrunk to the point that the very idea we even imagined we might be significant on this scale now seems preposterous."[4] She quite calmly takes the risk of appearing ridiculous, but not without certain weapons in her arsenal. In her essays, she frequently, although not exclusively, buttresses her arguments with what she sees to be the implications of modern physics. In *Gilead*, however, neither she nor her protagonist argues. The evidence for mystery lies elsewhere, in metaphor, and what metaphor reveals about us without even trying.

Robinson frequently refers to herself as a Christian, and more specifically as a Calvinist.[5] Her polemics are also about the heart of her tradition. As we will see in *Gilead*, Christianity is not primarily the promise of an afterlife or a punitive moral code, and certainly not a literal account of the physical world.[6] It is a response to the hidden structures of the universe, a metaphysics.[7] These structures reveal themselves in the midst of daily life, for those who pay attention. This view pits her against those Christians whose religion centers on establishing the scientific accuracy of the Bible as well as those who de-emphasize the radical centrality of the human in the scheme of creation. It is, of course, completely possible, even essential, to enjoy her novel outside of any of these polemics. *Gilead* is not an argument about anything but

3. Robinson, *Absence*, 22. See also, *Absence*, 39, 53, 56.

4. Robinson, *Absence*, 75.

5. Robinson, *Givenness*, 116. Many of the essays in this book are expositions of Christian, specifically Calvinist, theology, as are many of the essays in her other collections.

6. Robinson, *Death of Adam*, 38–40.

7. Robinson, *Givenness*, 156, 168, 170–71. In Robinson, *Absence of Mind*, 126, she speaks of both Judaism and Christianity as anthropologies, ways of understanding the human.

a description of an inner life, and should be read as such. Still, if we read the novel in tandem with the essays, we see the stakes involved in portraying the inner life in the way Robinson does.

Gilead—Mystery Hidden and Revealed

Excess

The main protagonist of *Gilead* is John Ames, an elderly Calvinist minister, a Congregationalist, who has lived his whole life in the small town in Iowa after which the novel is named. We meet him through the journal entries he intends for the son of his old age, still a child, and which Ames, diagnosed with a fatal heart condition, is not destined to see grow into manhood. The journal he writes is a kind of spiritual testament. Through musing on this or that event of daily life, he wants to acquaint the grown man his son will be one day with his father's way of seeing and thinking.

One of these daily events occurs on a morning after the rain. A young couple is walking ahead of Ames. The young man spontaneously grabs a branch, and the water still on the leaves comes pouring down on both himself and the young woman. Both run away, laughing. The old man describes this brief moment, "like something from a myth,"[8] capturing in paradigmatic form the erotic energy of the young. Everyone has seen a variant of such a scene. From the perch of his old age, however, the vigor and the joy suddenly appear as a blessing, the water pouring from the branches a baptism, implying a hidden source behind the quickening of life the young couple feels. "It is easy to believe at such moments that water was made primarily for blessing, and only secondarily for growing vegetables or doing the wash. I wish I had paid more attention to it."[9]

The old man meditates on the difficulty of expressing what he saw.

> I almost wish I could have written that the sun just *shone* and the tree just *glistened*, and the water just *poured* out of it, and the girl just *laughed* . . . People talk that way when they want to call attention to a thing existing in excess of itself, so to speak, a sort of purity and lavishness, at any rate something ordinary in kind but exceptional in degree.[10]

8. Robinson, *Gilead*, 28.
9. Robinson, *Gilead*, 28.
10. Robinson, *Gilead*, 28.

Paying attention is key for the excess to reveal itself as such, but language falls short whenever it runs into excess, participating in the veiling even as it reveals. What is that excess? It seems to be life itself, suddenly seen for what it really is, an inexplicable abundance.

A second example of excess occurs during Ames's perilous journey to Kansas in the company of his father. A severe draught had turned large swaths of the terrain into wilderness, destroying most of the vegetation and driving away all but a few inhabitants. Father and son risked death several times in the month they spent there, looking for the grave of the patriarch of the family, Ames' grandfather. The latter had left in anger, unreconciled with his son, who is driven to pay his last respects. They finally find the grave in an abandoned cemetery. As Ames's father prays over the now properly-tended grave, the young John Ames (he is twelve at the time) notices "a full moon rising just as the sun was going down. Each of them was standing on its edge, with the most wonderful light between them."[11] He reports, over sixty years later, what a joy and assurance filled him at that moment. "[Y]ou learn what an amazing instrument you are, so to speak, what a power you have to experience beyond anything you might actually need."[12]

The two lights at the edge of the late afternoon sky become a metaphor for the excess that we human beings are, by our very nature. One light in the sky would suffice but there are two, filling the entire sky. We are not just our physical needs but "more," an amazing instrument of all sorts of passions and emotions, in excess of practical concerns. The expression of joy is such an excess, but so is Ames's father commitment to seek peace with his father, at great risk, and even when it is not practically possible. The excess that we are wears such an ordinary face that it remains hidden, although it is right under our noses. In privileged circumstances, symbolized by the image of the sun and the moon so brilliant in the sky at the same time, we notice it.

The "more" within the ordinary often appears in Ames's interactions with his parishioners. In his role as minister, he listens to them speak about their troubles. Sometimes he sees in these conversations the very game of life. "By 'life' I means something like energy (as the scientists use the word) or 'vitality,' and also something very different."[13] The difference between the physicists' object of study and what he

11. Robinson, *Gilead*, 14.

12. Robinson, *Gilead*, 49.

13. Robinson, *Gilead*, 44.

encounters lies in the presence of an "I," which he describes "as a kind of incandescence . . . like a flame on a wick, emanating itself in grief and guilt and joy and whatever else. But quick and avid and resourceful."[14] This presence is undetectable except in the face-to-face of personal exchange. The energy of an "I" differs from energy in the scientific sense, precisely in the mode through which it reveals itself.

In what we have read so far, human beings hold a privileged place in the cosmos in that they display, in a paradigmatic way, the "more" in the ordinary that we also find reflected in the rest of nature. They are at once witnesses to the excess and the incarnation of it themselves. We see this double dimension when Ames speaks once again about baptism, a ritual he has performed countless times in his ministry. "The sensation is of really knowing a creature, I mean really feeling its mysterious life and your own mysterious life at the same time."[15] We encounter mystery at both ends, so to speak, in the other and in ourselves. This hidden depth, Ames also refers to as the sacred. "It [baptism] doesn't enhance sacredness but it acknowledges it, and there is a power in that."[16] The power lies in drawing attention to this hidden dimension.

If every human being as such is an instance of the excess in the ordinary, the human face is an excess within excess. Several times, Ames goes back to a very painful moment of his youth, the loss of his first wife in childbirth, and the subsequent loss of his infant daughter. Within that enormous and unrelenting suffering, he refers to one aspect of it as a blessing, being able to hold his daughter once before she died.[17] He recalls that she opened her eyes and looked straight at him. Ames characterizes beholding his tiny daughter as a vision. Her face gave access to something as hidden as what the mystics see, and yet there it is, in plain sight. We confront it daily in every human face.

> I realize that there is nothing more astonishing than a human face . . . It has something to do with incarnation. You feel your obligation to a child when you have seen it and held it. Any human face is a claim on you, because you can't help but understand the singularity of it, the courage and loneliness of it. But

14. Robinson, *Gilead*, 44–45.
15. Robinson, *Gilead*, 23.
16. Robinson, *Gilead*, 23.
17. Robinson, *Gilead*, 17.

> this is truest of the face of an infant. I consider that to be one kind of vision as mystical as any.[18]

The reference to the Incarnation (in lower-case) points to the theology from which this sacred dimension in the ordinary comes, and yet Ames's discretion about it indicates that it is not necessary to have this theology to see it. The theology gives a language for what we all see, when we pay attention.

In all of these examples, the hiddenness revealed in the ordinary is inseparable from blessing. Ames refers to the ordeal in Kansas as a great blessing to him,[19] and alludes to blessing again when he speaks of the moon and the sun in the sky at the same time.[20] The raindrops falling on the young people on a sunny day make him reflect on blessing,[21] as is his holding of his daughter for the first and last time.[22] Blessing is never defined in any of these passages. Whatever he means by it is embedded in the examples he gives. We know the word to have a positive connotation, but each case reveals it in a new way—the abundance of life itself or the love between people, even when it comes to a sorry impasse. We don't know what the content of the blessing will be, but in every case, the gift of being blessed or blessing also lies in the very ability to perceive beyond the surface what animates it beneath or within, as though the very revelatory quality of daily life were an end in itself, a source of regeneration, like water. Blessing is life-giving, even if its source remains hidden, a mystery.

Mystery and Its Critics—Arguments and Counterarguments

Mystification

It is easy for a contemporary reader to dismiss John Ames's outlook as a mystification. Why see mystery or excess in matters that can be explained without any reference to them? The scene of the young couple in the morning after the rain, for instance, simply captures the wistfulness the old feel toward a life energy they no longer have. Such a critic

18. Robinson, *Gilead*, 66.
19. Robinson, *Gilead*, 17.
20. Robinson, *Gilead*, 48.
21. Robinson, *Gilead*, 28.
22. Robinson, *Gilead*, 17.

would say that seeing blessing in it, and a blessing which refers to baptism, and thus to a hidden source as the giver of life, is unnecessary, but even more so, beautifies what is basically a kind of envy. Furthermore, seeing us as exceptional in nature, motivated by more than physical or even practical concerns, as in the case of the father's commitment to tend to his own father's grave, or in the many passages about the mystery of the human face or the human person is again to beautify what is at heart driven by less noble drives. It is to ignore evolutionary theory, psychological research and primate studies, all of which, in one way or another, dismiss our singularity and find in what we feel to be our least self-interested motivations traces of our genetic programming or the desire for survival. To see the "more" in the ordinary is poetic icing on the prosaic cake at best, and an illusion at worse, not the serious encounter with reality that Ames claims it to be.

A version of this view of Ames, oddly enough, is presented within the novel itself, as is his response to it. Ames's older brother, Edward, considered brilliant from the time he was a child, goes off to study in Germany, and instead of becoming a minister, like his father and grandfather before him, becomes an atheist, passing to Ames some of the books that influenced him to leave religion behind. Even Ames's father, a pastor all his life, leaves the tradition after he retires, and urges him to do likewise, to give up his provincial ways. "I have become aware that we here lived within the limits of notions that were very old and even very local," he says. "I want you to understand that we do not have to remain loyal to them."[23]

Ames refuses to abandon the teachings with which he grew up. Wanting in the first place to preserve both his own and others' inner freedom, he is very mild-mannered in his defense, fully accepting that people are moved to make decisions on bases that elude others. "While I was at seminary I read every book he [Edward] had ever mentioned . . .Who knows where any mind comes from? It's all a mystery," he muses.[24] Yet he maintains that Edward's turning away from Christianity does not necessarily make him more independent-minded than someone who remains within it. It might, just as much, be merely a question of the fashions of the time, what is being read at universities, for instance, and he urges his

23. Robinson, *Gilead*, 235.

24. Robinson, *Gilead*, 125.

son to try to make a distinction between a genuine questioning prompted by specific circumstances, and following a fad.

> I'm not saying never doubt or question. The Lord gave you a mind so that you would make honest use of it. I'm saying you must be sure that the doubts and questions are your own, not, so to speak, the mustache and the walking stick that happen to be the fashion at any particular moment.[25]

Looked at from this angle, to accuse Ames of mystification, as a hypothetical modern reader might do, or of provincialism and backwardness, as his father does within the novel, may owe more to the current allergy to any reference to metaphysics than to any objective truth, outside time. The refusal of the hidden, of mystery, of the sacred—all three terms working in tandem in Ames's vocabulary—is itself the product of a historical moment, which will be left in the dust.

Transitory and Eternal

But isn't everything arbitrary then, depending on one's location in time and space, or what one has been exposed to? To a degree, yes, but Ames does not feel that remaining within a Christian worldview is *merely* arbitrary, even if its starting point might be the society one has been exposed to. The arbitrariness stops when the central terms penetrate into one's life and themselves remain living. Something alive, although it has a definite form, is always on the move.[26] This is, in fact, the way he talks about experience, fluid and unknowable because of the new dimensions one discovers in it. After fifty years of loneliness, broken finally through his second marriage to a woman he loves, he suddenly finds sweetness in his previous aloneness, which at the time was a heavy burden for him. "My point here is that you never do know the actual nature even of your own experience. Or perhaps it has no fixed and certain nature."[27] The events of your life are fixed, and yet your understanding of what it is you have

25. Robinson, *Gilead*, 179.

26. In one of her essays on Shakespeare, the subject of her dissertation, Robinson says, "[N]o great statement about reality, for example, that the heavens are attentive to our thoughts and actions and will determine the state of our souls, can be static, like simple information." Robinson, *Givenness*, 45.

27. Robinson, *Gilead*, 95.

lived remains fluid. Christianity, if truly interiorized, is so intimately part of one's experience that its teachings function in the same way.

Despite the fluidity of Christian teaching, its changing meanings over time,[28] Ames is quite adamant that nonetheless the truth of Christianity is eternal. The emphases may depend on a given historical moment, but not its specific mystery, which transcends any one expression of it.

> . . . I knew perfectly well . . . that the Lord absolutely transcends any understanding I have of Him, which makes loyalty to Him a different thing from loyalty to whatever customs and doctrines and memories I happen to associate with Him.[29]

What is it, then, that isn't based on any given doctrines or customs? The Lord himself, he says. But how does the Lord reveal himself if not in customs and doctrines?

In a recurring meditation on a moment in his childhood in which the community got together to salvage what could be salvaged from a church destroyed by lightning, Ames speaks of receiving a piece of ash-covered biscuit from his father, as if the love he experienced were inseparable from this charred object. The way this bitter cracker becomes a means for conveying love, a love that does not erase affliction but accompanies it, is what as an older man he understands Communion to be. In turn, Communion expresses the universal human condition: "Blessed and broken."[30] To be Christian is to recognize this mixture of love and sorrow as our very humanity, wherever and whenever it presents itself. His experience of this since childhood makes his adherence to Christianity a matter of self-evidence about who we are rather than a set of dogma one adheres to intellectually. Words always fall short.[31] To recognize the love manifesting itself somehow together with the suffering is to recognize the Lord.

28. *Gilead* can, in fact, be read as Robinson's illustration of the spontaneity and particularity of a living tradition. Its fluidity is evident in the three different emphases within Ames's own family. His grandfather was a social activist, interpreting faithfulness to Jesus as a standing with the most vulnerable, to the point of violently opposing their oppressors. His own father, in the face of the enormous carnage of the Civil War, became a pacifist. He himself, as the above passages indicate, emphasizes another central insight, echoing Robinson's own interpretation of Calvin. "[N]ature is a shining garment in which God is revealed and concealed." See Robinson, *When I Was a Child*, 9.

29. Robinson, *Gilead*, 234.

30. Robinson, *Gilead*, 69.

31. Robinson, *Gilead*, 114.

As a result, against the argument that he is simply conditioned to think in terms of mystery, Ames does not argue back on dogmatic or theoretical grounds. "In the matter of belief, I have always found that defenses have the same irrelevance about them as the criticisms they are meant to answer."[32] His proof, or better put, his evidence, comes from a life lived. "'Let Your works so shine upon men,' etc. [Matthew 5:16] It was Coleridge who said Christianity is a life, not a doctrine, or words to that effect."[33] On the level of what is really real, the way one's life is penetrated by the teachings, in this case, love, is the only verification that counts. One can be deluded, of course, but that is always the risk one runs when one chooses a path. The rightness of it is not established by winning a debate, although engaging in one is sometimes inevitable, even if the argument involves the marginal value of debate.

The Dangers of Contemplation

A second accusation against Ames's theology occurs within the novel as well, much more serious than the first, since even Ames agrees with it. How does his ability to see the hidden in the ordinary turn into action in the world, into a vision of social relations? How does it stop being limited to behavior like that of the ladies in his community, who bring food to members of their church in times of need? This is good, of course, but far from sufficient. It is through Ames's relationship with his godson, Jack Boughton, that this question arises. Jack had left the town of Gilead many years earlier, and now a man in his early forties, he has come back, to Ames's great discomfort. His godson's behavior in his youth had led to a very sorry series of circumstances. In the few conversations they have, Ames senses that Jack is seeking some help but distrusts the younger man's intentions at every point. It turns out, however, that Jack has come to see whether he can bring his family, his common law wife and child, to Gilead to start a life there. In Missouri, where they have lived together for seven years, they cannot get married because she is Black. In Iowa, they could marry, but he is not sure about being accepted even by his own father, Ames's closest friend and also a pastor. That is, among other things, what he has come to find out.

32. Robinson, *Gilead*, 178.

33. Robinson, *Gilead*, 179.

Ames's response shows an odd blindness. It is as if he has never given race any thought, even though, in mid-1950s America, it was staring him in the face. It is even stranger, given that his own grandfather, about which he talked often, and with respect, was a fiery abolitionist. Throughout his journal, Ames tells stories about the founding of Gilead as part of the Underground Railroad, his grandfather's loss of an eye as a Union soldier, and the years after the Civil War when, against the hostility of his own community and even his own family, the older John Ames had kept the flame of social justice alive. Among other reminiscences, Ames relates the vision of Jesus his grandfather reported, which set him on the abolitionist path. He had seen Jesus bound in chains and "Those irons had rankled right down to His bones."[34] The sight convinced him "that he had to come to Kansas and make himself useful to the cause of abolition."[35] This was the first of his grandfather's visions of Jesus, occurring at odd moments of the day for the rest of his life.[36]

Without dismissing these visions or his grandfather's social engagement, Ames nonetheless amends the sense of the sacred his grandfather had. Visions are much more daily affairs, available to everyone.

> I believe that the old man did indeed have far too narrow an idea of what a vision might be. He may, so to speak, have been too dazzled by the great light of his experience to realize that a great sun shines on us all.[37]

Visions of a supernatural kind may blind us to the sacred right under our noses, so present we do not distinguish it from everything else. As a result, we often encounter the hidden depth of the ordinary after the fact, in our memory, as our experience grows. The great sun that shines over all of us remains invisible to the naked eye.

> Perhaps this is the one thing I wish to tell you. Sometimes the visionary aspect of any particular day comes to you in the memory of it, or it opens to you over time. For example, whenever I take a child into my arms to be baptized, I am, so to speak, comprehended in the experience more fully, having seen more of life, knowing better what it means to affirm the sacredness of

34. Robinson, *Gilead*, 49.
35. Robinson, *Gilead*, 49.
36. Robinson, *Gilead*, 97.
37. Robinson, *Gilead*, 91.

> the human creature. I believe that there are visions that come to us only in memory, in retrospect.[38]

A way of seeing not through our senses alone—a vision—is required because the light remains hidden even as it shines, a central motif of Ames's theology. "Even the Holy of Holies was broken open. The deep darkness vanished into ordinary daylight, and the mystery of God was only made more splendid."[39] The mystery remains a mystery even in broad daylight.

It is ironic, then, that Ames misses the significance of what is under his nose, what his grandfather, with all his supernatural visions saw right away. Ames mentions that the last African American Church in Gilead was set on fire when he was a child, but, even as an old man, he does not see the significance of this event. When the last remaining African American families leave town a few decades later, he accepts it without delving into the reasons. When he mentions the fire to his godson, it is to minimize it. "Oh yes, but that was *many* years ago, when I was a boy. And it was only a small fire. There was very little damage."[40] Only when he is confronted with whether Jack and his family can live in Gilead does he notices the failure of the town to live up to its promise. "I woke up this morning thinking that this town might as well be standing on the absolute floor of hell for all the truth there is in it, and the fault is mine as much as much as anyone's."[41] He is astonished that he and Jack's father had never spoken about racial issues. "It just didn't come up."[42]

We do not need to see in Ames's blindness Robinson's dismissal of his theology of mystery. A better explanation for it might be, not so much his theology, but his inability to live up to what it requires. The word "sin" does not occur often in the novel, but we note that toward the end, Ames emphasizes much more than in the earlier parts the failing of human beings to see the light. "Light is constant, we just turn over in it," which could mean turning one's back to it.[43] The same theme is repeated a bit later, even more emphatically. "Wherever you turn your eyes the world can shine like a transfiguration. You don't have to bring

38. Robinson, *Gilead*, 91.
39. Robinson, *Gilead*, 133.
40. Robinson, *Gilead*, 171.
41. Robinson, *Gilead*, 233.
42. Robinson, *Gilead*, 221.
43. Robinson, *Gilead*, 210.

a thing to it except a little willingness to see. Only who could have the courage to see it?"[44] It is not good enough to pay attention, as he emphasized earlier. One must act. Action requires courage. Those who acted courageously, like his grandfather and others of his generation, risked their reputations, their peace, and their very lives in choosing to stand with those who were most destitute.[45]

Courage does not necessarily pass from one generation to another, although the light remains constant. Even a gentle and learned man like Ames, with his abolitionist heritage, falls victim to an inexcusable indifference, and becomes aware of it only too late. "What have I to leave you, "he says to his son, "but the ruins of old courage, and the lore of old gallantry and hope?"[46] By the end of the novel, seeing the sacred in the ordinary, in the human being above all, means more than contemplating the wonder of excess. It translates into action on the social scale on behalf of defending downtrodden human beings. Ames ends his journal with the hope that his son will take up the mantle. "I'll pray that you grow up a brave man in a brave country. I will pray you find a way to be useful."[47] Making oneself useful is the term people of his grandfather's generation used to describe their militancy on behalf of the poor and enslaved.

The emphasis on sin in the latter part of the novel is accompanied by an increasing emphasis on love. Light is not merely the mystery of existence, the gift of it. It is, insistently, love. Speaking of his love for his son, he says, " . . . I could never thank God sufficiently for the splendor He has hidden from the world—your mother excepted, of course—and revealed to me in your sweetly ordinary face."[48] The love he feels for his son reveals the love that God bestows upon him by granting him the possibility to love in the first place. His love for his wife and son becomes not just a gift but a glimpse into God's love for mankind. "I might seem to be comparing something great and holy with a minor and ordinary thing, that is, love of God with mortal love. But I just don't see them as separate things at all. If we can be divinely fed with a morsel and divinely blessed with a touch, then the terrible pleasure we find in a particular face can certainly instruct us in the nature of the very grandest love."[49] Thus, to fail to see, as Ames

44. Robinson, *Gilead*, 245.
45. Robinson, *Gilead*, 246.
46. Robinson, *Gilead*, 246.
47. Robinson, *Gilead*, 247.
48. Robinson, *Gilead*, 237.
49. Robinson, *Gilead*, 204.

and his generation did, the inherent racism within the Church, is to fail to honor the gifts put into their hands,[50] which become actualized in extending oneself to the marginalized and dehumanized.

Despite the failures of several generations of American Christians, Ames ends on a note of hope, made possible by the very nature of love. It follows no rules, and falls where it wills. "There is no justice in love, no proportion in it, and there need not be, because in any specific instance it is only a glimpse or a parable of an embracing, incomprehensible reality."[51] Because it does not subordinate itself to causal explanations or to foreseeable consequences, it can reappear when one least counts on it. As a result, love can break through even death. In the last two pages of the book, Ames expresses hope both in the resurrection of Gilead as a place of peace between all people,[52] and in his own resurrection. Both depend on an infusion of love, human love and God's love, inseparable from each other. "I love this town. I think sometimes of going into the ground here as a last wild gesture of love—I too will smolder away until the great and general incandescence."[53] The fire might look extinguished but the embers are merely waiting for the next breath of love. This is a state of affairs not realized but hoped for. The evidence for this hope lies in the unexpected igniting of human love, foreshadowing the unexpectedness of where it can appear next. Light, in these last examples, the great incandescence, has turned into love.

If we return to Robinson's' avoidance of the word "transcendence" and her preference for the word "mystery," we see perhaps more clearly than at the outset how the ordinary, the daily reveal the sheer excess that life is—human life in particular. By the same token, the ordinary reveals the love inherent in the cosmos, although we fail so often in our response to it, in our ability to receive and give it. Being and love are inexhaustible, and only metaphor, as we shall see, can hint at this whole never exhausted in any one manifestation.

50. Robinson, *Gilead*, 246.

51. Robinson, *Gilead*, 238.

52. Robinson, *Gilead*, 242.

53. Robinson, *Gilead*, 247.

Mystery and the Centrality of Metaphor

As we have repeatedly noted, *Gilead* is permeated by imagery of light and dark. The light is everywhere, coinciding with darkness, in that it cannot be seen with the naked eye. It is hidden in the visible. Put another way, the metaphor of light indicates a reality intertwined in the physical world and yet beyond it, "a reality embracing this one but exceeding it."[54] If that is the way things are, acceding to the real requires capturing this intertwining, even if momentarily. This, I would suggest, is the way metaphor functions in *Gilead*. In Ames's usage, metaphor provides a glimpse into an infinitely varied intertwining. We have already seen this in the metaphor of water, which refers simultaneously to baptism and to the awakening of erotic energy, each pointing to the other, both revealing the gift of life, and of regeneration. It is difficult to separate the physical from the "more than physical" in this complex web, and that is the point. Similarly, in the last image mentioned, a dying fire is both an image for the dead awaiting resurrection, and an image for the revival of the town of Gilead, which are metaphors for each other. The multiple meanings within a single image point to a nonlinear fullness, a "more" not exhausted by the examples given.

The imagery of fire reappears in a long, extended metaphor, bringing in new nuances and aspects. Ames, and his close friend Boughton, Jack's father, also a Protestant minister, are sitting on the porch one evening, watching a myriad of fireflies dart in the dark around them. Boughton cites a verse from the Book of Job, "Man is born to trouble as the sparks fly upward."[55] This leads Ames to a series of associations which at first recall the image of a dying fire, from which the sparks will fly when stirred.

> And really, it was that night as if the earth were smoldering. Well, it was and is. An old fire will make a dark husk for itself and settle in on its core, as is the case for this planet. I believe the same metaphor may describe the human individual as well. Perhaps Gilead. Perhaps civilization. Prod a little and the sparks will fly.[56]

Ames spins out his usual theme of a core of light buried within darkness. The earth's dark crust hides the fire within; humans and their

54. Robinson, *Gilead*, 143.
55. Robinson, *Gilead*, 72.
56. Robinson, *Gilead*, 72

culture go through the darkness of decline and death but, like a fire with hidden embers, have the possibility of reviving. All these phenomena reflect one another. In each case, something that has gone dark releases light when prodded.

The reference to suffering in the verse from the Book of Job seems oblique, at best. It returns, however.

> I don't know whether the verse put a blessing on the fireflies or the fireflies put a blessing on the verse, or if both of them together put a blessing on trouble, but I have loved them both a good deal ever since.[57]

Many meanings lie intertwined within this sentence, replete with metaphors. The fireflies here are the multiple troubles of human beings, but they are also the light that accompanies suffering, as if the dark and the light were inseparable, and the fireflies and the night sky just one indivisible whole. Equally indivisible are the spiritual and the natural world. Did the writers of the Bible experience the blessing in trouble first and then turn to nature to express it, or is it that the natural phenomena around us come first, making us understand the spiritual dimension of suffering, or is there a continual back and forth between them, such that we see the meaning of suffering only through that interpenetration? In any case, for Ames, the perpetual back and forth between the physical world and the spiritual world is key. Metaphor, as Ames deploys it, reproduces this in its very form. It is not merely unifying different categories we normally do not juxtapose. It is also the intricate mix of visible and invisible, of the ordinary and of mystery, each modality pointing to the other.

A last example of the metaphor of light repeats the intertwining of material and spiritual, this time directly referring to the centrality of metaphor as the vehicle for what is real. Everything can be a metaphor for anything else.

> The moon looks wonderful in this warm evening light, just as a candle flame looks beautiful in the light of morning. Light within light. It seems like a metaphor for something. So much does. Ralph Waldo Emerson is excellent on this point.[58]

57. Robinson, *Gilead*, 72.

58. Robinson, *Gilead*, 119.

A candle in morning light accentuates the ambient light of which it is an instance. Ames proceeds to list a multiplicity of contexts to which the metaphor of light against light applies.

> It seems to me to be a metaphor for the human soul, the singular light within the great general light of existence. Or it seems like poetry within language. Perhaps wisdom within experience. Or marriage within friendship and love.[59]

Poetry within language—metaphor—expresses the hidden dimension, always there but taken for granted or not really seen without it. It is like a candle in daylight.

The reference to Emerson is not gratuitous. In Ames's understanding of metaphor, we can hear echoes of Emerson's own views in his essay *Nature*: "The world is emblematic. Parts of speech are metaphors because the whole of nature is a metaphor for the human mind."[60] Or, in another: "There seems to be a necessity in spirit to manifest itself in material forms . . . the visible creation is the terminus of the circumference of the invisible world."[61] Or yet again "every object rightly seen unlocks a new faculty of the soul."[62] And yet what is purely a matter of nature and mind in these quotations involves, for Ames, a God who revealed Himself not only in nature but also, emphatically, in the Bible. He finishes his thoughts on the candle in daylight and metaphor with a reference to the book of Genesis. Hagar and Ishmael in the wilderness become like "a specific moment of divine Providence within the whole providential regime of Creation."[63]

The divine, for Ames, despite the echoes of both Ludwig Feuerbach, whom he cites approvingly a number of times,[64] and Emerson, does not coincide with nature, but lies infinitely beyond it. There is something absolutely other, "a reality embracing this one but exceeding it."[65] We cannot know it. Our minds are not a reflection of it because "our human circumstance creates in us a radically limited and peculiar

59. Robinson, *Gilead*, 119.
60. Emerson, *Emerson*, 20.
61. Emerson, *Emerson*, 21.
62. Emerson, *Emerson*, 22.
63. Robinson, *Gilead*, 119.
64. Robinson, *Gilead*, 23–24, 145.
65. Robinson, *Gilead*, 143.

notion of what existence is."[66] Our minds and the reality in which we swim do not match. We get glimpses of it, but it remains fundamentally ungraspable, too multiple and intertwined for our concepts. Metaphor gives us an inkling of its inexhaustibility, but, to use one of Ames's metaphors, even though the light is constant, we turn over in it. We cannot see the real in its constancy, but only intermittently, and when we do see it, it is precisely in its unlikeness to us.

In a passage describing a time in his youth when he would get up before dawn to fetch water and wood, Ames conveys this unlikeness.

> I remember walking out into the dark and feeling as if the dark were a great, cool sea and the houses and the sheds and the woods were all adrift in it, just about to ease off their moorings. I always felt like an intruder then, and I still do, as if the darkness had a claim on everything, one that I violated just by stepping out of my door.[67]

The dark has turned into a metaphor for Reality, a huge sea in which the order we know floats. We are part of this sea, of course, but usually not privy to a view of it, and when we do get a glimpse of it, we feel we have intruded, gone beyond our proper limits. In glimpsing the great sea, within and without, we also see that the order we have built is without foundation, just floating along, and easily undone. Metaphor can point to the boundless fluidity of what lies beyond and within our order, as it does here, but it cannot make us become permanently aware of it. Metaphor can point to fluidity but not contain it. A glimpse of that enormous and calm sea has its disorienting aspects, as it does in the image above. But, at other points in *Gilead*, the dark points to a love and regeneration that in their unexpectedness and power of renewal suggest something other than the dread that filled Pascal in his famous *pensée*. "The eternal silence of these infinite spaces fills me with dread."[68] The awe Ames feels in that still dark early morning, laced with estrangement, is only one aspect of his confrontation with mystery.

66. Robinson, *Gilead*, 143.

67. Robinson, *Gilead*, 74.

68. Pascal, *Pensées*, 66.

Part 2—Robinson's Essays: Mystery in Another Key

Setting *Gilead* in the context of Robinson's essays will require a number of different approaches. In the first place, we need to understand better her refusal of what she calls materialism. Attendant to that, and at times central, are her references to modern physics, whose implications, on her view, place it squarely on the side of mystery. Robinson's reliance on physics to support her understanding about mystery is not unproblematic. I will devote some space to a critique, as well as to her possible rejoinders. The conclusion will address the role of a novel like *Gilead* in a universe of discourse that denies its premises.

The Centrality of Self

We began with the proposition that *Gilead,* while contemplative, can nonetheless be situated within Robinson's polemics in her essays. In the broadest sense, the novel, in the key place it gives to the self, is a retort to those spokespeople for the sciences who deny the self's centrality or even its reality. In *Gilead,* "that miraculous thing, our felt experience of life"[69] remains our sole entryway to the real, even if our entryway is limited and partial. After all, Ames's constant referral to light and dark is not just an aesthetic appreciation of nature but a fleeting glimpse into the fundaments of the cosmos, and even of what lies beyond it. Most readers today would probably label this elevation of the self "as sadly mystical and execrably unscientific," as William James imagined the response to his own defense of subjectivity more than a century earlier.[70] How Romantic can one get, the term Romantic here denoting a rear guard and unsuccessful attempt to present a speculative counter-vision, in this case, of a self, in opposition to the rigor of the sciences, which denies it a fundamental reality.

In giving such a central place to the self in the novel, not just as a study in the psychology of a character but as a vehicle for metaphysics, Robinson dismisses this dismissal. She opposes those for whom the self is nothing but a screen for forces that scientists can discover through their instruments. This "nothing but" is central to what she means by

69. Robinson, *When I Was a Child,* 8.

70. James, *The Will to Believe,* 52.

materialism, "by which I mean a discipline of exclusive attention to the reality that can be tested by scientists."[71] As mentioned previously, she is not so much attached to this term, which often coexists with positivism or reductionism or parascience, as she is intent in exposing the metaphysical conviction central to all of them: Anything the sciences do not discover through their methods is either not worth knowing or does not exist.[72] She begs to differ, most emphatically where the self is concerned.

In her essays, Robinson argues that consciousness eludes scientific instruments. Speaking about the cultural origins of fear, and the fact that fMRIs only get to the end product, the physical sensation, she says, ". . . the workings of the mind, or brain, are not of a kind existing instruments are designed to capture."[73] This would imply that future instruments might do so. In other places, however, she makes clear that scientific instruments cannot capture the mind or self-consciousness in principle. If, as some neuroscientists and evolutionary biologists or their spokespeople claim, we have no evidence for the existence of a self, a felt unity amidst all the fluctuations,[74] it is because these scientists are simply not looking in the right place and in the right way. "We know things in the ways we encounter them,"[75] she points out, or, as she says elsewhere, we know things at the scale we choose to observe them.[76]

A perfect example of operating on the wrong scale is to seek to say something meaningful about our subjectivity through instruments examining our neurons. To discover human interiority, we need to turn to where it has expressed itself, "to open the archives of all that humankind has thought and done, to see how the mind describes itself, to weigh the kind of evidence supposed science tacitly disallows."[77] That evidence is far from homogeneous. The reduction of our inner workings to basic survival mechanisms in the evolutionary struggle, for instance, adds to the host of other suppositions. When it comes to the question of what is real, including the reality of the mind, scientists have a voice, but no privileged access. "It [Science]is human, and has always been one strategy among others in the more general project of human self-awareness

71. Robinson, *Givenness*, 13.
72. Robinson, *Absence*, 33–34.
73. Robinson, *Givenness*, 77.
74. Robinson, *Givenness*, 262–3.
75. Robinson, *Givenness*, 13.
76. Robinson, *Absence*, 126.
77. Robinson, *Absence*, 16.

and self-assertion."[78] Although she objects to the reductionistic view of ourselves, she objects even more to its brushing aside of all the other ones, as if it alone can lay claim to objectivity. "I am not prepared to concede objectivity to the arbitrarily reductionist model of reality that has so long claimed, and been granted, this virtue."[79] In other words, the reductionistic view is not a view from nowhere. It is one more situated position among others.

Modern Physics and Christianity— Analogous Mysteries

In dismissing materialism, Robinson often turns to modern physics. With their very instruments, physicists have discovered that matter at the microcosmic level eludes our understanding.

> We know now that there is another reality, beyond the grasp of our comprehension yet wholly immanent in all of Being, powerful in every sense of the word, invisible to our sight, silent to our hearing, foolish to our wisdom, yet somehow steadfast, allowing us our days and years.[80]

Despite the echoes of a religious language here, what she means by "beyond the grasp of our comprehension" in this instance are the subatomic particles of the physicists. They do not even appear as separate before human beings measure them, and when they do appear, one photon or electron immediately influences a second one to which it was initially joined, at a rate faster than the speed of light.[81] These particles are "entangled" at any distance. If that is the case, why should the operations of the mind not be similarly "entangled," as entangled as metaphor, in fact? Entanglement is basic. Is not the mind —with its inescapable resort to metaphor—in the image of the matter that eludes the physicists? "Indeed, there is now a suggestion of the pervasive importance to the deep structures of reality of something of a kind with

78. Robinson, *When I Was a Child*, 16. Also, see Robinson, *Absence*, 124. "It [Science] is not a final statement about reality but a highly fruitful mode of inquiry into it."

79. Robinson, *Givenness*, 9.

80. Robinson, *Givenness*, 224.

81. Robinson, *Absence*, 113.

consciousness."[82] The infinite intertwining that is our mind reflects the cosmic entanglement and vice-versa.

Robinson is well aware that modern physicists, like all scientists, want to dispel mystery, disentangle more and more of the cosmos, and this, in her estimation, is absolutely how it should be. The discovery of mystery should be earned, appearing each time anew. "To be clear, I am not talking about the 'black box' approach that reifies ignorance . . . It is always premature to say that something cannot be known or cannot be described or explained."[83] She is convinced that contemporary quantum physics will indeed be transformed by new discoveries. Still, these will reveal a reality that eludes our conceptual grasp even more than the quantum particles of today. She finds this exhilarating, proclaiming herself happy to have been born in an age of such exciting improbabilities as black holes, dark matter, anti-matter, parallel universes and the rest. "I am deeply grateful to have lived in the era of cosmic exploration. I am thrilled by those photographs of deep space, as many of us are."[84] The quest to know is provoked by the unknown, which reemerges as its conclusion. "And our wealth of ignorance grows and multiplies. Much more is known about the atom now than was known fifty years ago, and all the brilliant probing has brought on a cascade of new, more elegant, more pregnant mystery."[85] She speaks of "the primordial human tropism toward mystery [which] may well have provided the impetus to all that we have learned."[86]

It is worth pondering the parallel Robinson draws between the mystery of physics and the mystery experienced by someone like Ames in *Gilead*. He apprehends a reality incommensurate with what we can ever comprehend. We bathe in it yet it exceeds our awareness by far, except at privileged moments. His stepping out of his house before dawn is such a moment. The darkness around him appears as a vast cool sea, in which the visible world is floating, and to which he remains a stranger, even when beholding it. A strikingly similar image of our situation in the cosmos occurs in one of Robinson's essays, this time a translation of the discoveries of modern physics.

82. Robinson, *Absence*, 36.
83. Robinson, *Givenness*, 199.
84. Robinson, *When I Was a Child*, 15.
85. Robinson, *Givenness*, 199.
86. Robinson, *When I Was a Child*, 197.

> It is as if we were a quiet city in the heart of a raging sea, no foundation touching the sea floor, no spire rising out of the waves. Some gentle spell prevents us from grasping our situation, and this is all right because the same gentle spell shelters us from it. We know what we need to know to live in this city. Cows give milk, hammers drive nails, books should be returned to the library. But we know now that the overwhelmingly preponderant forms and theaters of existence are utterly alien to such business.[87]

We live in a daily world, the quiet city, that behaves according to concepts that allow us to understand it and manipulate it. But within and beyond it lies the microcosmic world, with no objects, no time and no space. That other dimension, although we live in it, utterly exceeds our understanding. We are aliens in a raging sea. It gets even odder. We don't even know how these two dimensions fit together. Which one is the real world? If space, time, and causality are unreal, how is it that we cannot ignore the laws regulating them without perishing? And yet those laws do not operate at the more fundamental level. How is it that we, functioning with concepts applicable only to the quiet city, have discovered a reality that does not fit these concepts or any concepts, for that matter?[88]

Robinson argues that the mystery at the heart of quantum mechanics frees us to affirm a reality not captured by scientific instruments, a conclusion derived from findings produced by these very instruments. The assurance that the world can be made transparent to our devices, part of the materialist credo, is thus challenged, allowing a return to an imagination of mystery, including that of Christianity. "For these reasons, I am grateful to science for freeing me to consider essential elements of Christianity without bringing the prejudices of what is still called modern thought to bear on them."[89] Science, as Robinson sees it, returns to being "the invaluable handmaiden of theology in that it tells us how astonishing and gigantically elusive are all the particulars of existence. And nothing is more unfathomable than ourselves."[90] Physics,

87. Robinson, *Givenness*, 211. In a more recent essay, Robinson associates the raging sea of the scientist with the chaos found in biblical texts, as in Psalm 89, and with a chaos whose boundaries God chose to contain, as in the book of Job 38:8–11. See Robinson, "A Theology of the Present Moment," 10–11.

88. Robinson, *Givenness*, 212.

89. Robinson, *Givenness*, 212–3.

90. Robinson, *Givenness*, 198–9.

then, does not prove any dogma, but inspires new ways of emphasizing traditional Christian teachings.

It, for instance, allows Robinson to introduce the cool dark sea in *Gilead*, as a metaphor for the transcendence of God vis-a-vis his creation. This, in turn, allows her to reformulate the central teaching of Christianity—the Incarnation. Christ transcends matter and yet is present within matter. He is hidden within and also everywhere without, although we have to have eyes to see. Does not the matter that physicists discover defy our understanding of matter while at the same time producing the daily matter we know? "On scrutiny the physical is as elusive as anything to which a name can be given. The physical as we have come to know it frays away into dark matter, antimatter, and by implication on beyond them and beyond our present power of inference."[91] It is no longer a question of a matter we understand, the domain of physics, and a spirit that eludes our understanding, the domain of Christianity. Both now dwell in the realm of mystery—beyond cause and effect, space and time—and require the interference of a particular attentiveness to come into view at all.

She often claims that Christian theologians, and ordinary followers have been blocked from any cosmic formulation of Christianity or from reclaiming its mysteries,[92] not only from fear of appearing ridiculous, given the authority of science, but also from having internalized the basic premises of the materialism associated with it.[93] Speaking of the new physics, she says that "it entirely discredits the antimetaphysics that has prevailed in Christian thought for some time, the huge and damaging concessions made to a crudely restricted notion of the possible."[94] These theologians have left the physical world out of their considerations, and soft-pedal the Incarnation, with the centrality of the human in the cosmos that it implies.[95] Modern physics can help undo that, revealing the implications of Creation and Incarnation from a new angle.

She suggests, for instance, that the very arbitrariness of our order, the quiet city, may indicate what Christianity has always maintained, that our world has indeed been created with us in mind, by a Being that vastly exceeds that world. "Providential is fairly exactly what

91. Robinson, *Givenness*, 8.

92. Robinson, *Givenness*, 151.

93. Robinson, *Givenness*, 164.

94. Robinson, *Givenness*, 188.

95. Robinson, *Givenness*, 190–92.

Jonathan Edwards [the eighteenth-century American Protestant theologian] meant by arbitrary."[96] In other words, the very fact that we live in a kind of bubble—laws that function according to causality, time and space —in a raging sea that does not—may be a sign of our centrality in the scheme of creation. "I take the Christian mythos to be a special revelation of a general truth, that truth being the ontological centrality of humankind in the created order, with its theological corollary, the profound and unique sacredness of human beings as such."[97]

Similarly, subatomic physics, in presenting the basic stuff of the universe as not just bits or tiny particles subject to precise laws but as an intertwined whole that operates in ways that defy conceptual grasp, opens up a new/old way of affirming the Incarnation. Human beings, in their intertwined spirit and matter, are a microcosm of the inseparability into parts of the whole that is reality.[98] She is not saying that physicists' new discoveries about the fundaments have a direct corollary in Christian theology, but that they invite us to think that what scientists classically called the physical does not correspond to the strangeness of the basic stuff of the world. That strangeness makes possible a new kind of metaphysics.

These are tricky arguments and she knows it. "I run the risk here of seeming to theologize science or to use scientific speculation to vindicate theology."[99] In other words, she could easily be seen as reading a divine meaning into physics or as relying on the authority of science for the truth of Christianity, or at least as arguing that Christianity has to be in analogy with the sciences of the time in order to be correct. This would be but another way to demote Christianity as the source of truth. She is careful, however, to say what physics can and can't do for Christianity.

> Physics has shown us a volatile, intricate, elusive substratum of reality that makes the usefulness of the old nuts and bolts physics seem uncanny rather than obvious and inevitable. *This new view of the cosmos does not supply or support a new Christian metaphysics* . . . The basis for a new metaphysics is ready to hand

96. Robinson, *Givenness*, 221.

97. Robinson, *Givenness*, 222.

98. For human beings as microcosm, see her treatment of Nicholas of Cusa, Robinson, *Givenness*, 204–5. Her treatment of the way matter is understood in modern physics and the opening it gives to rethinking the Incarnation occurs throughout her essays. See for instance, Robinson, *Givenness*, 188–225, 231–2.

99. Robinson, *Absence*, 122. A similar sentiment is expressed in Robinson, *Givenness*, 237.

> in biblical and traditional theology. *The terms that will make it Christian are established in passages like Colossians 1:15–20, notable for the collapse of time and locus, which modern physics permits us or requires us to respect as an ontological fact to be reckoned with.*[100] (My italics)

A reality beyond time and space is already present in Scriptures. Christians did not need to wait for twentieth-century physics. The latter, however, permits thinking of the Christian affirmation of mystery not only as descriptive of our inner reality but also of the cosmos as a whole.

Objections to Robinson's Use of Physics and Her Counter-objections

William James

Still, despite the nuances, is not Robinson's reliance on physics as a way forward for Christian theology a difficult position to hold? If we follow William James in some of his essays, he argues that scientific findings change so much in the course of time that the metaphysics they seem inevitably to inspire at one point in time may turn out to be wrong as discoveries progress.

> Think how many absolutely new scientific conceptions have arisen in our own generation, how many new problems have been formulated that were never thought of before, and then cast an eye on the brevity of science's career . . . Whatever else be certain, this at least is certain—that the world of our present natural knowledge *is* enveloped in a larger world of *some* sort of whose residual properties we at present can frame no positivist idea.[101]

James knows that many scientists believe that a point will come when we will have a positivist idea of that larger world, when our scientific theories and the world will coincide for good. But, James points out, we are not there yet and don't even know whether we ever will be. The trust in science's ability to explain all there is remains a kind of faith, inherently implying a risk. He therefore urges those who want to believe in

100. Robinson, *Givenness*, 188. Colossians 1:15–20 speaks of Christ as intertwined with all of creation, "for in him all things were created, in heaven and on earth, visible and invisible . . . "

101. James, *Will to Believe*, 53–54.

the truths of Christianity to take a similar risk. They should wait, not for scientific confirmation, but rather for the verification that comes from their own experiences, as they act on Christian teachings. This is the only verification that counts in matters that cannot be established by the kind of evidence, always provisional, that science provides. "If religious hypotheses about the universe be in order at all, the active faiths of individuals in them, expressing themselves in life, are the experimental tests by which they are verified, and the only means by which their truth or falsehood can be wrought out."[102] Those who swear by materialism have, after all, done the same thing, he claims. Materialism is not a proven fact. It is a position staked on transitory results, which are often contested, even in their own time.

> He [Professor Clifford] calls it 'guilt' and 'sin' to believe even the truth without 'scientific evidence.' But what is the use of being a genius, unless with the same scientific evidence as other men, one can reach more truth than they? Why does Clifford fearlessly proclaim his belief in the conscious-automaton theory, although the proofs before him are the same which makes Mr. Lewes reject it? Why does he believe in the primordial units' mind-stuff, although the 'proofs' before him are the same which make Mr. Bain reject it?[103]

James, in showing how unstable scientific convictions about the nature of reality are, was not denying that science provides useful knowledge. Rather, he questioned the certainty with which people accepted science as the sole provider of a final truth about the metaphysical realm, as in the example above, about the nature of consciousness or the nature of matter. To get back to Robinson, the same argument could also be made today regarding quantum theory. What if some of the physicists working to establish a correlation between our concepts of cause and effect and the subatomic world turn out to be right? Is it not dangerous to rely on scientific findings when it comes to absolute truth, even when they seem to be analogous to Christian truths?

Robinson, much influenced by James, whom she quotes favorably throughout her essays, would certainly agree that the evidence for Christianity lies in our personal interaction with the ordinary world around us. "Faith takes its authority from subjective experience, from an inward

102. James, *Will to Believe*, xi–xii.

103. James, *Will to Believe*, 92.

sense of the substance and meaning of experience."[104] As her protagonist in *Gilead* sees it, if we pay attention, we see the incarnation confirmed in the "more" of a human face, in the mystery of love, in the way nature suggests an intertwined whole, over and over again. The language of the Christian tradition shapes human experience which, in turn, shapes the meaning of that language. Nothing else is needed.

Why then invoke physics at all? The answer, for Robinson, seems to lie in the conventions within which our self is inevitably entangled, evident in the most prosaic activities. "Anyone who has brought up children knows the overwhelming power of the larger culture."[105] As much as Robinson lays emphasis on the individual subject, she does not mean that we are gloriously independent of our environment. Our self is porous, "vulnerable to influences of every kind."[106] Religious thought, like everything else, has been subject to the influence of a kind of scientific thought for the last two to three hundred years.[107] Robinson is well aware of that weight on herself. The combined materialism and neo-capitalism of her own era[108] are not easily defeated by a novelistic representation of a person like John Ames. "As a fiction writer, I feel smothered by this collective fiction, this Reality . . . Maybe I can hit it on the head, put an end to it. This is not a realistic hope."[109] Who will take *Gilead*'s language of mystery and blessing and sacred seriously, as more than depiction of a time far away and long ago, when that language might have ruled experience? She strengthens the case for mystery by appealing to a parallel mystery in quantum physics. But James's critique of relying on science to support a metaphysical claim remains.

Dominique Janicaud

Robinson's view of physics as restoring mystery is also vulnerable from another direction, illustrated through the writings of the French philosopher Dominique Janicaud. For him, the problem is not that science continually changes and thus cannot provide stable ground for

104. Robinson, *Givenness*, 80.

105. Robinson, *Death of Adam*, 79.

106. Robinson, *Givenness*, 263. A similar sentiment is expressed in Robinson, *Absence*, 118.

107. Robinson, *Givenness*, 211.

108. Robinson, *Death of Adam*, 29–30

109. Robinson, *Death of Adam*, 77.

a metaphysics, but that science does not change enough. It is just as deterministic today as it was in the nineteenth century, only more so. He rejects the claims of scientists and philosophers, among others, Ilya Prirogine and Isabelle Stengers, who claim that modern physics reenchants the world.[110] "The cold, inert determined universe of classical science yields to fresh visions of nature and the cosmos. '*Life, destiny, freedom, spontaneity*' become the themes of this symphony of the new world."[111] Janicaud argues instead that these scientists merely provide a screen for the extension of science's power over the world.[112] Even if not completely intentionally, they attempt to shore up confidence in science in a public that might be moving away from it. "The New Science [the claim that modern physics is a break with classical science and its reductionism] becomes a scientistic myth, useful for remobilizing intellectuals posing to desert the scientific community, or, more globally, in order that an ill-informed public that scares easily regains its confidence in science, scientists, their institutions, and their projects."[113]

For Janicaud, to think that modern physics leaves room for the unpredictable and incalculable is a sheer idealization of an institution—the big science that modern physics embodies—which engages in projects on an enormous scale. He mentions "high-precision electronic materials, the use of perfected radars and lasers, surveillance and telecommunications through satellites, unprecedented archival information systems etc."[114] The ordinary person is yet more in the grip of a science/technology that leaves no room for particularity or the mystery it supposedly reveals. Quantum physics is, after all, all about the most precise quantifications, and produces extremely efficient results.[115] "Never more than today has there been such total calculation, and at such an unprecedented level of precision and exhaustiveness."[116] The realm of the calculable becomes endless, and that includes quantifying our own interiority and inwardness. "The last stage of this is technology's seizing control of consciousness and language itself."[117]

110. The book Janicaud is referring to is Prirogine and Stengers, *Order out of Chaos.*

111. Janicaud, *Powers*, 146.

112. Janicaud, *Powers*, 150–51.

113. Janicaud, *Powers*, 152.

114. Janicaud, *Powers*, 150.

115. Janicaud, *Powers*, 149.

116. Janicaud, *Powers*, 45.

117. Janicaud, *Powers*, 82.

This is certainly a powerful critique of the liberation Robinson sees in quantum physics. Yet, in some ways, Janicaud also provides fodder for Robinson's appeal to physics, if very indirectly. Despite his view that quantum mechanics is in a continuum with the sciences that preceded it, and not the hoped-for break in the project of eliminating the human as anything but matter to be explained and manipulated, Janicaud does retain some hope that the human may still triumph. He asks whether "the imponderable factor called 'human'" does not throw spokes in the wheels of total control, along with the unpredictable results of technology itself, sometimes turning against itself. He speaks of a "supplementary play, characteristic of human beings," that eludes control.[118] Play leads us back to his discussion of language. Although he comes from an intellectual tradition quite different from Robinson's, they cross paths on this topic. We will soon see how, in the case of Robinson, this may lead back to her view of physics.

Language, Physics and Gilead

Janicaud draws a contrast between natural language and what he calls techno-discourse. The first is inseparable from the symbol, embodying "a living, mysterious, multiple, unpredictable relation to the world."[119] The symbolic is "fragile, infinitely diverse and suggestively opaque."[120] "Techno-discourse," on the other hand, at its deepest level, is "the taking control of the symbolic by the functional,"[121] the conversion of the world into "an immense informational fortification."[122] Information is intended to make meaning transparent, universal, as a computer language might be.[123] What becomes universal instead is technology's "own processes and procedures,"[124] destroying the very multiplicity of associations of natural language, and its unpredictable transpositions. He claims that techno-discourse increasingly replaces the suggestiveness and diversity of the symbol, although not completely. "Natural

118. Janicaud, *Powers*, 182–3.
119. Janicaud, *Powers*, 90–91.
120. Janicaud, *Powers*, 88.
121. Janicaud, *Powers*, 75.
122. Janicaud, *Powers*, 83.
123. Janicaud, *Powers*, 87.
124. Janicaud, *Powers*, 87.

languages have not yet been destroyed; rather, they are shaped, even increasingly stifled by a computerized language."[125] It may be, however, that natural language, with its spontaneity and suggestiveness, has a role in resisting, even when it doesn't do so ideologically, the endless reduction to one-dimensionality. What else if not language exhibits the "supplementary play" Janicaud mentioned above?

For Robinson, too, a big part of the impact of the reductionistic/materialistic model on our culture is the language that accompanies it. Speaking of neuroscientists, she says, "These methods are as much a matter of vocabulary as of technology, though the two interact and reinforce each other."[126] That vocabulary has as one of its features "accounts of subjective experience that are impossible to affirm on the basis of subjective experience."[127] If we read Robinson through Janicaud, then, it is not so much the science of physics that liberates but *the symbolic,* or to use her expression, *the metaphorical language* it inspires. Whatever the technology modern physics gives rise to, it simultaneously allows for the creation of a language that competes with techno-discourse. That "entanglement," that "spooky action at a distance," those black holes all evoke the hidden dimension and multiplicity of meanings without which metaphor cannot function.

To elucidate how this competition between techno-discourse and the language of symbol/metaphor may work, I will interrelate three features of artistic language, as Robinson describes them in her essays. We begin with the common problem of finding an adequate expression for an experience that always exceeds that expression. That tension, when honored, produces art.

> . . . As a writer, I continuously attempt to make inroads on the vast terrain of what cannot be said . . . That is to say, the unnamed is overwhelmingly present and real for me. And this is truer because the moment it stops being a standard for what I do say is the moment my language goes slack and my imagination disengages itself."[128]

This struggle with what cannot be expressed flows into a second aspect of language, revealed in the task of the novelist, as she describes it,

125. Janicaud, *Powers,* 87.

126. Robinson, *Givenness,* 7.

127. Robinson, *Givenness,* 79.

128. Robinson, *When I Was a Child,* 20.

which is a way "to probe anomalies that emerge in the assumed world when it is under scrutiny."[129] The artist discovers anomalies not so much because she has an ideological ax to grind, but because finding a way of describing experience challenges convention, as if unintentionally. The anomalies emerge in the process of finding an adequate language. This, in turn, leads to the third aspect of language, the reader's appropriation of it. "Reading, above the level of the simplest information, is an act of great inwardness and subjectivity . . . Great respect for a text and great respect for, and pleasure in, the reader's subjectivity flourished together."[130] In the act of reading a work of art, broadly defined, one detects an underlying whole hidden in a detail, intertwining patterns that, *unlike information, which bypasses subjective confirmation*, require one's own experience to come to light.

The point of *Gilead*, then, would not be to convert its readers into users of the language of blessing and mystery but to make them exercise their inner life, in the very encounter with Ames's language, in the act of recognition or rejection that his experience evokes in them. From this angle, and with a wink in the direction of Janicaud, *Gilead* is not a nostalgic glance at a bygone time as much as the introduction of a multivalent metaphoric language into the one-dimensionality of information that assaults us. Or, to stick more closely to Robinson's own language, it is a way of introducing what can only be confirmed by experience into a language that asks us to bypass that experience. If artistic language cannot argue against the authority of the sciences, it can, below and beyond argument, activate the very inwardness that at least some of these sciences, or their spokespeople, deny.

While modern physics has nothing to say about inwardness, the subatomic world it brings to light no longer excludes the mystery—the hidden, inaccessible depth—which makes us come up with a term like inwardness in the first place. People will keep on writing and reading novels and poetry regardless of physics, but we can read Robinson as saying that physics helps us to take our own unfathomability more seriously. After all, it too works within the unfathomable. Is she right or are the critics? In any case, both her novels and her essays keep the issue alive.

129. Robinson, *Givenness*, 218.

130. Robinson, *Death of Adam*, 9.

The Appeal to Expert Authority

One last scruple remains about Robinson's reliance on physics, its persistence a witness to the very problem that Robinson's polemics with materialism raise. Where is Robinson's authority to speak about modern physics at all? Unlike a d'Espagnat who is himself a theoretical physicist or, to cite a very well-regarded popularizer of quantum, Carlo Rovelli,[131] also a quantum physicist, she cannot back her evaluations with the technical vocabulary and the charts and formula that they both employ, even if sparingly. But if we bracket our scruples for a moment, it is worth entertaining the possibility that Robinson's greatest contribution lies precisely in not being intimidated by her lack of expert knowledge.[132] After emphasizing the central role of universities as dispensers of what we need to know, she remarks, "Surely, it was never intended that the universities should do the thinking, or the knowing for the rest of us."[133] Her university education has given her tools, among them the art of reading carefully and the knowledge of what is out there to read. She has taken this instruction to heart, reading widely, among which popular books and articles about the natural sciences, often written by scientists themselves, and also many classics, the works of Nietzsche, Darwin, Freud, and Calvin, among many others. She interprets them without the mediation of a huge specialized literature, giving pride of place to her primary reading. As she sees it, in the area of understanding who we are as human beings, there are no experts, only (well-read) interlocutors. One's interpretations of texts can be mistaken, of course, and hers is certainly not exempt from this criticism, but this does not translate into excluding on principle those who are not narrowly specialized.

It is worth underscoring that Robinson's refusal of experts is limited to those who claim to explain away our thoughts and feelings through the authority derived from scientific method, bypassing the expression of those they are explaining. "A central tenet of the modern world view is that we do not know our own minds, our own motives, our own desires. And—an important corollary—certain well-qualified others *do*

131. See 108, footnote 4; 129, footnote 98.

132. Robinson, *Death of Adam*, 10. "The idea is well established now that people have areas of competence from which they should not stray, and into which others should not stray. This results in a sort of intellectual desertification . . ."

133. Robinson, *Death of Adam*, 7.

know them."[134] Her counter position is not that we do know ourselves. On the contrary, "nothing is more unfathomable than ourselves."[135] But, if we remain a mystery, it is a mystery to whose multiple dimensions we have access through our own and others' expression. Given this, she refuses to give authority to those who claim to erase that mystery, and its inherent multiplicity, on the basis of a privileged knowledge. "Every one of us has privileged access to the unique source of insight on this question, a living mind."[136]

Conclusion

If we have introduced William James at various points in this essay, it is because, in many ways, Robinson's voice echoes his. While engaging in scientific experiments himself, James argued not only for the limits of the scientific enterprise when it comes to truth about ourselves and the universe but also for the very necessity of arguing for those limits in a world overly convinced of the powers of science.[137] Robinson's feisty forays against the authority of the sciences to define or dismiss our interiority, illustrate, if nothing else, that when it comes to our view of who has the best take on our subjectivity, we still live in James's nineteenth-century world. From Robinson's perspective that world is surviving out of a misplaced trust in a premise surpassed by the very science that gave rise to it in the first place. In continuing to accept its authority, we live in a past altogether more past than the darkness in which we float conveyed in *Gilead.*

If we attempt to take some distance from the debate in which both James and Robinson are engaged, and see it as an instance of religious history, the interest of Robinson's work remains at least two-fold. In the first place, regardless of whether modern physics does make more plausible the multi-dimensionality and sheer elusiveness of the self, her work, as well as that of many others, shows that quantum has become a site for our religious imagination, our imagination of a reality that we cannot assimilate, the site of mystery, to use Robinson's choice word. This religious imagination shapes not only New Age sensibilities and a new understanding of

134. Robinson, *Absence*, 59.

135. Robinson, *Givenness*, 199.

136. Robinson, *Givenness*, 217.

137. James, *Will to Believe*, x–xiii.

Buddhism, both of which are often invoked as echoes of quantum physics, but also the reinterpretation of Christianity.

Secondly, it is worth remarking that Robinson's defense of the centrality of felt experience is unusually optimistic. Her work suggests that we encounter mystery as long as we read not just for information, but as a resource for our own understanding of ourselves, with all the unexpected outcomes this might produce. This in turn means that as long as there is natural language, replete with metaphor, and interpreters of that language, the mystery remains. The mystery appears, for instance, in the process of interiorization. Why does one person derive one meaning while another a very different one? If that mystery remains, our inwardness can be threatened, even severely threatened, but not altogether taken out of the picture. The affirmation of this mystery, that is of the secret of interiority, may be the act of faith required in modern circumstances. Given the dominance of the reductionistic view and some of its consequences, it is worth remembering that, both for James and for Robinson, an act of faith is verified in daily life through actions that continue to yield evidence. It should make us pay more attention to such an ordinary phenomenon as metaphor, to the way language is deployed around us, and, perhaps most of all, to the education that makes thinking about such matters available.

Postcript

Mystery, Once Again

I finished these lines in November of 2022, when ChatGPT began to receive much coverage in the press.[138] So much has been written about it since, in an incessant flow. But here is a reminder of what it can do once again. If queried about Marilynne Robinson's notion of mystery, for example, the Chat or one of its competitors would produce a short essay about it. If asked to write the beginning of a novel in the style of *Gilead*, it would do so. From one angle, it seems to belie everything that Robinson

138. In the first few days of December in *The New York Times* alone, we have Roose, "The Brilliance and Weirdness of ChatboxGPT; Krugman, "Does ChatGPT Mean Robots Can Take Away Our Jobs?" "Can ChatboxGPT Make this Podcast?" Metz, "Chatbots Can Amaze but Also Lie." In t*he New Yorker*, we have Kang, "Could an A.I. Chatbot Rewrite My Novel?" In *The Atlantic Monthly*, there are four, dating from Dec. 6 to Dec. 9. It would be impossible to list the thousands of articles that continue to appear on this topic.

has written about artistic language. The computer program runs through immense data bases, calculates which words or parts of words statistically follow others, and produces a text. The terminology used to explain how it functions involves "neural networks" and "large language models." As one technology journalist explains it, "Identifying billions of distinct patterns in the way people connect words, numbers and symbols, these systems learned how to generate text on their own."[139] The algorithms leading to these results bypass the struggle with the inexpressible and the discovery of anomaly. On the contrary, the text that emerges, in the speed with which it appears, in the flatness of the language within it, becomes an instance of the techno-discourse that Janicaud warned about.

Looked at from Robinson's perspective, however, this particular device is only one more instance of the mystery, or to use Ames's language, of the "excess" that we are. How strange that we humans create a technology that could someday replace the speech that comes from our own interiority, and produce one that simply relies on algorithms. What is the practical need for such a machine? And if we are to speak of mystery, what about all the questions that ChatGPT raises about the nature of creativity, among others? In the many articles I have read on this new application, all ponder this question directly or indirectly, as if a prompt to ChatGPT on creativity would not do. Creativity seems to be something we want to exercise, feeling it in the obstacles and triumphs of producing something of our own on our own person. The very device that plays dangerously close to eliminating mystery, reveals the mystery we are from yet another angle. This does not mean that the dangers of having our interiority erased are not real. Artificial intelligence, for instance, may displace the authority of our own speech. After all, it pits billions of patterns against our lone voice. It may dull our need to create, in the name of efficiency and productivity. Reading Robinson's work, however, helps us not to be too easily intimidated. The mystery that we are reemerges in the very attempt to eliminate it, if we pay attention.

Short Reflection on Robinson and Péguy

In Robinson's work, perhaps more than in any other author in this volume, we return to a warrior stance characteristic of Péguy. Nonetheless, she, like him, also recognizes that not even the best argument can defeat,

139. Metz, "Chatbots Can Amaze," B3.

once and for all, the narratives around the sciences. In recognition of this, her novels simply take for granted the reality of the self, revealing its many dimensions, the mystery that it is. In *Gilead* and her other works of fiction, the self is reaffirmed in our own act of reading, not as the conclusion of a logical chain. This is not to say that her creative work arose to combat the sciences, as if it were a stealth weapon in a war of ideas. It is no doubt quite the opposite. The mystery of the creative process comes first, propelling her arguments. Bathing in this mystery, rather than merely polemicizing, is, in the end, what we are called to do. This may be the only winning strategy, and yet one cannot help but argue as well, if only to clear one's mind.

On the other hand, the bridge Robinson draws between the sciences and the humanities does not closely resemble Péguy's. As we have seen, she relies on the findings of modern science, quantum physics in particular, in a way that he does not. The different eras in which they lived might account for this difference. Quantum was not yet on the horizon in the early twentieth century, although both Bergson[140] and Duhem[141] were already talking in Péguy's time about a non-deterministic, non-atomistic view of nature, derived from the latest findings of physics. For Péguy, the link between the natural sciences and the humanities remained intuition, a method rather than a specific finding. As we have seen, that method was central to the humanities in a way it could never be central to the sciences, and thus the determination of what is real lies squarely, in the case of Péguy, within the method associated with the humanities.

Despite this difference, Robinson and Péguy do intersect at a crucial point. For both authors, beyond their polemics against the narratives accompanying the natural sciences, the bridge to the natural sciences is unmistakably present. Insofar as scientists make mystery accessible to us, they stand before the same dark, cool sea that Ames perceived in that predawn morning, or before that tricky Reality whose inexhaustibility Péguy never ceased to demonstrate. Robinson may or may not draw correct implications regarding the link between modern physics and Christian theology but she is certainly not mistaken in claiming that the latest scientific discoveries, far from making Reality transparent

140. Bergson, *Creative Evolution*, 201, 203, in which the philosopher speaks of physics as increasingly moving away from describing matter as divided into units, as we perceive it through our senses alone, and that "we cannot reason about the parts as we reason about the whole."

141. Duhem, "Physics of a Believer," 44–133.

to our concepts, illuminate its mystery in new ways. She would add, and it is a crucial addition, that it requires the mystery of the human subject to perceive mystery at all.

Epilogue

Confessions of a Pedagogue

As I completed writing this book, I came across an author, Meghan O'Gieblyn, whose point of departure and, sometimes, of arrival differs substantially from my own. Nonetheless, many passages in both of her books to date arrested my attention, none perhaps as pertinent as the following as a way of entering into the themes of this book.

> But the stories that captivated and unsettled me were those that remained irreducible. In those, there were no codes to be cracked, no definitive meaning to be exposed—just the faintest sense that the surface of the text was undergirded by a vast system of roots that must remain forever invisible.[1]

I have tried in all that preceded to point to "a vast system of roots" in the works I interpreted. Each of them holds so many intertwined meanings that a careful reader can only hint at the underlying web. If lucky, she draws the next reader in. The invisibility of the web provokes ever new attempts to get at it through the surface that reveals it.

Much undergirds such a method of reading. Each author in this study alludes to an invisible web comparable to O'Gieblyn's, reflected both in reality and in the human expressions that try to capture it. For Péguy, his very style of repetition embodies a reality always on the move, never caught, slipping out of one's grasp again and again, in parallel to the inexhaustibility of great texts. DeLillo shows us the infinite web we

1. Meghan O'Gieblyn, *Interior States*, 121. The title is a play on words, simultaneously referring to the self and to the Midwest, where the author is from.

bathe in, the language we speak. We define words but they escape into metaphor, expanding their boundaries, in this sense imitating our own humanity, limited and yet of unsuspected depths. D'Espagnat suggests the existence of a Veiled Reality, absolute, beyond space and time. Yet, as he sees it, poets, musicians, mystics—and, perhaps, their interpreters—give us glimpses of it. Szymborska speaks of "the great Silence up on high," eluding any one expression, demanding that the poet start over and over, messing up every system. Robinson's *Gilead* is suffused with the metaphor of a light buried in darkness, and that darkness is the vast sea in which we swim. It is up to us to "read" this intertwining, in both texts and events. None of this adds up to one coherent metaphysics. D'Espagnat's Veiled Reality is not the same as Szymborska's Silence up on high. Nor is Robinson's dark cool sea the same as DeLillo's ocean of language. For every author, however, the name they give to what O'Gieblyn called "a vast system of roots that must remain invisible" has implications for reading. It allies reading with a metaphysics, a pursuit of the real.

This is a most ponderous statement. Let me turn to a parody of it that makes the same point but with humor. In the television series *Severance*, the protagonists are office workers in a huge corporation whose job is to detect strange patterns amid the vast series of numbers appearing on their computer screens all day long.[2] They get prizes for detecting a higher percentage of these numerical patterns than their fellow employees. In one episode, one of them unintentionally brings a forbidden object, a book from the world outside the corporation, into the office. Several of the protagonists start to read it in secret, and it fosters in them a desire they did not know they had, to find out who they really are outside the role dictated to them in the work place. According to the conceit of the show, this is no small matter for their brains have been surgically manipulated, "severed," so that while at their jobs, they completely forget about the life they live outside the perimeters of the work place, and vice versa. Thus, the need to keep books out, for they bring in a dose of reality otherwise kept firmly at bay.

The parodic dimension of *Severance* is that the forbidden book is composed of the most insipid phrases. It is a self-help manual. If parody is a playful deformation of what it is imitating, *Severance* pokes fun at our lofty ideas about reading, while still affirming its salvific qualities. Really, a revolution based on a self-help book? Not Marx or Fanon? Self-discovery,

2. Stiller, *Severance*, "The You You Are."

but not through Shakespeare or Tolstoy? What will people claim next, that *Severance*, a lowly television series, can capture our reality and transform us? The humor makes me want to clarify a suggestion I made in various places regarding the centrality of classical works in a good education. *Je m'explique*, as Péguy would say. The "classical," while it undeniably refers to works that have remained in the collective memory for generations, is not limited to the genial creations of yore. It also refers to a paradigmatic way of encapsulating a reality. As the contemporary works I have included in *The Thought at the Back of the Mind* suggest, classical expression is being born as we speak. Still, I did not include a self-help book. There is a hierarchy among works that cannot be erased. In short, it is better to live in a world in which self-help books are not our only choices. *Severance* itself is proof that that other world still exists.

I would just add that this way of understanding reading suggests that the skills often cited to justify the humanities—enhancing clear expression and critical thinking, for example—emerge from a more basic task. Interpreting human expressions gives us access to what is real, always receding from our grasp and yet revealing enough to orient us. Someone might object that the world is strewn with interpretations that have wreaked havoc upon us. There is no protection against that, except counter readings. I offer the interpretations in this book as counter readings to certain narratives that would eliminate the intuition, the metaphors, and the humor so central to touching what is real, a real, all the authors here proclaim, both intimate to us and beyond our grasp.

Doubts and Affirmations

I might as well admit that occasionally doubts assail me. After all, this book is based on the proposition that the narratives emanating from the natural sciences exert great authority in our culture, shaping our image of ourselves as humans, even when we are not always aware of it. Is this authority as pervasive as I and the authors, as I interpret them, have claimed? At the present moment, we hear of the diminished status of the natural sciences, the mounting reports of retracted scientific papers, the cases of political and economic pressures on scientific results etc. It may very well be that we are turning a corner, but if so, we have not turned it fully. Increased mistrust of the institutions associated with the sciences does not seem to have dented in the least the dreams of omniscience and omnipotence we saw expressed in several of the chapters in this book. The vast amount of resources poured into reversing the aging process, into duplicating our every capacity, into building huge science edifices with six miles of corridors do not indicate a major shift in the power of the narratives this book treats. The demand for big data and evidence-based teaching, with its accompanying quantitative evaluations, also suggest that the cachet of the scientific method is still required to legitimate knowledge, to the inclusion of other paths. In any case, *The Thought at the Back of the Mind* was not addressing this or that individual's "beliefs" about science but a reality that surrounds us, and that we have internalized, even when we rebel against it.

Two very recent works help to clarify, one last time, the nature of the scientific authority this book discussed, and its presence in our midst. Benjamin Labatut's *The Maniac* presents twentieth-century science, most particularly quantum physics, as a derailment of reason, a derailment so extreme that reason veers into the irrational and the catastrophic.[3] He begins with a short study of the physicist Paul Ehrenfest, who saw in quantum physics a turn to a mathematical thinking abstracted from any other human faculty, including the imagination.[4] He foresaw only horror as a result, expressing forebodings of "a strange new rationality that was beginning to take shape. . . a profoundly inhuman form of intelligence that was completely indifferent to mankind's deepest needs; this deranged reason, this specter haunting the soul of science . . . both logic driven and utterly irrational . . . enrapturing the cleverest men and women with whispered promises of superhuman power and godlike control."[5] To illustrate Ehrenfest's premonitions, Labatut then turns to the polymath, John von Neumann, behind so many of today's scientific developments. As Labatut has another scientist describe von Neumann, "He wanted to mathematize everything, to spark revolutions in biology, economics, neurology, and cosmology. To transform all areas of human thought and grab science by the throat by unleashing the power of unlimited computation."[6] *The Maniac* concludes with one of the practical

3. Labatut's book presents itself as a "nonfiction novel," which creates difficulties as to pinning down any one position put in the mouth of the scientists he describes as his own. On the other hand, the epigram is certainly his choice. It is a citation from a thirteenth-century poet, describing the terror induced by the soul's faculty of reason.

4. Labatut, *Maniac*, 10, 16.

5. Labatut, *Maniac*, 22.

6. Labatut, *Maniac*, 158.

consequences of such thinking, the creation of a machine, AlphaGo, built on some of the pioneering work of von Neumann and others.

As is well known, AlphaGo beat the world champion of the East Asian game of Go, considered to be the most complex in the world. This was hitherto deemed impossible, given that the game demanded an intuitive grasp, built over years of training, irreducible to mathematical computations. AlphaGo, capable of projecting possible future plays at unimaginable rates, shattered this assumption. It beat the champion, Lee Sedol, four out of five games. The A.I. has only improved since those initial matches, playing millions of games against itself, and making billions of small improvements in the process.[7]

In Labatut's rendering, we see that AlphaGo, in winning, has also transformed the game. It has made obsolete not only intuition, but also the interhuman dynamic between players, which required the cultivation of virtue—a particular fighting spirit and an esthetic sensibility, among others. All that mattered after AlphaGo's triumph was the ability to calculate outcomes, independently of a player's memory and personal qualities. It is not that the machine duplicated the human. It pushed it aside as an inferior mechanism. *In Labatut's novel, the derailment of reason lies in an artificial substitution that misses the very object it is imitating.* It is not, to repeat, that science/technology duplicates us. Rather, the machine dismisses us, making it seem as if we are utterly replaced. Labatut quotes Von Neumann: "You insist that there is something a machine cannot do. If you tell me precisely what a machine cannot do, then I can always make a machine that will do just that."[8] But, for Sedol, as Labatut presents it, it isn't so. In an interview the great Go player says:

> I started playing when I was five. Back then it was all about courtesy and manners. It was more like learning an art form than a game. As I grew up, Go started to be seen as a mind game, but what I learned was an art. Go is a work of art made by two people. Now it is totally different. After the advent of AI, the concept of Go itself has changed.

Along with ethics, another key dimension disappears, the very element of play. As Sedol goes on to say, the machine does not defeat its human opponent. It crushes him.[9] Play involves an element of risk, of

7. Labatut, *Maniac*, 324.
8. Labatut, *Maniac*, 349.
9. Labatut, *Maniac*, 350.

unpredictability, encountered in a personal way. No risk exists if the machine cannot be beaten. Lee Sedol resigned a couple of years after his match with AlphaGo, even though he could still beat human opponents, for the game was being played in imitation of the computer's ability to calculate. We have defeated ourselves.

William Egginton's *The Rigor of Angels*, on the other hand, foregrounds not a reason derailed but a reason properly limited. Egginton argues that modern physics and the scientific method that gave rise to it are our best defense against totalitarian visions, fanaticism, claims to omniscience or omnipotence. Quantum mechanics has definitely shown us, according to him, that we cannot know a reality independent of our observation of it. When we take something to be absolute, independent of our observations, we merely mistake a human construct for the thing in itself. Thus, when we assert the independent reality of a God, a self, or the reality of spacetime, "we sacrifice the core of what has made the scientific method so extraordinarily successful: its profound humility . . . "[10] Egginton goes on to say that science's culmination in quantum physics has definitively established that there is no realm beyond what appears to us, and what appears to us are only relations, not essences. Science, then, in Egginton's reading, does not merely deal with appearances. *It tells us there is nothing beyond appearances*. In other words, the scientific method seals our understanding of what is ultimate, of what is real, a point the subtitle of his book makes clear, *Borges, Heisenberg, Kant and the Ultimate Nature of Reality*. Natural science, in his book, remains the royal road to knowledge, providing us with the tools to dispel illusions.[11] To be sure, Immanuel Kant and Jorge Luis Borges, in Egginton's interpretation, expressed views remarkably similar to those of Werner Heisenberg, but it is Heisenberg's work that gets the last word, as if the works of the philosopher and the artist were mere anticipations or echoes of what the scientific method conclusively established.

My point, in quickly alluding to these books, diametrically opposed in their views, is that both authors treat the natural sciences as sources of a metaphysics, of a very powerful story about our relationship to what is ultimate. In the case of Labatut, that metaphysics is catastrophic in its drive to omniscience and omnipotence. It is not a mere theory, but descends, for instance, into weaponry, foreign policy, economic policies,

10. Egginton, *Rigor of Angels*, 274.

11. Egginton, *Rigor of Angels*, 277–282.

and the world of games. The latter might seem innocuous but it involves millions upon millions of people, if only as observers, and what they are observing is the disappearing of something essential to the human. For Egginton, on the contrary, the sciences protect us from illusions about what we can know, denying us any relation to an absolute reality. They shape what we can legitimately think, and, as a result, have an implication in the realm of action as well.

The Thought at the Back of the Mind aligns much more with Labatut's sense of dread about the narratives of omniscience emanating from the natural sciences than with Egginton's sense of the salutary powers of the scientific method. Yet, in a very different way from Egginton, I also claim, through my authors, that contemporary science, through its new discoveries about matter, and, even more importantly, through the reflection of some scientists on the limitations of the scientific method, provides a needed corrective to the very narratives that emanate from their work. This does not prevent me from having major disagreements with Egginton's claims about what the natural sciences can or cannot tell us. But the point remains that both authors view the natural sciences at the level of the questions in this book, at the level of that which organizes our sense of what is real. Catching that reality on the move, reflecting on where it is taking us, correcting ourselves as we go, keeps us in fighting form. *The Thought at the Back of the Mind* is not particularly irenic. Much hangs on how we define the human.

Bibliography

Adlee, Sally. *We Are Electric*. New York: Hachette, 2023.

Augustine of Hippo. *City of God*. Translated by Henry Bettenson. New York: Penguin, 2003.

Aviv, Rachel. *Strangers to Ourselves: Unsettled Minds and the Stories that Make Us*. New York: Farrar, Straus and Giroux, 2022.

Bakalar, Nikolas. "Is There a Ceiling on Life Expectancy?" *New York Times*, November 20, 2018, https://www.nytimes.com/2018/11/19/health/human-life-span.html.

Barańczak, Stanisław. "The Americanization of Wisława; or How I Was Translating 'An Opinion on the Question of Pornography' with One Young Californian." In *Wisława Szymborska's Poetry: Choice of Essays*, edited by Anna Nasiłowska, 229–42. Translated by Karolina Krasuska and Jędrzdej Burszta. New York: Peter Lang, 2015.

Bastaire, Jean. *Péguy contre Pétain, l'appel du 17 juin*. Paris: Salvator, 2000.

Begley, Adam. "The Art of Fiction CXXXV: Don DeLillo." In *Conversations with Don DeLillo*, edited by Thomas DePietro, 86–108. Jackson: University Press of Mississippi, 2005.

Bergson, Henri. *Creative Evolution*. Translated by Arthur Mitchell. Lavergne, TN: Harvard University Press, 2016.

———. *Introduction to Metaphysics*. Translated by T. E. Hulme. New York: Bobbs-Merrill, 1955.

The Bhagavadgita. Translated by Kees W. Bolle. Berkeley: University of California University, 1979.

Bojanowska, Edyta M. "Wisława Szymborska: Naturalist and Humanist." *Slavic and Eastern European Journal* 41:2 (1997) 199–223.

Bolle, Kees W. *The Freedom of Man in Myth*. Nashville: Vanderbilt University Press, 1993.

Burac. Robert. "Avertissement." In *Œuvres en prose complètes II*, by Charles Péguy, edited by Robert Burac, ix–xxv. Paris: Gallimard, 1988.

———. "Notices, notes et variantes." In *Œuvres en prose complètes II*, by Charles Péguy, edited by Robert Burac, 1353–1577. Paris: Gallimard, 1988.

———. *Le Sourire d'Hypathie: Essai sur le comique de Charles Péguy*. Paris: Honoré Champion, 1991.

Capa, Fritjof. *The Tao of Physics*. Berkeley: Shambhala, 1975.

Carey, Benedict. "Robert Provine, 76, an Authority on What Sets Off Giggles and Guffaws." *New York Times*, October 31, 2019, B15. https://www.nytimes.com/2019/10/28/obituaries/robert-provine-dead.html.

Carnino, Guillaume. *L'Invention de la science*. Paris: Seuil, 2015.

Carpenter, Bogdana. "Wisława Szymborska and the Importance of the Unimportant." *World Literature Today* 71:1 (1997) 8–12.

Cavanagh, Clare. "Poetry and Ideology: The Example of Wisława Szymborska." *Literary Imagination* 1:2 (1999) 174–90.

Certeau, Michel de. *Le Lieu de l'Autre: Histoire religieuse et mystique*. Paris: Gallimard/Seuil. 2005.

Chayka, Kyle. "The Uncanny Failures of A.I.-Generated Hands." *The New Yorker*, March 10, 2023. https://www.newyorker.com/culture/rabbit-holes/the-uncanny-failures-of-ai-generated-hands.

Chu Hsi. *Learning to be a Sage*. Translated by Daniel K. Gardner. Berkeley: University of California Press, 1990.

Cohen, Richard A., ed. *Face to Face with Levinas*. Albany, NY: State University of New York Press, 1986.

Collins, Lauren, "Living Proof." *The New Yorker*, February 17–24, 2020, 60–71. https://www.newyorker.com/magazine/2020/02/17/was-jeanne-calment-the-oldest-person-who-ever-lived-or-a-fraud.

Cowart, David. "DeLillo and the Power of Language." In *The Cambridge Companion to Don DeLillo*, edited by John N. Duvall, 151–65. New York: Cambridge University Press, 2008.

De Freytas-Tamura, Kimiko. "Wish of Girl, 14, to Be Frozen is Granted by British Judge." *New York Times*, November 19, 2016, A7. https://www.nytimes.com/2016/11/19/world/europe/frozen-girl-judge-last-wish.html.

DeLillo, Don. "In the Ruins of History." *Harper's Magazine*, December 2001, 33–41.

———. *Zero K*. New York: Scribner, 2016.

Duhem, Pierre. "Physique de Croyant." *Annales de Philosophie Chrétienne* 77:4 (Octobre-Novembre 1905) 44–67. http://ftp.colloquium.co.uk/"barrett/croyant.html.

Dupuy, Jean-Pierre. "Cybernetics is Antihumanism: Advanced Technologies and the Rebellion Against the Human Condition." In *H+–Transhumanism and Its Critics*, edited by Gregory R. Hansell and William Grassie, 227–48. Philadelphia: Metanexus Institute, 2011.

Duvall, John N. "Introduction: The Power of History and the Persistence of Memory." In *The Cambridge Companion to Don DeLillo*, edited by John N. Duvall, 1–10. Cambridge, U.K: Cambridge University Press, 2008.

Egginton, William. *The Rigor of Angels: Borges, Heisenberg, Kant, and the Ultimate Nature of Reality*. New York: Pantheon, 2023.

Emerson, Ralph Waldo. *Emerson on Transcendentalism*. Edited by Edward L. Ericson. New York: Ungar, 1987.

Espagnat, Bernard d'. *On Physics and Philosophy*. Princeton: Princeton University Press, 2006.

———. "The Quantum Theory and Reality." *Scientific American* 241:5 (1979) 158–81.

Friend, Tad. "Sam Altman's Manifest Destiny." *The New Yorker*, October 10, 2016. https://www.newyorker.com/magazine/2016/10/10/sam-altmans-manifest-destiny.

Galchen, Rivka. "How I Became a Vet." *The New Yorker*, March 13, 2023, 26–31. https://www.newyorker.com/magazine/2023/03/13/how-i-became-a-vet.

Gasché, Rodolphe. "Universalism and Spatial Form." In *Science and the Life-World: Essays on Husserl's Crisis of the European Sciences*, edited by David Hyder and Hans-Jorg Rheinberger, 116–35. Stanford: Stanford University Press, 2009.

Ghazzālī. *Al-Ghazali's Path to Sufism: His Deliverance from Error al-Munquidh al-Dalaf.* Translated by R. J. McCarthy, SJ. Louisville: Fons Vitae, 2000.

Goldstein, Dana. "Florida Colleges to Weigh Entrance Exams Based on Classics." *New York Times*, September 7, 2023, A22. https//:www.nytimes.com/2023/09/06/us/sat-alternative-florida-classical-learning-test.html.

Gombrowicz, Witold. *Diary.* Vols. 1–3. Translated by Lillian Vallee. Evanston, IL: North-western University Press, 1988–1993.

Grądziel, Joanna. "The World Trapped in a Poem. Self-Reflection and the Poetic Practice of Wislawa Szymborska." In *Wysława Szymborska's Poetry: Choice of Essays,* edited by Anna Nasiłowska, 83–96. Translated by Karolina Krasuska and Jędrzdej Burszta. New York: Peter Lang, 2015.

Grądziel-Wójcik, Joanna. "'Lekcje Biologii,' Czyli Miłosz Czyta Szymborską." *Ruch Literacki* 53(2012) 1 (310) 99–112.

Grassie, William. "Millenialism at the Singularity: Reflections on the Limits of Ray Kurzweil's Exponential Logic." In *H+-Transhumanism and Its Critics*, edited by Gregory R. Hansell, and William Grassie, 249–69. Philadelphia: Metanexus Institute, 2011.

Green, Emma. "Old School. Have the liberal arts gone conservative?" *The New Yorker,* March 18, 2024, 12–19.

Harari, Yuval Noah. *Homo Deus. A Brief History of Tomorrow*. New York: Harper, 2017.

Harmon, Amy. "Hoping to Transcend Death, via Cryonics." *New York Times*, September 13, 2015, A1. https://www.nytimes.com/2015/09/13/us/cancer-immortality-cryo genics.html.

———. "The Neuroscience of Immortality: Mileposts on a Long and Uncharted Road." *New York Times,* April 3, 2016. https://www.nytimes.com/interactive/2015/09/03/us/13immortality-explainer.html.

Harrison, Peter. *The Territories of Science and Religion*. Chicago: University of Chicago Press, 2015.

Heidegger, Martin. "The Origin of the Work of Art." In *Martin Heidegger, Basic Writings*, edited by David Farrell Krell, 149–87. New York: Harper & Row, 1977.

———. "The Question Concerning Technology." In *Martin Heidegger, Basic Writings*, edited by David Farrell Krell, 287–317. New York: Harper & Row, 1977.

Heisenberg, Werner. *Physics and Philosophy: The Revolution in Modern Science.* New York: Harper & Row, 1958.

Heller, Nathan. "The End of the English Major—Why Humanities Enrollments Are in Free Fall." *The New Yorker*, March 6, 2023, 28–39. htps://www.newyorker.com/magazine/2023/03/06/the-end-of-the-english-major.

Henderson, Bob. "The Quantum Mechanic." *New York Times Magazine*, June 28, 2020. https://www.nytimes.com/2020/06/25/magazine/angelo-bassi-quantum-mech anic.html.

Jacob, François. *Of Flies, Mice, and Men*. Cambridge: Harvard University Press, 1998.

James, William. *The Will to Believe and Other Essays in Popular Philosophy*. New York: Longmans, Green, 1904.

Janicaud, Dominique. *Powers of the Rational*. Translated by Peg Birmingham and Elizabeth Birmingham. Bloomington: Indiana University Press, 1994.

Jensen, Pablo. "La vérité scientifique et le saut du tigre." *Le Monde diplomatique* 741, n.12 (2015) 27–27. https://www.monde-diplomatique.fr/2015/12/JENSEN/54392.

Kafka, Franz. *Franz Kafka: The Complete Stories*. Edited by Nahum N. Glatzer. New York: Schocken, 1976.

Kaiser, David. *How the Hippies Saved Physics*. New York: Norton, 2011.

Kang, Caspian Jay. "Could an A.I. Chatbot Rewrite My Novel?" *The New Yorker*, December 9, 2022. https://www.newyorker.com/news/our-columnists/could-an-ai-chatbot-rewrite-my-novel.

Khullar, Dhruv. "Talking to Ourselves." *The New Yorker*, March 6, 2023, 16–22. https://www.newyorker.com/magazine/2023/03/06/can-ai-treat-mental-illness.

Klein, Ezra. "The Culture Creating A.I. Is Weird. Here's Why That Matters: Erik Davis Discusses the 'High Weirdness' that Has Shaped California and the Development of A.I." *New York Times*, May 2, 2023. Podcasts. apple/.../the culture creating a-i-is weird.

Klein, Naomi. "AI Machines Aren't 'Hallucinating' but Their Makers Are." *The Guardian*, May 8, 2023.

Krugman, Paul. "Does ChatGPT Mean Robots Can Take Away Our Jobs?" *New York Times*, December, 6, 2022. https://www.nytimes.com/2022/12/06/opinion/chatgpt-ai-skilled-jobs-automation.html.

Kumar, Manjit. *Quantum: Einstein, Bohr and the Great Debate about the Nature of Reality*. New York: Norton, 2011.

Labatut, Benjamìn. *The Maniac*. New York: Penguin, 2023.

Labouret, Denis. "Humour." In *Dictionnaire Charles Péguy*, edited by Salomon Malka, 160–63. Paris: Albin Michel, 2018.

Lalouette, Jacqueline. "La glorification de la science au xix siècle." In *La Vie intellectuelle en France, v.1:1. Des lendemains de la Révolution à 1914*, edited by Christophe Charles, and Laurent Jeanpierre, 429–49. Paris: Seuil, 2016.

———."La 'banqueroute de la science.'" In "*La Vie intellectuelle en France, v.1:1. Des lendemains de la Révolution à 1914*, edited by Christophe Charles, and Laurent Jeanpierre, 480–81. Paris: Seuil, 2016.

Latour, Bruno. "Charles Péguy: Time, Space, et 'le Monde Moderne.'" *New Literary History* 46:1 (Winter 2015) 41–62.

———. "'Nous sommes des vaincus.'" In *Charles Péguy*, edited by Camille Riquier, 11–30. Paris: Cerf, 2014.

Laudan, Larry. *Progress and Its Problems*. Berkeley: University of California Press, 1977.

Lem, Stanisław. *The Cyberiad: Fables for an Electronic Age*. Translated by Michael Kandel. New York: Seabury, 1974.

Levinas, Emmanuel. *Beyond the Verse*. Translated by Gary Mole. Bloomington: Indiana University Press, 1994.

———. *Hors sujet*. Paris: Fata Morgana, 1987.

———. *Nine Talmudic Readings by Emmanuel Levinas*. Translated by Annette Aronowicz. Bloomington: Indiana University Press, 2019.

———. *Proper Names*. Translated by Michael B. Smith. London: Athlone, 1996.

Lindley, David. *The Dream Universe: How Fundamental Physics Lost Its Way*. New York: Doubleday, 2020.

Liogier, Raphael. "Le transhumanisme." In *La Vie Intellectuelle en France II. De 1914 à nos jours*, edited by Christophe Charles, and Laurent Jeanpierre, 557–62. Paris: Seuil, 2016.

McGraw, Peter, and Joel Warner. *The Humor Code: The Global Search for What Makes Things Funny*. New York: Simon & Schuster, 2014.

Maguire, Matthew W. *Carnal Spirit, the Revolutions of Charles Péguy*. Philadelphia: University of Pennsylvania Press, 2019.

Manjoo, Farhad. "How Do You Know a Human Wrote This?" *New York Times*, July 29, 2020. https://www.nytimes.com/2020/07/29/opinion/gpt-3-ai-automation.html.

McClure, John A. "DeLillo and Mystery." In *The Cambridge Companion to Don DeLillo*, edited by John N. Duvall, 166–78. Cambridge, UK: Cambridge University Press, 2008.

Medawar, Peter Brian. *The Limits of Science*. New York: Harper and Row, 1984.

Metz, Cade, and Keith Collins. "All the Ways GPT-4 Is Impressive but Still Flawed." *New York Times*, March 15, 2023, B1, B6. https://www.nytimes.com/2023/03/14/technology/openai-new-gpt4.html.

———. "Chatbots Can Amaze but Also Lie." *New York Times*, December 12, 2022, B1. https://www.nytimes.com/2022/12/10/technology/ai-chat-bot-chatgpt.html.

Milbank, John. "Foreword: Charles Péguy and the Betrayal of Time." In Charles Péguy, *Notes on Bergson and Descartes: Philosophy, Christianity, and Modernity in Contestation*, xi–xxxviii. Translated by Bruce K. Ward. Eugene, OR: Cascade Books, 2019.

Milona, Elena, "Valery Novoselov: Investigating Jeanne Calment's Longevity Record." *Lifespan.io*, December 4, 2018. https://www.lifespan.io/news/valery-novoselov-investigating-jeanne-calments-longevity-record/.

Milosz, Czeslaw. *The Land of Ulro*. Translated by Louis Iribarne. New York: Farrar, Straus and Giroux, 1981.

———."On Szymborska." *New York Review of Books* 43:48 (1996) 17.

———."Poetry as Consciousness." In *Wisława Szymborska's Poetry: Choice of Essays*. Translated by Karolina Krasuska and Jędrzdej Burszta, edited by Anna Nasiłowka, 15–17. New York: Peter Lang, 2015.

———. *The Witness of Poetry*. Cambridge: Harvard University Press, 1983.

Milosz, Czeslaw, ed. *Postwar Polish Poetry*. Berkeley: University of California Press, 1983

Moravec, Hans. *Mind Children: The Future of Robot and Human Intelligence*. Cambridge, MA: Harvard University Press, 1990.

Nagel, Thomas. *Mind and Cosmos: Why the Materialist Neo-Darwinian Conception of Nature is Almost Certainly False*. Oxford: Oxford University Press, 2012.

Noble, David E. *The Religion of Technology*. New York: Penguin, 1999.

Noë, Alva. *Out of Our Heads. Why You Are Not Your Brain, and Other Lessons from the Biology of Consciousness*. New York: Hill and Wang, 2009.

Nuwer, Rachel. "Keeping Track of Oldest People in the World." *Smithsonian Magazine*, July 8, 2014. https://www.smithsonianmag.com/science-nature/keeping-track-oldest-people-world-180951976/

O'Gieblyn, Meghan. *Interior States: Essays*. New York: Anchor, 2018.

Olen, Helaine. "As Basic Health Care Grows Unaffordable, the Rich Seek Eternal Youth." *The Washington Post*, February 6, 2023. https://www.washingtonpost.com/opinons/2023/02/06/american=health-care=disparity-rich/.

Osnos, Evan. "Doomsday Prep for Super-Rich." *The New Yorker*, January 23, 2017, 1–29. https://www.newyorker.com/magazine/2017/01/30/doomsday-prep-for-the-super-rich.

Paligot, Carole Reynaud. "Médicine, biologie et racialisme." In *Vie intellectuelle en France, v. 1:1. Des lendemains de la Révolution à 1914*, edited by Christopher Charles and Laurent Jeanpierre, 453–68. Paris: Seuil, 2016.

Pascal, Blaise. *Pensées*. Translated by A. J. Krailsheimer. New York: Penguin, 1995.

Péguy, Charles. *Notes on Bergson and Descartes: Philosophy, Christianity, and Modernity in Contestation*. Translated by Bruce K. Ward. Eugene, OR: Cascade Books, 2019.

———. *Œuvres en prose complètes I*. Edited by Robert Burac. Paris: Gallimard, 1987.

———. *Œuvres en prose complètes II*. Edited by Robert Burac. Paris: Gallimard, 1988.

———. *Œuvres en prose complètes III*. Edited by Robert Burac. Paris: Gallimard, 1992.

Pióro, Tadeusz, "Rampa Pampa Pam: Szymborska in the USA." In *Wisława Szymborska's Poetry: Choice of Essays*, edited by Anna Nasiłowka, 213–16. Translated by Karolina Krasuska and Jędrzdej Burszta. New York: Peter Lang, 2015.

Plato, *The Collected Dialogues of Plato*. Edited by Edith Hamilton and Huntington Cairns. Princeton: Princeton University Press, 1961.

Polkinghorne, John. *Quantum Theory: A Very Short Introduction*. Oxford: Oxford University Press, 2002.

Prirogine, Ilya, and Stengers Isabelle. *Order Out of Chaos: Man's Dialogue with Nature*. New York: Bantam, 1984.

Provine, Robert. *Laughter: A Scientific Investigation*. New York: Penguin, 2000.

Regalado, Antonio. "Google's Long Strange Life-Span Trip." *MIT Technology Review*. December 15, 2016. https://www.technologyreview.com/2016/12/15/69305/googles-long-strange-life-span-trip/

Ringer, Fritz. *Fields of Knowledge. French Academic Culture in Comparative Perspective, 1890–1920*. New York: Cambridge University Press, 1992.

Riquier, Camille. "Péguy Bergsonien." In *Charles Péguy*, edited by Camille Riquier, 149–78. Paris: Cerf, 2014.

Robinet, André. *Péguy entre Jaurès, Bergson et l'Église*. Vichy: Seghers, 1968.

Robinson, Marilynne. *Absence of Mind: The Dispelling of Inwardness from the Modern Myth of the Self*. New Haven: Yale University Press, 2010.

———. *Death of Adam: Essays on Modern Thought*. New York: Picador, 2005.

———. *Gilead*. New York: Picador, 2004.

———. *The Givenness of Things: Essays*. New York: Picador, 2015.

———."A Theology of the Present Moment." *The New York Review of Books*, December 22, 2022. https://www.nybooks.com/articles/2022/12/22/a-theology-of-the-present-moment-marilynne-robinson/

———. *When I Was a Child I Read Books*. New York: Picador, 2012.

Roe, Glen H. *The Passion of Péguy: Literature, Modernity and the Crisis of Historicism*. Oxford: Oxford University Press, 2014.

Roose, Kevin. "The Brilliance and Weirdness of ChatGPT." *New York Times*, December 9, 2022, B1. https://www.nytimes.com/2022/12/05technology/chatgpt-ai-twitter.html.

Rovelli, Carlo. *Helgoland: Making Sense of the Quantum Revolution*. New York: Riverhead Books, 2021.

Schmidgen, Henning. "The Materiality of Things? Bruno Latour, Charles Péguy and the History of Science." *History of Human Sciences 26:1* (2012) 3–28.

Seabrook, John. "The Next Word. Where Will Predictive Texts Take Us?" *The New Yorker*, October 14, 2019, 52–63. https://www.newyorker.com/magazine/2019/10/14/can-a-machine-learn-to-write-for-the-new-yorker.

Shortall, Sarah. "Lost in Translation: Religion and the Writing of History." *Modern Intellectual History* 13:1 (2016) 273–86.

———. *Soldiers of God in a Secular World: Catholic Theology and Twentieth-Century French Politics*. Cambridge: Harvard University Press, 2021.

Sorel, Georges. "Les Préoccupations métaphysiques des physiciens modernes." *Revue de Métaphysique et de Morale* 13:6 (Novembre 1905) 859–89.

Stengers, Elizabeth. "La thèse que Péguy n'a jamais écrite." *In Charles Péguy*, edited by Camille Riquier, 32–67. Paris: Cerf, 2014.

Stiller, Ben, dir. *Severance*. Season 1, episode 9, "The You You Are." Aired on April 8, 2022, on Apple TV+.

Szymborska, Wysława. *Map: Collected and Last Poems*. Translated by Clare Cavanagh and Stanisław Barańczak. New York: Mariner, 2016.

———. *Monologue of a Dog*. Translated by Clare Cavanagh and Stanisław Barańczak. New York: Harcourt, 2002.

———. *Non-required Reading. Prose Pieces*. Translated by Clare Cavanagh. New York: Harcourt, 2002.

———. *Sounds, Feelings, Thoughts: Seventy Poems by Wislawa Szymborska*. Translated by Magnus J. Krynski and Robert A. Maguire. Princeton: Princeton University Press, 1981.

———. *Wszystkie lektury nadobowiązkowe*. Krakow: Znak, 2015.

Tallis, Raymond. *Aping Mankind: Neuromania, Darwinitis and the Misrepresentation of Humanity*. Durham: Acumen, 2011.

Tauber, Alfred I. *Science and the Quest for Meaning*. Waco, TX: Baylor University Press, 2009.

Toulmin, Stephen. *The Return to Cosmology*. Berkeley: University of California Press, 1982.

Ward, Bruce K. "Introduction." In Charles Péguy, *Notes on Bergson and Descartes: Philosophy, Christianity, and Modernity in Contestation*, 1–25. Translated by Bruce K. Ward. Eugene, OR: Cascade, 2019.

Weatherby, Leif. "ChatGPT Is an Ideology Machine." *Jacobin*, April 17, 2023. https://www.jacobin.com/2023/04/chatgpt-ai-language-models-ideology.

Zimmerman, Eileen. "Biotech Start-Up Invests in Anti-Aging Therapy." *New York Times*, August 1, 2022, B3. https://www.nytimes.com/2022/07/19/business/aging-protein-elevian.html.

Zinoman, Jason. "Are Comedian Bots Ready to Kill?" *New York Times*, August 20, 2023, AR 7. https://www.nytimes.com/2023/08/15/arts/television/comedy-artificial-intelligence-chatgpt.html.

Index

www.ingramcontent.com/pod-product-compliance
Lightning Source LLC
LaVergne TN
LVHW050619100826
845148LV00011B/1653
* 9 7 9 8 3 8 5 2 0 7 1 5 2 *